BOOK 5 – ALTERNATIVE INVESTMENTS AND PORTFOLIO MANAGEMENT

SCHWESERNOTES™ 2018 LEVEL II CFA® BOOK 5: ALTERNATIVE INVESTMENTS AND PORTFOLIO MANAGEMENT

©2017 Kaplan, Inc. All rights reserved.

Published in 2017 by Kaplan, Inc.

Printed in the United States of America.

ISBN: 978-1-4754-5982-1

Getting Started

CFA®

Level II CFA® Exam

Welcome

As the VP of Advanced Designations at Kaplan Schweser, I am pleased to have the opportunity to help you prepare for the CFA® exam. Getting an early start on your study program is important for you to sufficiently **prepare**, **practice**, and **perform** on exam day. Proper planning will allow you to set aside enough time to master the Learning Outcome Statements (LOS) in the Level II curriculum.

Now that you've received your SchweserNotes™, here's how to get started:

Step 1: Access Your Online Tools

Visit **www.schweser.com** and log in to your online account using the button located in the top navigation bar. After logging in, select the appropriate level and proceed to the dashboard where you can access your online products.

Step 2: Create a Study Plan

Create a study plan with the **Study Calendar** (located on the Schweser dashboard) and familiarize yourself with your financial calculator. Check out our calculator videos in the **Candidate Resource Library** (also found on the dashboard).

Step 3: Prepare and Practice

Read your SchweserNotes™ Volumes 1–5

At the end of each reading, you can answer the Concept Checker questions for better understanding of the curriculum.

Attend a Weekly Class

Attend live classes online or take part in our live classroom courses in select cities around the world. Our expert faculty will guide you through the curriculum with a structured approach to help you prepare for the CFA® exam. The Schweser **On-Demand Video Lectures**, in combination with the **Weekly Class**, offer a blended learning approach that covers every LOS in the CFA curriculum.

Practice with SchweserPro™ QBank

Maximize your retention of important concepts by answering questions in the **SchweserPro™ QBank** and taking several **Practice Exams**. Use **Schweser's QuickSheet** for continuous review on the go. (Visit **www.schweser.com/cfa** to order.)

Step 4: Attend a 3-Day, 5-Day, or WindsorWeek™ Review Workshop

Schweser's late-season review workshops are designed to drive home the CFA® material, which is critical for CFA exam success. Review key concepts in every topic, **perform** by working through demonstration problems, and **practice** your exam techniques.

Step 5: Perform

Take a **Live** or **Live Online Schweser Mock Exam** to ensure you are ready to **perform** on the actual CFA® exam. Put your skills and knowledge to the test and gain confidence before the exam.

Again, thank you for trusting Kaplan Schweser with your CFA exam preparation!

Sincerely,

Derek Burkett

Derek Burkett, CFA, FRM, CAIA
VP, Advanced Designations, Kaplan Schweser

The Kaplan Way

Prepare
Acquire new knowledge through demonstration and examples.

Practice
Apply new knowledge through simulation and practice.

Perform
Evaluate mastery of new knowledge and identify achieved outcomes.

Visit our website,
www.schweser.com/cfa-free-resources,
to view all the free materials we have to help you prepare.

 Question of the Day

 Kaplan Schweser Adaptive CFA® Review Mobile App

 How to Pass Videos

Contact us for questions about your study package, upgrading your package, purchasing additional study materials, or for additional information:

888.325.5072 (U.S.) | +1 608.779.8327 (Int'l.)

staff@schweser.com | www.schweser.com/cfa

READINGS AND LEARNING OUTCOME STATEMENTS

READINGS

The following material is a review of the Alternative Investments and Portfolio Management principles designed to address the learning outcome statements set forth by CFA Institute.

STUDY SESSION 15

Reading Assignments

Alternative Investments and Portfolio Management, CFA Program Curriculum, Volume 6, Level II (CFA Institute, 2017)

STUDY SESSION 16

Reading Assignments

Alternative Investments and Portfolio Management, CFA Program Curriculum, Volume 6, Level II (CFA Institute, 2017)

STUDY SESSION 17

Reading Assignments

Alternative Investments and Portfolio Management, CFA Program Curriculum, Volume 6, Level II (CFA Institute, 2017)

LEARNING OUTCOME STATEMENTS (LOS)

The CFA Institute Learning Outcome Statements are listed below. These are repeated in each topic review; however, the order may have been changed in order to get a better fit with the flow of the review.

STUDY SESSION 15

The topical coverage corresponds with the following CFA Institute assigned reading:

43. Private Real Estate Investments

The candidate should be able to:

a. classify and describe basic forms of real estate investments. (page 1)
b. describe the characteristics, the classification, and basic segments of real estate. (page 2)
c. explain the role in a portfolio, economic value determinants, investment characteristics, and principal risks of private real estate. (page 4)
d. describe commercial property types, including their distinctive investment characteristics. (page 6)
e. compare the income, cost, and sales comparison approaches to valuing real estate properties. (page 7)
f. estimate and interpret the inputs (for example, net operating income, capitalization rate, and discount rate) to the direct capitalization and discounted cash flow valuation methods. (page 9)
g. calculate the value of a property using the direct capitalization and discounted cash flow valuation methods. (page 9)
h. compare the direct capitalization and discounted cash flow valuation methods. (page 17)
i. calculate the value of a property using the cost and sales comparison approaches. (page 18)
j. describe due diligence in private equity real estate investment. (page 23)
k. discuss private equity real estate investment indexes, including their construction and potential biases. (page 23)
l. explain the role in a portfolio, the major economic value determinants, investment characteristics, principal risks, and due diligence of private real estate debt investment. (page 4)
m. calculate and interpret financial ratios used to analyze and evaluate private real estate investments. (page 24)

The topical coverage corresponds with the following CFA Institute assigned reading:

44. Publicly Traded Real Estate Securities

The candidate should be able to:

a. describe types of publicly traded real estate securities. (page 34)
b. explain advantages and disadvantages of investing in real estate through publicly traded securities. (page 35)
c. explain economic value determinants, investment characteristics, principal risks, and due diligence considerations for real estate investment trust (REIT) shares. (page 37)
d. describe types of REITs. (page 39)

e. Justify the use of net asset value per share (NAVPS) in REIT valuation and estimate NAVPS based on forecasted cash net operating income. (page 43)

f. describe the use of funds from operations (FFO) and adjusted funds from operations (AFFO) in REIT valuation. (page 46)

g. compare the net asset value, relative value (price-to-FFO and price-to-AFFO), and discounted cash flow approaches to REIT valuation. (page 47)

h. calculate the value of a REIT share using net asset value, price-to-FFO and price-to-AFFO, and discounted cash flow approaches. (page 48)

The topical coverage corresponds with the following CFA Institute assigned reading:
45. Private Equity Valuation
The candidate should be able to:

a. explain sources of value creation in private equity. (page 62)

b. explain how private equity firms align their interests with those of the managers of portfolio companies. (page 63)

c. distinguish between the characteristics of buyout and venture capital investments. (page 64)

d. describe valuation issues in buyout and venture capital transactions. (page 68)

e. explain alternative exit routes in private equity and their impact on value. (page 72)

f. explain private equity fund structures, terms, valuation, and due diligence in the context of an analysis of private equity fund returns. (page 73)

g. explain risks and costs of investing in private equity. (page 78)

h. Interpret and compare financial performance of private equity funds from the perspective of an investor. (page 80)

i. calculate management fees, carried interest, net asset value, distributed to paid in (DPI), residual value to paid in (RVPI), and total value to paid in (TVPI) of a private equity fund. (page 83)

j. calculate pre-money valuation, post-money valuation, ownership fraction, and price per share applying the venture capital method 1) with single and multiple financing rounds and 2) in terms of IRR. (page 85)

k. demonstrate alternative methods to account for risk in venture capital. (page 90)

The topical coverage corresponds with the following CFA Institute assigned reading:
46. Commodities and Commodity Derivatives: An Introduction
The candidate should be able to:

a. compare characteristics of commodity sectors. (page 109)

b. compare the life cycle of commodity sectors from production through trading or consumption. (page 111)

c. contrast the valuation of commodities with the valuation of equities and bonds. (page 112)

d. describe types of participants in commodity futures markets. (page 113)

e. Analyze the relationship between spot prices and expected future prices in markets in contango and markets in backwardation. (page 114)

f. compare theories of commodity futures returns. (page 114)

g. describe, calculate, and interpret the components of total return for a fully collateralized commodity futures contract. (page 116)

h. contrast roll return in markets in contango and markets in backwardation. (page 117)

i. describe how commodity swaps are used to obtain or modify exposure to commodities. (page 117)

j. describe how the construction of commodity indexes affects index returns. (page 119)

STUDY SESSION 16

The topical coverage corresponds with the following CFA Institute assigned reading:

47. The Portfolio Management Process and the Investment Policy Statement

The candidate should be able to:

a. explain the importance of the portfolio perspective. (page 130)

b. describe the steps of the portfolio management process and the components of those steps. (page 130)

c. explain the role of the investment policy statement in the portfolio management process and describe the elements of an investment policy statement. (page 131)

d. explain how capital market expectations and the investment policy statement help influence the strategic asset allocation decision and how an investor's investment time horizon may influence the investor's strategic asset allocation. (page 131)

e. define investment objectives and constraints and explain and distinguish among the types of investment objectives and constraints. (page 132)

f. contrast the types of investment time horizons, determine the time horizon for a particular investor, and evaluate the effects of this time horizon on portfolio choice. (page 136)

g. Justify ethical conduct as a requirement for managing investment portfolios. (page 137)

The topical coverage corresponds with the following CFA Institute assigned reading:

48. An Introduction to Multifactor Models

The candidate should be able to:

a. describe arbitrage pricing theory (APT), including its underlying assumptions and its relation to multifactor models. (page 144)

b. define arbitrage opportunity and determine whether an arbitrage opportunity exists. (page 145)

c. calculate the expected return on an asset given an asset's factor sensitivities and the factor risk premiums. (page 146)

d. describe and compare macroeconomic factor models, fundamental factor models, and statistical factor models. (page 148)

e. explain sources of active risk and interpret tracking risk and the information ratio. (page 153)

f. describe uses of multifactor models and interpret the output of analyses based on multifactor models. (page 155)

g. describe the potential benefits for investors in considering multiple risk dimensions when modeling asset returns. (page 160)

The topical coverage corresponds with the following CFA Institute assigned reading:

49. Measuring and Managing Market Risk

The candidate should be able to:

a. explain the use of value at risk (VaR) in measuring portfolio risk. (page 167)

b. compare the parametric (variance–covariance), historical simulation, and Monte Carlo simulation methods for estimating VaR. (page 168)

c. estimate and interpret VaR under the parametric, historical simulation, and Monte Carlo simulation methods. (page 168)

d. describe advantages and limitations of VaR. (page 171)

e. describe extensions of VaR. (page 172)

f.   describe sensitivity risk measures and scenario risk measures and compare these measures to VaR. (page 173)

g.   demonstrate how equity, fixed-income, and options exposure measures may be used in measuring and managing market risk and volatility risk. (page 173)

h.   describe the use of sensitivity risk measures and scenario risk measures. (page 174)

i.   describe advantages and limitations of sensitivity risk measures and scenario risk measures. (page 176)

j.   describe risk measures used by banks, asset managers, pension funds, and insurers. (page 176)

k.   explain constraints used in managing market risks, including risk budgeting, position limits, scenario limits, and stop-loss limits. (page 178)

l.   explain how risk measures may be used in capital allocation decisions. (page 179)

STUDY SESSION 17

The topical coverage corresponds with the following CFA Institute assigned reading:

50. Economics and Investment Markets

The candidate should be able to:

a.   explain the notion that to affect market values, economic factors must affect one or more of the following: 1) default-free interest rates across maturities, 2) the timing and/or magnitude of expected cash flows, and 3) risk premiums. (page 186)

b.   explain the role of expectations and changes in expectations in market valuation. (page 186)

c.   explain the relationship between the long-term growth rate of the economy, the volatility of the growth rate, and the average level of real short-term interest rates. (page 187)

d.   explain how the phase of the business cycle affects policy and short-term interest rates, the slope of the term structure of interest rates, and the relative performance of bonds of differing maturities. (page 189)

e.   describe the factors that affect yield spreads between non-inflation-adjusted and inflation-indexed bonds. (page 190)

f.   explain how the phase of the business cycle affects credit spreads and the performance of credit-sensitive fixed-income instruments. (page 191)

g.   explain how the characteristics of the markets for a company's products affect the company's credit quality. (page 191)

h.   explain how the phase of the business cycle affects short-term and long-term earnings growth expectations. (page 192)

i.   explain the relationship between the consumption-hedging properties of equity and the equity risk premium. (page 192)

j.   describe cyclical effects on valuation multiples. (page 192)

k.   describe the implications of the business cycle for a given style strategy (value, growth, small capitalization, large capitalization). (page 193)

l.   describe how economic analysis is used in sector rotation strategies. (page 193)

m.   describe the economic factors affecting investment in commercial real estate. (page 194)

The topical coverage corresponds with the following CFA Institute assigned reading:

51. Analysis of Active Portfolio Management

The candidate should be able to:

a. describe how value added by active management is measured. (page 200)

b. calculate and interpret the information ratio (ex post and ex ante) and contrast it to the Sharpe ratio. (page 203)

c. State and interpret the fundamental law of active portfolio management including its component terms—transfer coefficient, information coefficient, breadth, and active risk (aggressiveness). (page 206)

d. explain how the information ratio may be useful in investment manager selection and choosing the level of active portfolio risk. (page 208)

e. compare active management strategies (including market timing and security selection) and evaluate strategy changes in terms of the fundamental law of active management. (page 208)

f. describe the practical strengths and limitations of the fundamental law of active management. (page 211)

The topical coverage corresponds with the following CFA Institute assigned reading:

52. Algorithmic Trading and High-Frequency Trading

The candidate should be able to:

a. define algorithmic trading. (page 216)

b. distinguish between execution algorithms and high-frequency trading algorithms. (page 216)

c. describe types of execution algorithms and high-frequency trading algorithms. (page 217)

d. describe market fragmentation and its effects on how trades are placed. (page 219)

e. describe the use of technology in risk management and regulatory oversight. (page 220)

f. describe issues and concerns related to the impact of algorithmic and high-frequency trading on securities markets. (page 221)

Private Real Estate Investments

Exam Focus

This topic review concentrates on valuation of real estate. The focus is on the three valuation approaches used for appraisal purposes, especially the income approach. Make sure you can calculate the value of a property using the direct capitalization method and the discounted cash flow method. Make certain you understand the relationship between the capitalization rate and the discount rate. Finally, understand the investment characteristics and risks involved with real estate investments.

LOS 43.a: Classify and describe basic forms of real estate investments.

CFA® Program Curriculum, Volume 6, page 7

Forms of Real Estate

There are four basic forms of real estate investment that can be described in terms of a two-dimensional quadrant. In the first dimension, the investment can be described in terms of public or private markets. In the private market, ownership usually involves a direct investment like purchasing property or lending money to a purchaser. Direct investments can be solely owned or indirectly owned through partnerships or **commingled real estate funds** (CREF). The public market does not involve direct investment; rather, ownership involves securities that serve as claims on the underlying assets. Public real estate investment includes ownership of a **real estate investment trust** (REIT), a **real estate operating company** (REOC), and mortgage-backed securities.

The second dimension describes whether an investment involves debt or equity. An equity investor has an ownership interest in real estate or securities of an entity that owns real estate. Equity investors control decisions such as borrowing money, property management, and the exit strategy.

A debt investor is a lender that owns a mortgage or mortgage securities. Usually, the mortgage is collateralized (secured) by the underlying real estate. In this case, the lender has a superior claim over an equity investor in the event of default. Since the lender must be repaid first, the value of an equity investor's interest is equal to the value of the property less the outstanding debt.

Each of the basic forms has its own risk, expected returns, regulations, legal issues, and market structure.

Private real estate investments are usually larger than public investments because real estate is indivisible and illiquid. Public real estate investments allow the property to remain undivided while allowing investors divided ownership. As a result, public real estate investments are more liquid and enable investors to diversify by participating in more properties.

Real estate must be actively managed. Private real estate investment requires property management expertise on the part of the owner or a property management company. In the case of a REIT or REOC, the real estate is professionally managed; thus, investors need no property management expertise.

Equity investors usually require a higher rate of return than mortgage lenders because of higher risk. As previously discussed, lenders have a superior claim in the event of default. As financial leverage (use of debt financing) increases, return requirements of both lenders and equity investors increase as a result of higher risk.

Typically, lenders expect to receive returns from promised cash flows and do not participate in the appreciation of the underlying property. Equity investors expect to receive an income stream as a result of renting the property and the appreciation of value over time.

Figure 1 summarizes the basic forms of real estate investment and can be used to identify the investment that best meets an investor's objectives.

Figure 1: Basic Forms of Real Estate Investment

	Debt	Equity
Private	Mortgages	Direct investments such as sole ownership, partnerships, and other forms of commingled funds
Public	Mortgage-backed securities	Shares of REITs and REOCs

LOS 43.b: Describe the characteristics, the classification, and basic segments of real estate.

CFA® Program Curriculum, Volume 6, page 9

REAL ESTATE CHARACTERISTICS

Real estate investment differs from other asset classes, like stocks and bonds, and can complicate measurement and performance assessment.

- **Heterogeneity.** Bonds from a particular issue are alike, as are stocks of a specific company. However, no two properties are exactly the same because of location, size, age, construction materials, tenants, and lease terms.
- **High unit value.** Because real estate is indivisible, the unit value is significantly higher than stocks and bonds, which makes it difficult to construct a diversified portfolio.

- **Active management.** Investors in stocks and bonds are not necessarily involved in the day-to-day management of the companies. Private real estate investment requires active property management by the owner or a property management company. Property management involves maintenance, negotiating leases, and collection of rents. In either case, property management costs must be considered.
- **High transaction costs.** Buying and selling real estate is costly because it involves appraisers, lawyers, brokers, and construction personnel.
- **Depreciation and desirability.** Buildings wear out over time. Also, buildings may become less desirable because of location, design, or obsolescence.
- **Cost and availability of debt capital.** Because of the high costs to acquire and develop real estate, property values are impacted by the level of interest rates and availability of debt capital. Real estate values are usually lower when interest rates are high and debt capital is scarce.
- **Lack of liquidity.** Real estate is illiquid. It takes time to market and complete the sale of property.
- **Difficulty in determining price.** Stocks and bonds of public firms usually trade in active markets. However, because of heterogeneity and low transaction volume, appraisals are usually necessary to assess real estate values. Even then, appraised values are often based on similar, not identical, properties. The combination of limited market participants and lack of knowledge of the local markets makes it difficult for an outsider to value property. As a result, the market is less efficient. However, investors with superior information and skill may have an advantage in exploiting the market inefficiencies.

The market for REITs has expanded to overcome many of the problems involved with direct investment. Shares of a REIT are actively traded and are more likely to reflect market value. In addition, investing in a REIT can provide exposure to a diversified real estate portfolio. Finally, investors don't need property management expertise because the REIT manages the properties.

PROPERTY CLASSIFICATIONS

Real estate is commonly classified as residential or non-residential. Residential real estate includes single-family (owner-occupied) homes and multi-family properties, such as apartments. Residential real estate purchased with the intent to produce income is usually considered commercial real estate property.

Non-residential real estate includes commercial properties, other than multi-family properties, and other properties such as farmland and timberland.

Commercial real estate is usually classified by its end use and includes multi-family, office, industrial/warehouse, retail, hospitality, and other types of properties such as parking facilities, restaurants, and recreational properties. A *mixed-use development* is a property that serves more than one end user.

Some commercial properties require more management attention than others. For example, of all the commercial property types, hotels require the most day-to-day attention and are more like operating a business. Because of higher operational risk, investors require higher rates of return on management-intensive properties.

Farmland and timberland are unique categories (separate from commercial real estate classification) because each can produce a saleable commodity as well as have the potential for capital appreciation.

LOS 43.c: Explain the role in a portfolio, economic value determinants, investment characteristics, and principal risks of private real estate.

LOS 43.l: Explain the role in a portfolio, the major economic value determinants, investment characteristics, principal risks, and due diligence of private real estate debt investment.

CFA® Program Curriculum, Volume 6, pages 13 and 61

REASONS TO INVEST IN REAL ESTATE

Current income. Investors may expect to earn income from collecting rents and after paying operating expenses, financing costs, and taxes.

Capital appreciation. Investors usually expect property values to increase over time, which forms part of their total return.

Inflation hedge. During inflation, investors expect both rents and property values to rise.

Diversification. Real estate, especially private equity investment, is less than perfectly correlated with the returns of stocks and bonds. Thus, adding private real estate investment to a portfolio can reduce risk relative to the expected return.

Tax benefits. In some countries, real estate investors receive favorable tax treatment. For example, in the United States, the depreciable life of real estate is usually shorter than the actual life. As a result, depreciation expense is higher, and taxable income is lower resulting in lower income taxes. Also, REITs do not pay taxes in some countries, which allow investors to escape double taxation (e.g., taxation at the corporate level and the individual level).

PRINCIPAL RISKS

Business conditions. Numerous economic factors—such as gross domestic product (GDP), employment, household income, interest rates, and inflation—affect the rental market.

New property lead time. Market conditions can change significantly while approvals are obtained, while the property is completed, and when the property is fully leased. During the lead time, if market conditions weaken, the resultant lower demand affects rents and vacancy resulting in lower returns.

Cost and availability of capital. Real estate must compete with other investments for capital. As previously discussed, demand for real estate is reduced when debt capital is scarce and interest rates are high. Conversely, demand is higher when debt capital is easily obtained and interest rates are low. Thus, real estate prices can be affected by capital market forces without changes in demand from tenants.

Unexpected inflation. Some leases provide inflation protection by allowing owners to increase rent or pass through expenses because of inflation. Real estate values may not keep up with inflation when markets are weak and vacancy rates are high.

Demographic factors. The demand for real estate is affected by the size and age distribution of the local market population, the distribution of socioeconomic groups, and new household formation rates.

Lack of liquidity. Because of the size and complexity of most real estate transactions, buyers and lenders usually perform due diligence, which takes time and is costly. A quick sale will typically require a significant discount.

Environmental issues. Real estate values can be significantly reduced when a property has been contaminated by a prior owner or adjacent property owner.

Availability of information. A lack of information when performing property analysis increases risk. The availability of data depends on the country, but generally more information is available as real estate investments become more global.

Management expertise. Property managers and asset managers must make important operational decisions—such as negotiating leases, property maintenance, marketing, and renovating the property—when necessary.

Leverage. The use of debt (leverage) to finance a real estate purchase is measured by the loan-to-value (LTV) ratio. Higher LTV results in higher leverage and, thus, higher risk because lenders have a superior claim in the event of default. With leverage, a small decrease in net operating income (NOI) negatively magnifies the amount of cash flow available to equity investors after debt service.

Other factors. Other risk factors, such as unobserved property defects, natural disasters, and acts of terrorism, may be unidentified at the time of purchase.

In some cases, risks that can be identified can be hedged using insurance. In other cases, risk can be shifted to the tenants. For example, a lease agreement could require the tenant to reimburse any unexpected operating expenses.

The Role of Real Estate in a Portfolio

Real estate investment has both bond-like and stock-like characteristics. Leases are contractual agreements that usually call for periodic rental payments, similar to the coupon payments of a bond. When a lease expires, there is uncertainty regarding renewal and future rental rates. This uncertainty is affected by the availability of competing space, tenant profitability, and the state of the overall economy, just as stock prices are affected by the same factors. As a result, the risk/return profile of real estate as an asset class, is usually between the risk/return profiles of stocks and bonds.

Role of Leverage in Real Estate Investment

So far, our discussion of valuation has ignored debt financing. Earlier we determined that the level of interest rates and the availability of debt capital impact real estate prices. However, the percentage of debt and equity used by an investor to finance real estate does not affect the property's value.

Investors use debt financing (leverage) to increase returns. As long as the investment return is greater than the interest paid to lenders, there is positive leverage and returns are magnified. Of course, leverage can also work in reverse. Because of the greater uncertainty involved with debt financing, risk is higher since lenders have a superior claim to cash flow.

LOS 43.d: Describe commercial property types, including their distinctive investment characteristics.

CFA® Program Curriculum, Volume 6, page 19

Commercial Property Types

The basic property types used to create a low-risk portfolio include office, industrial/warehouse, retail, and multi-family. Some investors include hospitality properties (hotels and motels) even though the properties are considered riskier since leases are not involved and performance is highly correlated with the business cycle.

It is important to know that with all property types, location is critical in determining value.

Office. Demand is heavily dependent on job growth, especially in industries that are heavy users of office space like finance and insurance. The average length of office leases varies globally.

In a *gross lease*, the owner is responsible for the operating expenses, and in a *net lease*, the tenant is responsible. In a net lease, the tenant bears the risk if the actual operating expenses are greater than expected. As a result, rent under a net lease is lower than a gross lease.

Some leases combine features from both gross and net leases. For example, the owner might pay the operating expenses in the first year of the lease. Thereafter, any increase in the expenses is passed through to the tenant. In a multi-tenant building, the expenses are usually prorated based on square footage.

Understanding how leases are structured is imperative in analyzing real estate investments.

Industrial. Demand is heavily dependent on the overall economy. Demand is also affected by import/export activity of the economy. Net leases are common.

Retail. Demand is heavily dependent on consumer spending. Consumer spending is affected by the overall economy, job growth, population growth, and savings rates. Retail lease terms vary by the quality of the property as well as the size and importance of the tenant. For example, an anchor tenant may receive favorable lease terms to attract them to the property. In turn, the anchor tenant will draw other tenants to the property.

Retail tenants are often required to pay additional rent once sales reach a certain level. This unique feature is known as a *percentage lease* or *percentage rent*. Accordingly, the lease will specify a minimum amount of rent to be paid without regard to sales. The minimum rent also serves as the starting point for calculating the percentage rent.

For example, suppose that a retail lease specifies minimum rent of $20 per square foot plus 5% of sales over $400 per square foot. If sales were $400 per square foot, the minimum rent and percentage rent would be equivalent ($400 sales per square foot × 5% = $20 per square foot). In this case, $400 is known as the natural breakpoint. If sales are $500 per square foot, rent per square foot is equal to $25 [$20 minimum rent + $5 percentage rent ($500 – $400) × 5%]. Alternatively, rent per square foot is equal to $500 sales per square foot × 5% = $25 because of the natural breakpoint.

Multi-family. Demand depends on population growth, especially in the age demographic that typically rents apartments. The age demographic can vary by country, type of property, and locale. Demand is also affected by the cost of buying versus the cost of renting, which is measured by the ratio of home prices to rents. As home prices rise, there is a shift toward renting. An increase in interest rates will also make buying more expensive.

LOS 43.e: Compare the income, cost, and sales comparison approaches to valuing real estate properties.

CFA® Program Curriculum, Volume 6, page 25

REAL ESTATE APPRAISALS

Since commercial real estate transactions are infrequent, appraisals are used to estimate value or assess changes in value over time in order to measure performance. In most cases, the focus of an appraisal is *market value*; that is, the most probable sales price a typical investor is willing to pay. Other definitions of value include *investment value*, → for a particular investor value the value or worth that considers a particular investor's motivations; *value in use*, the value to a particular user such as a manufacturer that is using the property as a part of its business; and *assessed* value that is used by a taxing authority. For purposes of valuing collateral, lenders sometimes use a more conservative *mortgage lending value*.

for ex. Banks

Valuation Approaches

Appraisers use three different approaches to value real estate: the cost approach, the sales comparison approach, and the income approach.

The premise of the *cost approach* is that a buyer would not pay more for a property than it would cost to purchase land and construct a comparable building. Consequently, under the cost approach, value is derived by adding the value of the land to the current replacement cost of a new building less adjustments for estimated depreciation and obsolescence. Because of the difficulty in measuring depreciation and obsolescence, the cost approach is most useful when the subject property is relatively new. The cost approach is often used for unusual properties or properties where comparable transactions are limited.

The premise of the *sales comparison approach* is that a buyer would pay no more for a property than others are paying for similar properties. With the sales comparison approach, the sale prices of similar (comparable) properties are adjusted for differences with the subject property. The sales comparison approach is most useful when there are a number of properties similar to the subject that have recently sold, as is usually the case with single-family homes.

The premise of the *income approach* is that value is based on the expected rate of return required by a buyer to invest in the subject property. With the income approach, value is equal to the present value of the subject's future cash flows. The income approach is most useful in commercial real estate transactions.

Highest and Best Use

The concept of highest and best use is important in determining value. The highest and best use of a vacant site is not necessarily the use that results in the highest total value once a project is completed. Rather, the highest and best use of a vacant site is the use that produces the highest implied land value. The implied land value is equal to the value of the property once construction is completed less the cost of constructing the improvements, including profit to the developer to handle construction and lease-out.

> **Example: Highest and best use**
>
> An investor is considering a site to build either an apartment building or a shopping center. Once construction is complete, the apartment building would have an estimated value of €50 million and the shopping center would have an estimated value of €40 million. Construction costs, including developer profit, are estimated at €45 million for the apartment building and €34 million for the shopping center. Calculate the highest and best use of the site.

©2017 Kaplan, Inc.

Answer:

The shopping center is the highest and best use for the site because the €6 million implied land value of the shopping center is higher than the €5 million implied land value of the apartment building as follows:

	Apartment Building	Shopping Center
Value when completed	€50,000,000	€40,000,000
Less: Construction costs	45,000,000	34,000,000
Implied land value	€5,000,000	€6,000,000

Note that the highest and best use is not based on the highest value when the projects are completed but, rather, the highest implied land value.

LOS 43.f: Estimate and interpret the inputs (for example, net operating income, capitalization rate, and discount rate) to the direct capitalization and discounted cash flow valuation methods.

LOS 43.g: Calculate the value of a property using the direct capitalization and discounted cash flow valuation methods.

CFA® Program Curriculum, Volume 6, pages 27 and 29

INCOME APPROACH

The income approach includes two different valuation methods: the direct capitalization method and the discounted cash flow method. With the *direct capitalization method*, value is based on capitalizing the first year NOI of the property using a capitalization rate. With the *discounted cash flow method*, value is based on the present value of the property's future cash flows using an appropriate discount rate.

Value is based on NOI under both methods. As shown in Figure 2, NOI is the amount of income remaining after subtracting vacancy and collection losses, and operating expenses (e.g., insurance, property taxes, utilities, maintenance, and repairs) from potential gross income. NOI is calculated before subtracting financing costs and income taxes.

Figure 2: Net Operating Income

```
    Rental income if fully occupied
  + Other income
  = Potential gross income
  - Vacancy and collection loss
  = Effective gross income
  - Operating expense
  = Net operating income
```

Example: Net operating income

Calculate net operating income (NOI) using the following information:

Property type	Office building
Property size	200,000 square feet
Gross rental income	€25 per square foot
Other income	€75,000
Vacancy and collection loss	5% of potential gross income
Property taxes and insurance	€350,000
Utilities and maintenance	€875,000
X Interest expense	€400,000
X Income tax rate	40%

NO

Answer:

Gross rental income	€5,000,000 [200,000 SF × €25]
Other income	75,000
Potential gross income	€5,075,000
Vacancy and collection losses	(253,750)[5,075,000 × 5%]
Operating expenses	(1,225,000)[350,000 + 875,000]
Net operating income	€3,596,250

Note that interest expense and income taxes are not considered operating expenses.

The Capitalization Rate

The **capitalization rate**, or cap rate, and the discount rate are not the same rate although they are related. The discount rate is the required rate of return; that is, the risk-free rate plus a risk premium.

ONLY

The cap rate is applied to first-year NOI, and the discount rate is applied to first-year and future NOI. So, if NOI and value is expected to grow at a constant rate, the cap rate is lower than the discount rate as follows:

$$\text{cap rate} = \text{discount rate} - \text{growth rate}$$

NOI if it is expected to grow at constant Rate

Using the previous formula, we can say the growth rate is implicitly included in the cap rate.

The cap rate can be defined as the current yield on the investment as follows:

$$\text{cap rate} = \frac{NOI_1}{\text{value}}$$

Since the cap rate is based on first-year NOI, it is sometimes called the *going-in cap rate.*

By rearranging the previous formula, we can now solve for value as follows:

$$\text{value} = V_0 = \frac{NOI_1}{\text{cap rate}}$$

If the cap rate is unknown, it can be derived from recent comparable transactions as follows:

$$\text{cap rate} = \frac{\text{NOI}_1}{\text{comparable sales price}} \text{(Value)}$$

It is important to observe several comparable transactions when deriving the cap rate. Implicit in the cap rate derived from comparable transactions are investors' expectations of income growth and risk. In this case, the cap rate is similar to the reciprocal of the price-earnings multiple for equity securities.

Example: Valuation using the direct capitalization method

Suppose that net operating income for an office building is expected to be $175,000, and an appropriate cap rate is 8%. Estimate the market value of the property using the direct capitalization method.

Answer:

The estimated market value is:

$$\text{Cap} = \frac{\text{NOI}}{\text{Value}} \%$$

$$V_0 = \frac{\text{NOI}_1}{\text{cap rate}} = \frac{\$175,000}{8\%} = \$2,187,500$$

When tenants are required to pay all expenses, the cap rate can be applied to rent instead of NOI. Dividing rent by comparable sales price gives us the *all risks yield* (ARY). In this case, the ARY is the cap rate and will differ from the discount rate if an investor expects growth in rents and value.

Net lease

→ No Operating Expenses and No collection loss and Vacancy loss

$$\text{value} = V_0 = \frac{\text{rent}_1}{\text{ARY}}$$

All Risk Yield

If rents are expected to increase at a constant rate each year, the internal rate of return (IRR) can be approximated by summing the cap rate and growth rate.

Stabilized NOI

Recall the cap rate is applied to first-year NOI. If NOI is not representative of the NOI of similar properties because of a temporary issue, the subject property's NOI should be stabilized. For example, suppose a property is temporarily experiencing high vacancy during a major renovation. In this case, the first-year NOI should be stabilized; NOI should be calculated as if the renovation is complete. Once the stabilized NOI is capitalized, the loss in value, as a result of the temporary decline in NOI, is subtracted in arriving at the value of the property.

Example: Valuation during renovation

On January 1 of this year, renovation began on a shopping center. This year, NOI is forecasted at €6 million. Absent renovations, NOI would have been €10 million. After this year, NOI is expected to increase 4% annually. Assuming all renovations are completed by the seller at their expense, estimate the value of the shopping center as of the beginning of this year assuming investors require a 12% rate of return.

Answer:

The value of the shopping center after renovation is:

$$\frac{\text{stabilized NOI}}{\text{cap rate}} = \frac{10{,}000{,}000}{(12\% - 4\%)} = €125{,}000{,}000$$

Using our financial calculator, the present value of the temporary decline in NOI during renovation is:

N = 1; I/Y = 12, PMT = 0; FV = 4,000,000; CPT → PV = €3,571,429

(In the previous computation, we are assuming that all rent is received at the end of the year for simplicity).

The total value of the shopping center is:

Value after renovations	€125,000,000
Loss in value during renovations	(3,571,429)
Total value	€121,428,571

The gross income multiplier, another form of direct capitalization, is the ratio of the sales price to the property's expected gross income in the year after purchase. The gross income multiplier can be derived from comparable transactions just like we did earlier with cap rates.

$$\text{gross income multiplier} = \frac{\text{sales price}}{\text{gross income}}$$

Once we obtain the gross income multiplier, value is estimated as a multiple of a subject property's estimated gross income as follows:

value = gross income × gross income multiplier

A shortfall of the gross income multiplier is that it ignores vacancy rates and operating expenses. Thus, if the subject property's vacancy rate and operating expenses are higher than those of the comparable transactions, an investor will pay more for the same rent.

Discounted Cash Flow Method

Recall from our earlier discussion, we determined the growth rate is implicitly included in the cap rate as follows:

cap rate = discount rate – growth rate

Rearranging the above formula we get:

discount rate = cap rate + growth rate

So, we can say the investor's rate of return includes the return on first-year NOI (measured by the cap rate) and the growth in income and value over time (measured by the growth rate).

$$\text{value} = V_0 = \frac{NOI_1}{(r-g)} = \frac{NOI_1}{\text{cap rate}}$$

where:
r = rate required by equity investors for similar properties
g = growth rate of NOI (assumed to be constant)
r – g = cap rate

 *Professor's Note: This equation should look very familiar to you because it's just a modified version of the constant growth dividend discount model, also known as the Gordon growth model, from the equity valuation portion of the curriculum.*

If no growth is expected in NOI, then the cap rate and the discount rate are the same. In this case, value is calculated just like any perpetuity.

$$\frac{NOI}{r}$$

Terminal Cap Rate

Using the discounted cash flow (DCF) method, investors usually project NOI for a specific holding period and the property value at the end of the holding period rather than projecting NOI into infinity. Unfortunately, estimating the property value at the end of the holding period, known as the *terminal value* (also known as *reversion* or *resale*), is challenging. However, since the terminal value is just the present value of the NOI received by the next investor, we can use the direct capitalization method to estimate the value of the property when sold. In this case, we need to estimate the future NOI and a future cap rate, known as the *terminal* or *residual cap rate*.

The terminal cap rate is not necessarily the same as the going-in cap rate. The terminal cap rate could be higher if interest rates are expected to increase in the future or if the growth rate is projected to be lower because the property would then be older and might be less competitive. Also, uncertainty about future NOI may result in a higher terminal cap rate. The terminal cap rate could be lower if interest rates are expected to be lower or if rental income growth is projected to be higher. These relationships are easily mastered using the formula presented earlier (cap rate = discount rate – growth rate).

Since the terminal value occurs in the future, it must be discounted to present. Thus, the value of the property is equal to the present value of NOI over the holding period and the present value of the terminal value.

Example: Valuation with terminal value

Because of existing leases, the NOI of a warehouse is expected to be $1 million per year over the next four years. Beginning in the fifth year, NOI is expected to increase to $1.2 million and grow at 3% annually thereafter. Assuming investors require a 13% return, calculate the value of the property today assuming the warehouse is sold after four years.

Answer:

Using our financial calculator, the present value of the NOI over the holding period is:

N = 4; I/Y = 13, PMT = 1,000,000; FV = 0; CPT → PV = $2,974,471

The terminal value after four years is:

$$V_4 = \frac{NOI_5}{cap\ rate} = \frac{\$1,200,000}{(13\% - 3\%)} = \$12,000,000$$

The present value of the terminal value is:

N = 4; I/Y = 13, PMT = 0; FV = 12,000,000; CPT → PV = $7,359,825

The total value of the warehouse today is:

PV of forecast NOI	$2,974,471
PV of terminal value	7,359,825
Total value	$10,334,296

Note: We can combine the present value calculations as follows:

N = 4; I/Y = 13, PMT = 1,000,000; FV = 12,000,000; CPT → PV = $10,334,296

Valuation with Different Lease Structures

Lease structures can vary by country. For example, in the U.K., it is common for tenants to pay all expenses. In this case, the cap rate is known as the ARY as discussed earlier. Adjustments must be made when the contract rent (passing or term rent) and the current market rent (open market rent) differ. Once the lease expires, rent will likely be adjusted to the current market rent. In the U.K. the property is said to have *reversionary potential* when the contract rent expires.

One way of dealing with the problem is known as the *term and reversion approach* whereby the contract (term) rent and the reversion are appraised separately using different cap rates. The reversion cap rate is derived from comparable, fully let,

©2017 Kaplan, Inc.

properties. Because the reversion occurs in the future, it must be discounted to present. The discount rate applied to the contract rent will likely be lower than the reversion rate because the contract rent is less risky (the existing tenants are not likely to default on a below-market lease).

Example: Term and Reversion Valuation Approach

A single-tenant office building was leased six years ago at £200,000 per year. The next rent review occurs in two years. The estimated rental value (ERV) in two years based on current market conditions is £300,000 per year. The all risks yield (cap rate) for comparable fully let properties is 7%. Because of lower risk, the appropriate rate to discount the term rent is 6%. Estimate the value of the office building.

Answer:

Using our financial calculator, the present value of the term rent is:

N = 2; I/Y = 6, PMT = 200,000; FV = 0; CPT → PV = £366,679

The value of reversion to ERV is:

$$V_2 = \frac{ERV_3}{ERV \text{ cap rate}} = \frac{300,000}{7\%} = £4,285,714$$

The present value of the reversion to ERV is:

N = 2; I/Y = 7, PMT = 0; FV = 4,285,714; CPT → PV = £3,743,309

The total value of the office building today is:

PV of term rent	£366,679
PV of reversion to ERV	£3,743,309
Total value	£4,109,988

Except for the differences in terminology and the use of different cap rates for the term rent and reversion to current market rents, the term and reversion approach is similar to the valuation example using a terminal value.

A variation of the term and reversion approach is the *layer method*. With the layer method, one source (layer) of income is the contract (term) rent that is assumed to continue in perpetuity. The second layer is the increase in rent that occurs when the lease expires and the rent is reviewed. A cap rate similar to the ARY is applied to the term rent because the term rent is less risky. A higher cap rate is applied to the incremental income that occurs as a result of the rent review.

Example: Layer method

Let's return to the example that we used to illustrate the term and reversion valuation approach. Suppose the contract (term) rent is discounted at 7%, and the incremental rent is discounted at 8%. Calculate the value of the office building today using the layer method.

Answer:

The value of term rent (bottom layer) into perpetuity is:

$$\frac{\text{term rent}}{\text{term rent cap rate}} = \frac{200,000}{7\%} = £2,857,143$$

The value of incremental rent into perpetuity (at time t = 2) is:

$$\frac{\text{ERV}}{\text{ERV cap rate}} = \frac{(300,000 - 200,000)}{8\%} = £1,250,000$$

Using our financial calculator, the present value of the incremental rent (top layer) into perpetuity is:

N = 2; I/Y = 8, PMT = 0; FV = 1,250,000; CPT → PV = £1,071,674

The total value of the office building today is:

PV of term rent	£2,857,143
PV of incremental rent	1,071,674
Total value	£3,928,817

Using the term and reversion approach and the layer method, different cap rates were applied to the term rent and the current market rent after review. Alternatively, a single discount rate, known as the *equivalent yield*, could have been used. The equivalent yield is an average, although not a simple average, of the two separate cap rates.

Using the discounted cash flow method requires the following estimates and assumptions, especially for properties with many tenants and complicated lease structures:

- *Project income from existing leases.* It is necessary to track the start and end dates and the various components of each lease, such as base rent, index adjustments, and expense reimbursements from tenants.
- *Lease renewal assumptions.* May require estimating the probability of renewal.
- *Operating expense assumptions.* Operating expenses can be classified as fixed, variable, or a hybrid of the two. Variable expenses vary with occupancy, while fixed expenses do not. Fixed expenses can change because of inflation.
- *Capital expenditure assumptions.* Expenditures for capital improvements, such as roof replacement, renovation, and tenant finish-out, are lumpy; that is, they do not occur evenly over time. Consequently, some appraisers average the capital expenditures and deduct a portion each year instead of deducting the entire amount when paid.

- *Vacancy assumptions.* It is necessary to estimate how long before currently vacant space is leased.
- *Estimated resale price.* A holding period that extends beyond the existing leases should be chosen. This will make it easier to estimate the resale price because all leases will reflect current market rents.
- *Appropriate discount rate.* The discount rate is not directly observable, but some analysts use buyer surveys as a guide. The discount rate should be higher than the mortgage rate because of more risk and should reflect the riskiness of the investment relative to other alternatives.

Example: Allocation of operating expenses

Total operating expenses for a multi-tenant office building are 30% fixed and 70% variable. If the 100,000 square foot building was fully occupied, operating expenses would total $6 per square foot. The building is currently 90% occupied. If the total operating expenses are allocated to the occupied space, calculate the operating expense per occupied square foot.

Answer:

If the building is fully occupied, total operating expenses would be $600,000 (100,000 SF × $6 per SF). Fixed and variable operating expenses would be:

Fixed	$180,000 (600,000 × 30%)
Variable	420,000 (600,000 × 70%)
Total	$600,000

Thus, variable operating expenses are $4.20 per square foot ($420,000 / 100,000 SF) if the building is fully occupied. Since the building is 90% occupied, total operating expenses are:

Fixed	$180,000
Variable	378,000 (100,000 SF × 90% × $4.20 per SF)
Total	$558,000

So, operating expenses per occupied square foot are $6.20 (558,000 total operating expenses / 90,000 occupied SF).

LOS 43.h: Compare the direct capitalization and discounted cash flow valuation methods.

CFA® Program Curriculum, Volume 6, page 44

Under the direct capitalization method, a cap rate or income multiplier is applied to first-year NOI. Implicit in the cap rate or multiplier are expected increases in growth.

Under the discounted cash flow (DCF) method, the future cash flows, including the capital expenditures and terminal value, are projected over the holding period and discounted to present at the discount rate. Future growth of NOI is explicit in the DCF method.

Because of the inputs required, the DCF method is more complex than the direct capitalization method, as it focuses on NOI over the entire holding period and not just NOI in the first year. DCF does not rely on comparable transactions as long as an appropriate discount rate is chosen. Choosing the appropriate discount rate and terminal cap rate are crucial as small differences in the rates can significantly affect value.

Following are some common errors made using the DCF method:

- The discount rate does not adequately capture risk.
- Income growth exceeds expense growth.
- The terminal cap rate and the going-in cap rate are not consistent.
- The terminal cap rate is applied to NOI that is atypical.
- The cyclicality of real estate markets is ignored.

LOS 43.i: Calculate the value of a property using the cost and sales comparison approaches.

CFA® Program Curriculum, Volume 6, page 46

Cost Approach

The premise behind the cost approach is that a buyer is unlikely to pay more for a property than it would cost to purchase land and build a comparable building. The cost approach involves estimating the market value of the land, estimating the replacement cost of the building, and adjusting for depreciation and obsolescence. The cost approach is often used for unusual properties or properties where comparable transactions are limited.

Professor's Note: Depreciation for appraisal purposes is not the same as depreciation used for financial reporting or tax reporting purposes. Financial depreciation and tax depreciation involve the allocation of original cost over time. For appraisal purposes, depreciation represents an actual decline in value.

The steps involved in applying the cost approach are as follows:

Step 1: **Estimate the market value of the land.** The value of the land is estimated separately, often using the sales comparison approach.

Step 2: **Estimate the building's replacement cost.** Replacement cost is based on current construction costs and standards and should include any builder/developer's profit.

Professor's Note: Replacement cost refers to the cost of a building having the same utility but constructed with modern building materials. Reproduction cost refers to the cost of reproducing an exact replica of the building using the same building materials, architectural design, and quality of construction. Replacement cost is usually more relevant for appraisal purposes because reproduction cost may be uneconomical.

Step 3: **Deduct depreciation including physical deterioration, functional obsolescence,** نقاص **locational obsolescence, and economic obsolescence.** *Physical deterioration* is related to the building's age and occurs as a result of normal wear and tear over time. Physical deterioration can be curable or incurable. An item is curable if the benefit of fixing the problem is at least as much as the cost to cure. For example, replacing the roof will likely increase the value of the building by at least as much as the cost of the roof. The cost of fixing curable items is subtracted from replacement cost.

An item is incurable if the problem is not economically feasible to remedy. For example, the cost of fixing a structural problem might exceed the benefit of the repair. Since an incurable defect would not be fixed, depreciation can be estimated based on the **effective age** of the property relative to its total **economic life**. For example, the physical depreciation of a property with an effective age of 30 years and a 50-year total economic life is 60% (30 year effective age / 50 year economic life). To avoid double counting, the age/life ratio is multiplied by and deducted from replacement cost minus the cost of fixing curable items.

> *Professor's Note: The effective age and the actual age can differ as a result of above-normal or below-normal wear and tear. Incurable items increase the effective age of the property.*

Functional obsolescence is the loss in value resulting from defects in design that impairs a building's utility. For example, a building might have a bad floor plan. As a result of functional obsolescence, NOI is usually lower than it otherwise would be because of lower rent or higher operating expenses. Functional obsolescence can be estimated by capitalizing the decline in NOI.

Locational obsolescence occurs when the location is no longer optimal. For example, five years after a luxury apartment complex is completed, a prison is built down the street making the location of the apartment complex less desirable. As a result, lower rental rates will decrease the value of the complex. Care must be taken in deducting the loss in value because part of the loss is likely already reflected in the market value of the land.

Economic obsolescence occurs when new construction is not feasible under current economic conditions. This can occur when rental rates are not sufficient to support the property. Consequently, the replacement cost of the subject property exceeds the value of a new building if it was developed.

Example: The cost approach

Heavenly Towers is a 200,000 square foot high-rise apartment building located in the downtown area.

The building has an effective age of 10 years, while its total economic life is estimated at 40 years. The building has a structural problem that is not feasible to repair. The building also needs a new roof at a cost of €1,000,000. The new roof will increase the value of the building by €1,300,000.

The bedrooms in each apartment are too small and the floor plans are awkward. As a result of the poor design, rents are €400,000 a year lower than competing properties.

When Heavenly Towers was originally built, it was located across the street from a park. Five years ago, the city converted the park to a sewage treatment plant. The negative impact on rents is estimated at €600,000 a year.

Due to recent construction of competing properties, vacancy rates have increased significantly resulting in an estimated loss in value of €1,200,000.

The cost to replace Heavenly Towers is estimated at €400 per square foot plus builder profit of €5,000,000. The market value of the land is estimated at €20,000,000. An appropriate cap rate is 8%. Using the cost approach, estimate the value of Heavenly Towers.

Answer:

Replacement cost including builder profit [(200,000 SF × €400 per SF) + 5,000,000]	85,000,000
Curable physical deterioration – new roof	(1,000,000)
Replacement cost after curable physical deterioration	€84,000,000
Incurable physical deterioration – structural problem [(10-year effective age / 40 year life) × 84,000,000]	(21,000,000)
Incurable functional obsolescence – poor design [400,000 lower rent / 8% cap rate]	(5,000,000)
Locational obsolescence – sewage plant [600,000 lower rent / 8% cap rate]	(7,500,000)
Economic obsolescence – competing properties	(1,200,000)
Market value of land	20,000,000
Estimated value using the cost approach	€69,300,000

Because of the difficulty in measuring depreciation and obsolescence, the cost approach is most useful when the subject property is relatively new.

The cost approach is sometimes considered the upper limit of value since an investor would never pay more than the cost to build a comparable building. However, investors must consider that construction is time consuming and there may not be enough demand for another building of the same type. That said, market values that exceed the implied value of the cost approach are questionable.

Sales Comparison Approach

The premise of the sales comparison approach is that a buyer would pay no more for a property than others are paying for similar properties in the current market. Ideally, the comparable properties would be identical to the subject but, of course, this is impossible since all properties are different. Consequently, the sales prices of similar (comparable) properties are adjusted for differences with the subject property. The differences may relate to size, age, location, property condition, and market conditions at the time of sale. The values of comparable transactions are adjusted upward (downward) for undesirable (desirable) differences with the subject property. We do this to value the comparable as if it was similar to the subject property.

Example: Sales comparison approach

An appraiser has been asked to estimate the value of a warehouse and has collected the following information:

| | | Comparable Transactions | | |
Unit of Comparison	Subject Property	1	2	3
Size, in square feet	30,000	40,000	20,000	35,000
Age, in years	5	9	4	5
Physical condition	Average	Good	Average	Poor
Location	Prime	Prime	Secondary	Prime
Sale date, months ago		6	18	12
Sales price		$9,000,000	$4,500,000	$8,000,000

The appraiser's adjustments are based on the following:

- Each adjustment is based on the unadjusted sales price of the comparable.
- Properties depreciate at 2% per annum. Since comparable #1 is four years older than the subject, an upward adjustment of $720,000 is made [$9,000,000 × 2% × 4 years].
- *Condition adjustment*: Good: +5%, average: none; poor: –5%. Because comparable #1 is in better condition than the subject, a downward adjustment of $450,000 is made [$9,000,000 × 5%]. Similarly, an upward adjustment is made for comparable #3 to the tune of $400,000 [$8,000,000 × 5%].
- *Location adjustment*: Prime – none, secondary – 10%. Because both comparable #1 and the subject are in a prime location, no adjustment is made.
- Over the past 24 months, sales prices have been appreciating 0.5% per month. Because comparable #1 was sold six months ago, an upward adjustment of $270,000 is made [$9,000,000 × 0.5% × 6 months].

Answer:

Once the adjustments are made for all of the comparable transactions, the adjusted sales price per square foot of the comparable transactions are averaged and applied to the subject property as follows:

		Comparable Transactions		
Adjustments	Subject Property	1	2	3
Sales price		$9,000,000	$4,500,000	$8,000,000
Age		+720,000	−90,000	
Condition		−450,000	–	+400,000
Location		–	+450,000	–
Sale date		+270,000	+405,000	+480,000
Adjusted sales price		$9,540,000	5,265,000	$8,880,000
Size in square feet	30,000	40,000	20,000	35,000
Adjusted sales price per SF		$238.50	$263.25	$253.71
Average sales price per SF	$251.82			
Estimated value	$7,554,600			

The sales comparison approach is most useful when there are a number of properties similar to the subject that have been recently sold, as is usually the case with single-family homes. When the market is weak, there tend to be fewer transactions. Even in an active market, there may be limited transactions of specialized property types, such as regional malls and hospitals. The sales comparison approach assumes purchasers are acting rationally; the prices paid are representative of the current market. However, there are times when purchasers become overly exuberant and market bubbles occur.

RECONCILIATION OF VALUE

Because of different assumptions and availability of data, the three valuation approaches are likely to yield different value estimates. An important part of the appraisal process involves determining the final estimate of value by reconciling the differences in the three approaches.

An appraiser may provide more, or less, weight to an approach because of the property type or market conditions. For example, an appraiser might apply a higher weight to the value obtained with the sales comparison approach when the market is active with plenty of comparable properties. Alternatively, if the subject property is old and estimating depreciation is difficult, an appraiser might apply a lower weight to the cost method.

LOS 43.j: Describe due diligence in private equity real estate investment.

CFA® Program Curriculum, Volume 6, page 54

Real estate investors, both debt and equity, usually perform *due diligence* to confirm the facts and conditions that might affect the value of the transaction. Due diligence may include the following:

- Lease review and rental history.
- Confirm the operating expenses by examining bills.
- Review cash flow statements.
- Obtain an environmental report to identify the possibility of contamination.
- Perform a physical/engineering inspection to identify structural issues and check the condition of the building systems.
- Inspect the title and other legal documents for deficiencies.
- Have the property surveyed to confirm the boundaries and identify easements.
- Verify compliance with zoning laws, building codes, and environmental regulations.
- Verify payment of taxes, insurance, special assessments, and other expenditures.

Due diligence can be costly, but it lowers the risk of unexpected legal and physical problems.

LOS 43.k: Discuss private equity real estate investment indexes, including their construction and potential biases.

CFA® Program Curriculum, Volume 6, page 57

A number of real estate indices are used to track the performance of real estate including appraisal-based indices and transaction-based indices. Investors should be aware of how the indices are constructed as well as their limitations.

Appraisal-Based Indices

Because real estate transactions covering a specific property occur infrequently, indices have been developed based on appraised values. Appraisal-based indices combine valuations of individual properties that can be used to measure market movements. A popular index in the United States is the NCREIF Property Index (NPI). Members of NCREIF, mainly investment managers and pension fund sponsors, submit appraisal data quarterly, and NCREIF calculates the return as follows:

$$\text{return} = \frac{\text{NOI} - \text{capital expenditures} + (\text{end market value} - \text{beg market value})}{\text{beginning market value}}$$

The index is then value-weighted based on the returns of the separate properties. The return is known as a holding-period return and is equivalent to a single-period IRR.

Earlier, we found that the cap rate is equal to NOI divided by the beginning market value of the property. This is the current yield or income return of the property and is one component of the index equation. The remaining components of the equation produce the capital return. To have a positive capital return, the market value must increase by more than the capital expenditures.

The index allows investors to compare performance with other asset classes, and the quarterly returns can be used to measure risk (standard deviation). The index can also be used by investors to benchmark returns.

Property — Might not have appraised each quarter →

Appraisal-based indices tend to lag actual transactions because actual transactions occur before appraisals are performed. Thus, a change in price may not be reflected in appraised values until the next quarter or longer if a property is not appraised every quarter. Also, appraisal lag tends to smooth the index; that is, reduce its volatility, much like a moving average reduces volatility. Finally, appraisal lag results in lower correlation with other asset classes. Appraisal lag can be adjusted by unsmoothing the index or by using a transaction-based index.

Transaction-Based Indices

Two Indexes

Transaction-based indices can be constructed using a repeat-sales index and a hedonic index.

at least sold (1) Two Times

A *repeat-sales index* relies on repeat sales of the same property. A change in market conditions can be measured once a property is sold twice. Accordingly, a regression is developed to allocate the change in value to each quarter.

sold at least one (2) To capture the characteristic of Property

A *hedonic index* requires only one sale. A regression is developed to control for differences in property characteristics such as size, age, location, and so forth.

LOS 43.m: Calculate and interpret financial ratios used to analyze and evaluate private real estate investments.

CFA® Program Curriculum, Volume 6, page 62

Lenders often use the **debt service coverage ratio (DSCR)** and the **loan-to-value (LTV)** ratio to determine the maximum loan amount on a specific property. The maximum loan amount is based on the measure that results in the lowest debt.

The DSCR is calculated as follows:

Cap Rate Loan Payment ← instead of Value of Property

$$DSCR = \frac{\text{first-year NOI}}{\text{debt service}}$$

= loan Payment + Interest = Amortized Payment or only Interest Payment

Debt service (loan payment) includes interest and principal, if required. Principal payments reduce the outstanding balance of the loan. An interest-only loan does not reduce the outstanding balance. The LTV ratio is calculated as follows:

loan of Principal + Interest Payment or only Interest Payment

Amortized loan

$$LTV = \frac{\text{loan amount}}{\text{appraisal value}}$$

Example: Maximum loan amount

A real estate lender agreed to make a 10% interest-only loan on a property that was recently appraised at €1,200,000 as long as the debt service coverage ratio is at least 1.5 and the loan-to-value ratio does not exceed 80%. Calculate the maximum loan amount assuming the property's NOI is €135,000.

Answer:

Using the LTV ratio, the property will support a loan amount of €960,000 [1,200,000 value × 80% LTV ratio].

Using the DSCR, the property will support a debt service payment of €90,000 [135,000 NOI / 1.5]. The corresponding loan amount would be €900,000 [90,000 payment / 10% interest rate].

In this case, the maximum loan amount is the €900,000, which is the lower of the two amounts.

At €900,000, the LTV is 75% [900,000 loan amount / 1,200,000 value] and the DSCR is 1.5 [135,000 NOI / 90,000 payment].

When debt is used to finance real estate, equity investors often calculate the **equity dividend rate**, also known as the cash-on-cash return, which measures the cash return on the amount of cash invested.

$$\text{equity dividend rate} = \frac{\text{first year cash flow}}{\text{equity}}$$

The equity dividend rate only covers one period. It is not the same as the IRR that measures the return over the entire holding period.

Example: Equity dividend maximum loan amount

Returning to the previous example, calculate the equity dividend rate (cash-on-cash return) assuming the property is purchased for the appraised value.

Answer:

The €1,200,000 property was financed with €900,000 debt and €300,000 equity. First-year cash flow is €45,000 (135,000 NOI – 90,000 debt service payment). Thus, the equity dividend rate is 15% (45,000 first year cash flow / 300,000 equity).

In order to calculate the IRR with leverage, we need to consider the cash flows over the entire holding period including the change in value of the original investment. Since the property was financed with debt, the cash flows that are received at the end of the holding period (i.e., net sales proceeds) are reduced by the outstanding mortgage balance.

Example: Leveraged IRR

Returning to the last example, calculate the IRR if the property is sold at the end of six years for €1,500,000. Assume that NOI growth is zero.

Answer:

135K - 90K = 45K

Over the holding period, annual cash flows of €45,000 are received and, at the end of six years, the sale proceeds of €1,500,000 are reduced by the outstanding mortgage balance of €900,000. Recall that the loan was interest only and, hence, the entire original mortgage amount of €900,000 was outstanding at the end of the holding period. Using our financial calculator, the leveraged IRR is 24.1% as follows:

$$N = 6; \; PV = (300,000), \; PMT = 45,000; \; FV = 600,000; \; CPT \rightarrow I/Y = 24.1\%$$

b/c Equity

1500000 - 900000 = 600000

We can see the effects of leverage by calculating an unleveraged IRR. In this case, the initial cash outflow is higher because no debt is incurred. The annual cash flows are higher because there is no debt service, and the terminal cash flow is higher because no mortgage balance is repaid at the end of the holding period.

Returning to the last example, the unleveraged IRR is 14.2% as follows:

$$N = 6; \; PV = (1,200,000), \; PMT = 135,000; \; FV = 1,500,000; \; CPT \rightarrow I/Y = 14.2\%$$

Notice the leveraged IRR of 24.1% is higher than the unleveraged IRR of 14.2%. As a result, the equity investor benefits by financing the property with debt because of positive leverage. Remember, however, that leverage will also magnify negative returns.

Interest Paymt Only Loan

PV: 1200000
Pmt: 135K

KEY CONCEPTS

LOS 43.a

There are four basic forms of real estate investment; private equity (direct ownership), publicly traded equity (indirect ownership), private debt (direct mortgage lending), and publicly traded debt (mortgage-backed securities).

LOS 43.b

Real estate investments are heterogeneous, have high unit values, have high transaction costs, depreciate over time, are influenced by the cost and availability of debt capital, are illiquid, and are difficult to value.

Real estate is commonly classified as residential and non-residential. Income-producing properties (including income-producing residential properties) are considered commercial real estate.

LOS 43.c

Reasons to invest in real estate include current income, capital appreciation, inflation hedge, diversification, and tax benefits.

Risks include changing business conditions, long lead times to develop property, cost and availability of capital, unexpected inflation, demographic factors, illiquidity, environmental issues, property management expertise, and the effects of leverage.

Real estate is less than perfectly correlated with the returns of stocks and bonds; thus, adding real estate to a portfolio can reduce risk relative to the expected return.

LOS 43.d

Commercial property types, and the demand for each is driven by:
- Office—Job growth
- Industrial—The overall economy
- Retail—Consumer spending
- Multi-family—Population growth

LOS 43.e

Cost approach. Value is derived by adding the value of the land to the replacement cost of a new building less adjustments for estimated depreciation and obsolescence.

Sales comparison approach. The sale prices of similar (comparable) properties are adjusted for differences with the subject property.

Income approach. Value is equal to the present value of the subject's future cash flows over the holding period.

LOS 43.f

NOI is equal to potential gross income (rental income fully leased plus other income) less vacancy and collection losses and operating expenses.

The cap rate, discount rate, and growth rate are linked.

cap rate = discount rate (r) – growth rate (g)

If the cap rate is unknown, it can be derived from recent comparable transactions as follows:

$$\text{cap rate} = \frac{NOI_1}{\text{comparable sales price}}$$

The discount rate is the required rate of return of the investor.

discount rate = cap rate + growth rate

LOS 43.g

Direct capitalization method:

$$\text{value} = V_0 = \frac{NOI_1}{\text{cap rate}}$$

Discounted cash flow method:

Step 1: Forecast the terminal value at the end of the holding period (use direct capitalization method if NOI growth is constant).

Step 2: Discount the NOI over the holding period and the terminal value to present.

LOS 43.h

Under the direct capitalization method, a cap rate is applied to first-year NOI. Implicit in the cap rate is an expected increase in growth.

Under the DCF method, the future cash flows, including the capital expenditures and terminal value, are projected over the holding period and discounted to present at the discount rate. Future growth of NOI is explicit to the DCF method. Choosing the appropriate discount rate and terminal cap rate are crucial as small differences in the rates can significantly affect value.

LOS 43.i

Steps involved with applying the cost approach.

Step 1: Estimate the market value of the land.
Step 2: Estimate the building's replacement cost.
Step 3: Deduct physical deterioration (estimate incurable using effective age/economic life ratio), functional obsolescence, locational obsolescence, and economic obsolescence.

With the sales comparison approach, the sales prices of similar (comparable) properties are adjusted for differences with the subject property. The differences may relate to size, age, location, property condition, and market conditions at the time of sale. Once the adjustments are made, the adjusted sales price per square foot of the comparable transactions are averaged and applied to the subject property.

LOS 43.j

Investors perform due diligence to confirm the facts and conditions that might affect the value of the transaction. Due diligence can be costly, but it lowers risk of unexpected legal and physical problems. Due diligence involves reviewing leases, confirming expenses, performing inspections, surveying the property, examining legal documents, and verifying compliance.

LOS 43.k

Appraisal-based indices tend to lag transaction-based indices and appear to have lower volatility and lower correlation with other asset classes.

LOS 43.l

Investors use debt financing (leverage) to increase returns. As long as the investment return is greater than the interest paid to lenders, there is positive leverage and returns are magnified. Leverage results in higher risk.

dscr   As long $NOI > Mortgage\ Payment$

LOS 43.m

Lenders often use the debt service coverage ratio and the loan-to-value ratio to determine the maximum loan amount on a specific property. Investors use ratios such as the equity dividend rate (cash-on-cash return), leveraged IRR, and unleveraged IRR to evaluate performance.

$$\frac{DVD}{Equity}$$

$$Return = \frac{NOI - Capital\ Expenditure + (end\ Value - begin\ Value)}{Begin\ Value}$$

CONCEPT CHECKERS

1. Which form of investment is *most appropriate* for a first-time real estate investor that is concerned about liquidity and diversification?
    A. Direct ownership of a suburban office building.
    B. Shares of a real estate investment trust.
    C. An undivided participation interest in a commercial mortgage.

2. Which of the following real estate properties is *most likely* classified as commercial real estate?
    A. A residential apartment building.
    B. Timberland and farmland.
    C. An owner-occupied, single-family home.

3. A real estate investor is concerned about rising interest rates and decides to pay cash for a property instead of financing the transaction with debt. What is the *most likely* effect of this strategy?
    A. Inflation risk is eliminated.
    B. Risk of changing interest rates is eliminated.
    C. Risk is reduced because of lower leverage.

4. Which of the following *best describes* the primary economic driver of demand for multi-family real estate?
    A. Growth in savings rates.
    B. Job growth, especially in the finance and insurance industries.
    C. Population growth.

5. Which real estate valuation method is likely the *most appropriate* for a 40-year-old, owner-occupied single-family residence?
    A. Cost approach.
    B. Sales comparison approach.
    C. Income approach.

6. The Royal Oaks office building has annual net operating income of $130,000. A similar office building with net operating income of $200,000 recently sold for $2,500,000. Using the direct capitalization method, the market value of Royal Oaks is *closest* to:
    A. $1,200,000.
    B. $1,625,000.
    C. $2,500,000.

7. Using the discounted cash flow method, estimate the property value of a building with the following information:

NOI for next five years	$600,000
NOI in Year 6	$700,000
Holding period	5 years
Discount rate	10%
Terminal growth rate	2%

    A. $7,707,534.
    B. $8,350,729.
    C. $9,024,472.

8.   Which of the following *most accurately* describes the relationship between a discount rate and a capitalization rate?
A. The capitalization rate is the appropriate discount rate less NOI growth.
B. The appropriate discount rate is the capitalization rate less NOI growth.
C. The capitalization rate is the present value of the appropriate discount rate.

9.   You are provided the following data for a property:

Building size	50,000 square feet
Replacement cost	€75 per square foot
Actual age	10 years
Effective age	12 years
Total economic life	20 years
Economic obsolescence	€400,000
Land market value	€900,000

Using the cost approach, the estimated property value of the building is *closest* to:
A. €1,100,000.
B. €2,000,000.
C. €2,375,000.

10.   You just entered into a contract to purchase a recently renovated apartment building, and you are concerned that some of the contractors have not been paid. In performing your due diligence, which of the following procedures should be performed to alleviate your concern?
A. Have the property surveyed.
B. Have an environmental study performed.
C. Search the public records for outstanding liens.

11.   Which of the following statements about real estate indices is *most accurate*?
A. Transaction-based indices tend to lag appraisal-based indices.
B. Appraisal-based indices tend to lag transaction-based indices.
C. Transaction-based indices appear to have lower correlation with other asset classes as compared to appraisal-based indices.

12.   Which of the following statements about financial leverage is *most accurate*?
A. Debt financing increases the appraised value of a property because interest expense is tax deductible.
B. Increasing financial leverage reduces risk to the equity owner.
C. For a property financed with debt, a change in NOI will result in a more than proportionate change in cash flow.

13.   A lender will make a 10%, interest-only loan on a property as long as the debt service coverage ratio is at least 1.6 and the loan-to-value ratio does not exceed 80%. The maximum loan amount, assuming the property just appraised for $1,500,000 and NOI is $200,000, is *closest* to:
A. $1,050,000.
B. $1,200,000.
C. $1,500,000.

ANSWERS – CONCEPT CHECKERS

1. **B** Of the three investment choices, REITs are the most liquid because the shares are actively traded. Also, REITs provide quick and easy diversification across many properties. Neither the direct investment nor the mortgage participation is liquid, and significant capital would be required to diversify the investments.

2. **A** Residential real estate (i.e., an apartment building) purchased with the intent to produce income is usually considered commercial real estate property. Timberland and farmland are unique categories of real estate.

3. **C** An all-cash transaction eliminates financial leverage and lowers risk. Inflation risk is typically lower with a real estate investment, but the risk is not totally eliminated. If interest rates rise, non-leveraged property values are still impacted. Investors require higher returns when rates rise. Resale prices also depend on the cost and availability of debt capital.

4. **C** Demand for multi-family properties depends on population growth, especially in the age demographic that typically rents apartments.

5. **B** The sales comparison approach is likely the best valuation approach because of the number of comparable transactions. The cost approach is not as appropriate because of the difficulty in estimating depreciation and obsolescence of an older property. The income approach is not appropriate because an owner-occupied property does not generate income.

6. **B** The cap rate of the comparable transaction is 8% (200,000 NOI / 2,500,000 sales price). The value of Royal Oaks is $1,625,000 (130,000 NOI / 8% cap rate).

7. **A** The terminal value at the end of five years is $8,750,000 [700,000 year 6 payment / (10% discount rate – 2% growth rate)]. The terminal value is discounted to present and added to the present value of the NOI during the holding period. You can combine both steps using the following keystrokes:

   N = 5; I/Y = 10; PMT = 600,000; FV = 8,750,000; CPT → PV = $7,707,534

8. **A** The capitalization rate is the discount rate (required rate of return on equity, r) less the constant growth rate in net operating income, g (i.e., cap rate = r – g).

9. **B**

Replacement cost	€3,750,000 [50,000 SF × €75 per SF]
Physical deterioration	(2,250,000)[3,750,000 × (12 eff age / 20 life)]
Economic obsolescence	(400,000)
Land value	900,000
Total value	€2,000,000

10. **C** The public records should be searched for outstanding liens filed by contractors involved in the renovation. An existing lien can result in legal problems for the purchaser and the lender. A survey will not identify outstanding liens. A survey confirms the property boundaries and identifies any easements.

11. **B** Appraisal-based indices tend to lag transaction-based indices because actual transactions occur before appraisals are performed (appraisals are based on transaction data). Appraisal-based indices, not transaction-based indices, appear to have lower correlations with other asset classes.

12. **C**   Financial leverage magnifies the effect of changing NOI on cash flow because the interest expense owed to lenders is a fixed cost. The use of debt financing does not affect the value of property. Leverage increases (not decreases) risk.

13. **B**   Using the DSCR, the property will support a debt service payment of $125,000 (200,000 NOI / 1.6); thus, the loan amount would be $1,250,000 ($125,000 payment / 10% interest rate). However, using the LTV ratio, the property will only support a loan amount of $1,200,000 (1,500,000 value × 80% LTV). Thus, the maximum loan amount is $1,200,000, which is the lower of the two amounts.

To access other content related to this topic review that may be included in the Schweser package you purchased, log in to your Schweser.com online dashboard. Schweser's OnDemand Video Lectures deliver streaming instruction covering every LOS in this topic review, while SchweserPro™ QBank provides additional quiz questions to help you practice and recall what you've learned.

The following is a review of the Alternative Investments principles designed to address the learning outcome statements set forth by CFA Institute. Cross-Reference to CFA Institute Assigned Reading #44.

PUBLICLY TRADED REAL ESTATE SECURITIES

EXAM FOCUS

For the exam, be able to describe the different types of publicly traded real estate securities, and understand the advantages and disadvantages of investing in real estate through publicly traded securities. Be able to explain the types of REITs, as well as their economic value determinants, investment characteristics, principal risks, and due diligence considerations. Understand the various approaches to REIT valuation, and be able to calculate the value of a REIT share.

LOS 44.a: Describe types of publicly traded real estate securities.

CFA® Program Curriculum, Volume 6, page 80

Publicly traded real estate securities can take several forms: real estate investment trusts (REITs), real estate operating companies (REOCs), and residential or commercial mortgage-backed securities (MBS).

We can categorize publicly traded real estate securities into two broad groups, debt and equity.

EQUITY

Publicly traded real estate equity securities represent ownership stakes in properties. Equity REITs and REOCs fall into this category.

Equity REITs (Real estate investment trusts): REITs are tax-advantaged companies (trusts) that are for the most part exempt from corporate income tax. Equity REITs are actively managed, own income-producing real estate, and seek to profit by growing cash flows, improving existing properties, and purchasing additional properties. REITs often specialize in a particular kind of property, while still diversifying holdings by geography and other factors.

REOCs (Real estate operating companies): REOCs are not tax-advantaged; rather, they are ordinary (i.e., taxable) corporations that own real estate. A business will form as a REOC if it is ineligible to organize as REIT. For example, the firm may intend to develop and sell real estate rather than generating cash from rental payments, or the firm may be based in a country that does not allow tax-advantaged REITs.

Debt

MBS (mortgage-backed securities) and mortgage REITs fall into this category.

Residential or commercial mortgage-backed securities (MBS): Residential or commercial mortgage-backed securities are publicly traded asset-backed securitized debt obligations that receive cash flows from an underlying pool of mortgage loans. These loans may be for commercial properties (in the case of CMBS) or on residential properties (in the case of RMBS). Real estate debt securities represent a far larger aggregate market value than do publicly traded real estate equity securities.

MBS > REITs

Mortgage REITs: Mortgage REITs invest primarily in mortgages, mortgage securities, or loans that are secured by real estate.

LOS 44.b: Explain advantages and disadvantages of investing in real estate through publicly traded securities.

CFA® Program Curriculum, Volume 6, page 85

Advantages

Investments in REITs and REOCs offer a number of advantages compared to direct investments in physical real estate:

- **Superior liquidity.** Investors in publicly traded real estate securities enjoy far greater liquidity than do investors in physical real estate, because REIT and REOC shares trade daily on a stock exchange. The low liquidity of a direct real estate investment stems from the relatively high value of an individual real estate property and the unique nature of each property.
- **Lower minimum investment.** While a direct investment in a real estate property may require a multi-million dollar commitment, REIT or REOC shares trade for much smaller dollar amounts.
- **Limited liability.** The financial liability of a REIT investor is limited to the amount invested. Other types of investment in real estate, such as a general partnership interest, have potential liabilities greater than the investor's initial investment.
- **Access to premium properties.** Some prestigious properties, such as high-profile shopping malls or other prominent or landmark buildings, are difficult to invest in directly. Shares in REITs that have invested in these properties represent one way to take an ownership stake in these assets.
- **Active professional management.** While a direct investment in properties requires a degree of real estate investment expertise and property management skill, REIT and REOC investments do not. REITs and REOCs employ professional management to control expenses, maximize rents and occupancy rates, and sometimes to acquire additional properties.
- **Protections accorded to publicly traded securities.** REITs and REOCs must meet the same requirements applicable to other publicly traded companies, including rules related to financial reporting, disclosure, and governance. Investors benefit from these securities regulations and from having a board overseeing the management on behalf of investors. Additionally, having public investors monitor the actions of management and the board of directors leads to financial and operating efficiency.

- **Greater potential for diversification.** Because of the high cost of a single property, it is difficult to achieve adequate diversification though direct investments in real estate. Through REITs, however, an investor can diversify across property type and geographical location.

REIT-Specific Advantages   *ONLY REITS*

The following advantages apply to REITs, but not to REOCs:

- **Exemption from taxation.** As long as certain requirements are met, REITs enjoy favorable taxation, because a major part of REIT distributions are treated as a return of capital and are thus not taxable.
- **Predictable earnings.** The earnings of REITs tend to be relatively consistent over time, because REITs' rental income is fixed by contracts, unlike the income of companies in other industries.
- **High yield.** To maintain their tax-advantaged status, REITs are obligated to pay out most of their taxable income as dividends. Because of this high income payout ratio, the yields of REITs are higher than the yields on most other publicly traded equities.

DISADVANTAGES

Disadvantages of investing in real estate through publicly traded securities may include:

- **Taxes versus direct ownership.** Depending on local laws, investors that make direct investments in properties may be able to deduct losses on real estate from taxable income or replace one property for a similar property ("like-kind exchange" in the U.S.) without taxation on the gains. For investors in REITs or REOCs, these specific tax benefits are not available.
- **Lack of control.** REIT investors have comparatively little input into investment decisions compared to investors that make direct investments in real estate.
- **Costs of a publicly traded corporate structure.** There are clear benefits from maintaining a publicly traded REIT structure. However, there are also related costs, which may not be worthwhile for smaller REITs.
- **Price is determined by the stock market.** While the appraisal-based value of a REIT may be relatively stable, the market-determined price of a REIT share is likely to be much more volatile. While this relationship suggests a direct real estate investment is less risky, in reality much of this effect results from the underestimation of volatility that is associated with appraised values; appraisals tend to be infrequent and backward-looking, while the stock market is continuous and reflects forward-looking values.
- **Structural conflicts of interest.** When a REIT is structured as an UPREIT or a DOWNREIT there is the potential for conflict of interest. When the opportunity arises to sell properties or take on additional borrowing, a particular action may have different tax implications for REIT shareholders and for the general partners, which may tempt the general partners to act in their own interest, rather than in the interest of all stakeholders.

Price vs Real Value
↓
Market

Professor's Note: An UPREIT is an "umbrella partnership" REIT structure, where the REIT is the general partner and holds a controlling interest in a partnership that owns and operates the properties. UPREITs are the most common REIT structure in the United States. In a DOWNREIT, the REIT has an ownership interest in more than one partnership and can own properties both at the partnership level and at the REIT level.

The following disadvantage applies to REITs, but not to REOCs: ONLY REIT

- **Limited potential for income growth.** REITs' high rates of income payout limit REITs' ability to generate future growth through reinvestment. This limits future income growth and may dampen the share price of REITs.
- **Forced equity issuance.** In order to maintain financial leverage, REITs frequently participate in bond markets to refinance maturing debt. When credit is difficult to obtain (e.g., during the 2008 credit crisis), a REIT may be forced to issue equity at a disadvantageous price.
- **Lack of flexibility.** The rules that qualify REITs for favorable taxation also have a downside: REITs are prevented from making certain kinds of investments and from retaining most of their income. These limits may prevent REITs from being as profitable as they might otherwise be. REOCs, on the other hand, do not need to meet these requirements, and thus are free to retain income and devote those funds to property development when the REOC managers see attractive opportunities. REOCs are also not restricted in their use of leverage.

LOS 44.c: Explain economic value determinants, investment characteristics, principal risks, and due diligence considerations for real estate investment trust (REIT) shares.

CFA® Program Curriculum, Volume 6, page 90

Economic Value Determinants of REITs

National GDP growth is the largest driver of economic value for all REIT types. Overall growth in the economy means more jobs, more need for office space, more disposable income, more growth in shopping centers, more demand for hotel rooms from business and leisure travellers, and so on.

In addition to national GDP growth, there are four major economic factors that impact REITs, as shown in Figure 1.

Figure 1: Rank of Most Important Factors Affecting Economic Value for REIT Property Types

	Relative Importance of Factors Affecting REIT Economic Value			
REIT Type	*Population Growth*	*Job Creation*	*New Space Supply vs. Demand*	*Retail Sales Growth*
Shopping/Retail	3	2	3	1
Office	3	1	2	4
Residential	1	1	3	4
Healthcare	1	3	2	4
Industrial	2	4	3	1
Hotel	3	1	2	4
Storage	1	2	3	4

Note: 1 = most important, 4 = least important
Adapted from: Exhibit 6, Level II 2016 Volume 5, Alternative Asset Valuation and Fixed Income. John Wiley & Sons (P&T), pp. 94–95.

INVESTMENT CHARACTERISTICS OF REITS

- **Exemption from corporate-level income taxes:** As mentioned earlier, the defining characteristic of REITs is that they are exempt from corporate taxation. However, in order to gain this status, REITs are required to distribute almost all of the REITs' otherwise-taxable income, and a sufficient portion of assets and income must relate to rental income-producing real estate.
- **High dividend yield:** To maintain their tax-exempt status, REITs' dividend yields are generally higher than yields on bonds or other equities.
- **Low income volatility:** REITs' revenue streams tend to be relatively stable. This characteristic is due to REITs' dependence on interest and rent as income sources.
- **Secondary equity offerings:** Since REITs distribute most earnings, they are likely to finance additional real estate acquisitions by selling additional shares. For this reason, REITs issue equity more frequently than do non-real estate companies.

PRINCIPAL RISKS OF REITS

The most risky REITs are those that invest in property sectors where significant mismatches between supply and demand are likely (particularly health care, hotel, and office REITs), as well as those sectors where the occupancy rates are most likely to fluctuate within a short period of time (especially hotels). Other items to consider in assessing the riskiness of a REIT relate to the properties' financing, the leases that are in place, and the properties' locations and quality.

DUE DILIGENCE CONSIDERATIONS OF REITS

- **Remaining lease terms:** An analyst should evaluate the length of remaining lease terms in conjunction with the overall state of the economy—short remaining lease terms provide an opportunity to raise rents in an expansionary economy, while long remaining lease terms are advantageous in a declining economy or softening rental market. Initial lease terms vary with the type of property—industrial and office buildings and shopping centers generally have long lease terms, while hotels and multi-family residential real estate have short lease terms.

- **Inflation protection:** The level of contractual hedging against rising general price levels should be evaluated—some amount of inflation protection will be enjoyed if leases have rent increases scheduled throughout the term of the lease or if rents are indexed to the rate of inflation.
- **In-place rents versus market rents:** An analyst should compare the rents that a REIT's tenants are currently paying (in-place rents) with current rents in the market. If in-place rents are high, the potential exists for cash flows to fall going forward.

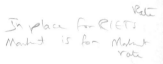
(handwritten margin note: In place for REITs. Rate. Market is for Market rate)

- **Costs to re-lease space:** When a lease expires, expenses typically incurred include lost rent, any new lease incentives offered, the costs of tenant-demanded improvements, and broker commissions.
- **Tenant concentration in the portfolio:** Risk increases with tenant concentration; a REIT analyst should pay special attention to any tenants that make up a high percentage of space rented or rent paid.
- **Tenants' financial health:** Since the possibility of a major tenant's business failing poses a significant risk to a REIT, it is important to evaluate the financial position of the REIT's largest renters.
- **New competition:** An analyst should evaluate the amount of new space that is planned or under construction. New competition could impact the profitability of existing REIT properties.
- **Balance sheet analysis:** Due diligence should include an in-depth analysis of the REIT's balance sheet, with special focus on the amount of leverage, the cost of debt, and the debt's maturity.
- **Quality of management:** Senior management's performance record, qualifications, and tenure with the REIT should be considered.

LOS 44.d: Describe types of REITs.

CFA® Program Curriculum, Volume 6, page 91

SUBTYPES OF EQUITY REITs

The following paragraphs provide more details on several subtypes of equity REITs.

1. **Retail or Shopping Center REITs.** REITs in this category invest in shopping centers of various sizes and sometimes in individual buildings in prime shopping neighborhoods. Regional shopping malls are large enclosed centers where anchor tenants have very long fixed-rate leases, while smaller tenants often pay a "percentage lease," which consists of a fixed rental price (the "minimum lease"), plus a percentage of sales over a certain level. Community shopping centers, such as "big-box centers," consist of stores that surround parking lots. These stores commonly pay pre-determined rents that increase on a schedule. Lease rates and sales per square foot are important factors for analysts to consider when examining a shopping center REIT.

2. **Office REITs.** Office REITs own office properties that typically lease space to multiple business tenants. Leases are long (generally 5 to 25 years) and rents increase over time. In addition to rent, tenants pay a share of property taxes, operating expenses, and other common costs proportional to the size of their unit (i.e., they are net leases). Because of the length of time that it takes to build this type of property, there is often a supply-demand mismatch, resulting in variations in occupancy rates and rents over the economic cycle. In analyzing office REITs, analysts must consider properties' location, convenience and access to transportation, and the quality of the space including the condition of the building.

3. **Residential (Multi-Family) REITs.** This category of REITs invests in rental apartments. Demand for rental apartments tends to be stable; however, lease periods are short (usually one year), so rental income fluctuates over time as competing properties are constructed. Variables that will affect rental income include the overall strength of the local economy and any move-in inducements offered. Factors to consider when analysing a residential REIT include local demographic trends, availability of alternatives (i.e., home ownership), any rent controls imposed by the local government, and factors related to the portfolio properties themselves, such as the age of the properties and how appealing they are to renters in the local market compared to other competing properties. Additionally, because rents are typically based on a gross lease, the impact of rising costs must be considered (under a gross lease, operating costs are paid by the landlord). Examples include rising fuel or energy costs, taxes, and maintenance costs.

4. **Health Care REITs.** Health care REITs invest in hospitals, nursing homes, retirement homes, rehab centers, and medical office buildings. REITs in many countries are barred from operating this kind of business themselves. In order to participate in this property sector while maintaining their tax-free status, REITs rent properties to health care providers. Leases in this sector are usually net leases. Health care REITs are relatively unaffected by the overall economy. However, other factors are important, such as government funding of health care, demographic shifts, new construction versus demand, increases in the cost of insurance, and the potential for lawsuits by residents.

5. **Industrial REITs.** Industrial REITs own properties used in activities such as manufacturing, warehousing, and distribution. The value of industrial properties is relatively stable and less cyclical compared to the value of other types of properties, due to long leases (5 to 25 years) which smoothes rental income. In analysing industrial REITs, an analyst needs to closely examine the local market for industrial properties; new properties coming on to the market and the demand for such space by tenants will affect the value of existing properties. Location and availability of transportation links (airports, roads, and ports) are also important considerations for industrial REITs.

6. **Hotel REITs.** A hotel REIT (like a health care REIT) usually leases properties to management companies, so the REIT receives only passive rental income. Hotels are exposed to revenue volatility driven by changes in business and leisure travel, and the sector's cyclical nature is intensified by a lack of long-term leases. In analysing hotel REITs, analysts compare a number of statistics against industry averages (operating profit margins, occupancy rates, and average room rates). One key metric that is closely followed is RevPAR, the revenue per available room, which is calculated by multiplying the average occupancy rate by the average room rate. Other closely-watched variables are the level of margins, forward bookings, and food and beverage sales. Expenses related to maintaining the properties are also closely monitored. Because of the time lag associated with bringing new hotel properties on-line (up to three years), the cyclical nature of demand needs to be considered. Because of the uncertainty in income, the use of high amounts of leverage in financing hotel properties is risky.

7. **Storage REITs.** Properties owned by storage REITs rent self-storage lockers (also known as mini-warehouses) to individuals and small businesses. Space is rented to users on a monthly basis and under a gross lease. In analysing storage REITs, it is important to look at the local factors that drive demand for storage, such as housing sales, new business start-ups, demographic trends in the surrounding area, as well as any other competing facilities that are under construction. Seasonal demand should also be considered.

8. **Diversified REITs.** Diversified REITs own more than one category of REIT. While they are uncommon in North America, some investors in Europe and Asia are drawn to the broad nature of these REITs. Because diversified REITs hold a range of property types, when analysing this class of REIT it is especially important to evaluate management's background in the kinds of real estate invested in.

Figure 2: Characteristics of REIT property subtypes

REIT Type	Characteristic			
	Economic Value Determinant	Investment Characteristics	Principal Risks	Due Diligence Considerations
Retail	• Retail sales growth • Job creation	• Stable revenue stream over the short term	• Depends on consumer spending	• Per-square-foot sales and rental rates
Office	• Job creation • New space supply vs. demand	• Long (5-25 yrs) lease terms • Stable year-to-year income	• Changes in office vacancy and rental rates	• New space under construction • Quality of office space (location, condition of building, and so on)
Residential	• Population growth • Job creation	• One-year leases • Stable demand	• Competition • Inducements • Regional economy • Inflation in operating costs	• Demographics and income trends • Age and competitive appeal • Cost of home ownership • Rent controls
Health care	• Population growth • New space supply vs. demand	• REITs lease facilities to health care providers. • Leases are usually net leases.	• Demographics • Government funding • Construction cycles • Financial condition of operators • Tenant litigation	• Operating trends • Government funding trends • Litigation settlements • Insurance costs • Competitors' new facilities vs demand
Industrial	• Retail sales growth • Population growth	• Less cyclical than some other REIT types • 5-25 year net leases • Change in income and values are slow	• Shifts in the composition of local and national industrial bases and trade	• Trends in tenants' requirements • Obsolescence of existing space • Need for new types of space • Proximity to transportation • Trends in local supply and demand
Hotel	• Job creation • New space supply vs. demand	• Variable income • Sector is cyclical because it is not protected by long-term leases	• Exposed to business-cycle • Changes in business and leisure travel • Exposure to travel disruptions	• Occupancy, room rates, and operating profit margins vs. industry averages • Revenue per available room (RevPAR) • Trends in forward bookings • Maintenance expenditures • New construction in local markets • Financial leverage
Storage	• Population growth • Job creation	• Space is rented under gross leases and on a monthly basis	• Ease of entry can lead to overbuilding.	• Construction of new competitive facilities • Trends in housing sales • Demographic trends • New business start-up activity • Seasonal trends in demand for storage facilities that can be significant in some markets

LOS 44.e: Justify the use of net asset value per share (NAVPS) in REIT valuation and estimate NAVPS based on forecasted cash net operating income.

Net Asset Value Per Share [handwritten]

CFA® Program Curriculum, Volume 6, page 98

NAVPS is the (per-share) amount by which assets exceed liabilities, using current market [handwritten: *for Asset*] values rather than accounting book values. NAVPS is generally considered the most appropriate measure of the fundamental value of REITs (and REOCs). If the market price of a REIT varies from NAVPS, this is seen as a sign of over- or undervaluation.

Estimating NAVPS Based on Forecasted Cash Net Operating Income

In the absence of a reliable appraisal, analysts will estimate the value of operating real estate by capitalizing the net operating income. This process first requires the calculation of a market required rate of return, known as the **capitalization rate** ("cap rate"), based on the prices of comparable recent transactions that have take place in the market.

$$\text{capitalization rate} = \frac{\text{net operating income}}{\text{property value}}$$

[handwritten: NOI for first Year (or) ONE YEAR / Value]

Note that the net operating income (NOI) refers to the *expected income in the coming year*. Once a cap rate for the market has been determined, this cap rate can be used to capitalize the NOI:

$$\text{property value} = \frac{\text{net operating income}}{\text{capitalization rate}}$$

In the example below, we show how NAVPS is calculated by capitalizing a rental stream. First, estimated first-year NOI is capitalized using a market cap rate. Next, we add the value of other tangible assets and subtract the value of liabilities to find total net asset value. Net asset value divided by the number of outstanding shares gives us NAVPS.

Note that in calculating cash NOI, we subtract non-cash rent. Non-cash rent is the difference between the average rent over the term of a lease contract (i.e. straight-line rent) versus the amount of cash rent actually received in a period.

[handwritten: difference Average Rent —]

Example: Computing NAVPS

Vinny Cestone, CFA, is undertaking a valuation of the Anyco Shopping Center REIT, Inc. Given the following financial data for Anyco, estimate NAVPS based on forecasted cash net operating income.

Select Anyco Shopping Center REIT, Inc. Financial Information (in millions)

Last 12-months NOI	$80
Cash and equivalents	$20
Accounts receivable	$15
Total debt	$250
Other liabilities	$50
Non-cash rents	$2
Full-year adjustment for acquisitions	$1
Land held for future development	$10
Prepaid/Other assets (excluding intangibles)	$5
Estimate of next 12 months growth in NOI	1.25%
Cap rate based on recent comparable transactions	8.0%
Shares outstanding	15

Answer:

	Last 12-months NOI	$80
–	Non-cash rents[1]	$2
+	Full-year adjustment for acquisitions[2]	$1
=	Pro forma cash NOI for last 12 months	$79
+	Next 12 months growth in NOI (@1.25%/yr)[3]	$1
=	Estimated next 12 months cash NOI	$80
÷	Cap rate[4]	8.0%
=	Estimated value of operating real estate[5]	$1,000
+	Cash and equivalents[6]	$20
+	Land held for future development	$10
+	Accounts receivable	$15
+	Prepaid/other assets (excluding intangibles)	$5
=	Estimated gross asset value	$1,050
–	Total debt[7]	$250
–	Other liabilities	$50
=	Net asset value	$750
÷	Shares outstanding	15
=	Net asset value per share[8]	$50.00

Notes:
(1) Non-cash rent (difference between average contractual rent and cash rent paid) is removed.
(2) NOI is increased to represent full-year rent for properties acquired during the year.
(3) Cash NOI is expected to increase by 1.25% over the next year.
(4) Cap rate is based on recent transactions for comparable properties.
(5) Operating real estate value = expected next 12-month cash NOI / 8% capitalization rate.
(6) Add the book value of other assets: cash, accounts receivable, land for future development, prepaid expenses, and so on. Certain intangibles, such as goodwill, deferred financing expenses, and deferred tax assets, if given, are ignored.
(7) Debt and other liabilities are subtracted to get to net asset value.
(8) NAVPS = NAV / number of outstanding shares

LOS 44.f: Describe the use of funds from operations (FFO) and adjusted funds from operations (AFFO) in REIT valuation.

CFA® Program Curriculum, Volume 6, page 105

Analysts calculate and use two measures, FFO and AFFO.

1. **Funds from operations:** FFO adjusts reported earnings and is a popular measure of the continuing operating income of a REIT or REOC. FFO is calculated as follows:

    Accounting net earnings
    (+) Depreciation expense
    (+) Deferred tax expenses (i.e., deferred tax liabilities)
    (−) Gains from sales of property and debt restructuring
    (+) Losses from sales of property and debt restructuring
    = Funds from operations

    Depreciation is added back under the premise that accounting depreciation often exceeds economic depreciation for real estate. Deferred tax liabilities and associated periodic charges are also excluded, under the idea that this liability will probably not be paid for many years, if ever. Gains from sales of property and debt restructuring are excluded because these are not considered to be part of continuing income.

2. **Adjusted funds from operations:** AFFO is an extension of FFO that is intended to be a more useful representation of current economic income. AFFO is also known as *cash available for distribution* (CAD) or *funds available for distribution* (FAD). The calculation of AFFO generally involves beginning with FFO and then subtracting non-cash rent and maintenance-type capital expenditures and leasing costs (such as improvement allowances to tenants or capital expenditures for maintenance).

    FFO (funds from operations)
    − Non-cash (straight-line) rent adjustment
    − Recurring maintenance-type capital expenditures and leasing commissions
    = AFFO (adjusted funds from operations)

    Straight-line rent refers not to the cash rent paid during the lease but rather to the average contractual rent over a lease period—the two figures differ by non-cash rent, which reflects contractually-increasing rental rates. Capital expenditures related to maintenance, as well expenses related to leasing the space in properties, are subtracted from FFO because they represent costs that must be expended in order to maintain the value of the properties.

    AFFO is considered a better measure of economic income than FFO because AFFO considers the capital expenditures that are required to sustain the property's economic income. However, FFO is more frequently cited in practice, because AFFO relies more on estimates and is considered more subjective.

LOS 44.g: Compare the net asset value, relative value (price-to-FFO and price-to-AFFO), and discounted cash flow approaches to REIT valuation.

CFA® Program Curriculum, Volume 6, page 111

REITs and REOCs are valued using several different approaches.

Net asset value per share: The net asset value method of valuation can be used either to generate an absolute valuation or as part of a relative valuation approach. Note, however, that net asset value is an indication of a REIT's assets to a buyer in the private market, which can be quite different from the value public market investors would attach to the REIT. For this reason, there have historically been significant differences (i.e., premiums or discounts) between NAV estimates and the prices at which REITs actually trade.

 Professor's Note: Relative valuation using NAVPS is essentially comparing NAVPS to the market price of a REIT (or REOC) share. If, in general, the market is trading at a premium to NAVPS, a value investor would select the investments with the lowest premium (everything else held constant).

Relative value (price-to-FFO and price-to-AFFO): There are three key factors that impact that price-to-FFO and price-to-AFFO of REITs and REOCs:

1. Expectations for growth of FFO or AFFO.

2. The level of risks inherent in the underlying real estate.

3. Risk related to the firm's leverage and access to capital.

Discounted cash flow approach: Dividend discount and discounted cash flow models of valuation are appropriate for use with REITs and REOCs, because these two investment structures typically pay dividends and thereby return a high proportion of their income to investors. DDM and DCF are used in private real estate in the same way that they are used to value stocks in general. For dividend discount models, an analyst will typically develop near-term, medium-term, and long-term growth forecasts and then use these values as the basis for two- or three-stage dividend discount models. To build a discounted cash flow model, analysts will generally create intermediate-term cash flow projections plus a terminal value that is developed using historical cash flow multiples.

 Professor's Note: We discuss dividend discount models extensively in the study session on equity valuation. Similar to price multiples in equity valuation, price multiples here depend on growth rate and risk. The first factor (above) focuses on growth rate, while the second and third factors above focus on risk.

LOS 44.h: Calculate the value of a REIT share using net asset value, price-to-FFO and price-to-AFFO, and discounted cash flow approaches.

CFA® Program Curriculum, Volume 6, page 113

We will demonstrate the calculation of the value of a REIT share using net asset value, price-to-FFO and price-to-AFFO, and discounted cash flow approaches with an example.

Example: Calculating the value of a REIT share

Lucinda Crabtree, CFA, is an asset manager that is interested in diversifying the portfolio she manages through an investment in an office building REIT.

Crabtree wants to value the potential investment using four different approaches as of the end of 2013, as follows:

Approach 1: Net asset value
Approach 2: Price-to-FFO
Approach 3: Price-to-AFFO
Approach 4: Discounted cash flow

Selected REIT Financial Information

	All amounts in $million
Estimated 12 months cash net operating income (NOI)	$80
Last year's actual funds from operations (FFO)	$70
Cash and equivalents	$65
Accounts receivable	$35
Debt and other liabilities	$400
Non-cash rents	$5
Recurring maintenance-type capital expenditures	$15
Shares outstanding	10 million shares
Expected annual dividend next year (2014)	$5.00
Dividend growth rate in 2015 and 2016	2%
Dividend growth rate (from 2017 into perpetuity)	1%
Assumed cap rate	8%
Office subsector average P/FFO multiple	10×
Office subsector average P/AFFO multiple	14×
Crabtree's applicable cost of equity capital	9%
Risk-free rate	2%

Approach 1: Value of a REIT share using net asset value approach

The value per share for this REIT using net asset value valuation is computed as follows:

Estimated cash NOI	80
Assumed cap rate	8%
Estimated value of operating real estate (80 / .08)	1,000
Plus: cash + accounts receivable	100
Less: debt and other liabilities	400
Net asset value	700
Shares outstanding	10
NAV / share	$70.00

$\frac{80}{0.08} = 1000$ Asset

Asset in B/S
Liability
Equity

The REIT share value using the net asset value approach is thus $70. Note that no adjustment for non-cash rents was required in this case because we began with an estimate of cash NOI.

Approach 2: Value of a REIT share using price-to-FFO approach

The value per share for this REIT using price-to-FFO valuation is computed as follows:

Funds from operations (FFO)	$70
Shares outstanding (millions)	10
FFO / share = $70 million / 10 million shares	$7.00

Per share

Applying the office subsector average P/FFO multiple of 10× yields a value per share of:

$$\$7.00 \times 10 = \$70.00$$

The REIT share value using the price-to-FFO approach is thus $70.

Approach 3: Value of REIT share using price-to-AFFO approach

Funds from operations (FFO)	$70
Subtract: non-cash rents	$5
Subtract: recurring maintenance-type capital expenditures	$15
Equals: AFFO	$50
Shares outstanding (million)	10
AFFO / share = $50 million / 10 million shares	$5
Property subsector average P/AFFO multiple	14×

AFFO

Per share

Applying the office subsector average P/AFFO multiple of 14× yields a value per share of $5 × 14 = $70.

The REIT share value using the price-to-AFFO approach is thus $70.

Approach 4: Value of REIT share using discounted cash flow approach

	2014	2015	2016	2017
Dividends per share	$5.00	↑ $5.10	↑ $5.20	↑ $5.25

Present value in 2016 of dividend stream beginning in 2017 = $5.25 / (0.09 − 0.01) = $65.63

These dividends are discounted at a rate of 9%.

value of a REIT share

= PV(dividends for years 1 through n) + PV(terminal value at the end of year n)

= $PV_{2014 \text{ dividend}}$ + $PV_{2015 \text{ dividend}}$ + $PV_{2016 \text{ dividend}}$ + $PV_{2017 \text{ and later dividends (terminal value)}}$

= $5.00 / (1.09) + $5.10 / (1.09)^2 + $5.20 / (1.09)^3 + $65.63 / (1.09)^3

= $63.61

The REIT share value using the discounted cash flow approach is thus $63.61.

Note that the calculated value of a REIT share is likely to vary, sometimes greatly, depending on which of these approaches is used.

KEY CONCEPTS

LOS 44.a

The main types of publicly traded real estate securities are:

- Real estate investment trusts (REITs) which are tax-advantaged companies that own income-producing real estate.
- Real estate operating companies (REOCs) which are non-tax-advantaged companies that own real estate.
- Mortgage-backed securities (MBS) which are investments in residential or commercial mortgages that are backed by real estate.

The main types of REITs are:

- Equity REITs which take ownership stakes in income-producing property.
- Mortgage REITs which invest primarily in mortgages, mortgage securities, or loans that use real estate as collateral.

LOS 44.b

Advantages of publicly traded real estate securities include:

- Superior liquidity.
- Lower minimum investment.
- Limited liability.
- Access to premium properties.
- Active professional management.
- Protections accorded to publicly traded securities.
- Greater potential for diversification.
- Exemption from taxation.
- Earnings predictability.
- High yield.

Disadvantages of publicly traded real estate securities include:

- Taxes versus direct ownership.
- Lack of control.
- Costs of a publicly traded corporate structure.
- Price is determined by the stock market.
- Structural conflicts of interest.
- Limited potential for income growth.
- Forced equity issuance.
- Lack of flexibility.

LOS 44.c:

Investment characteristics of REITs include:

- Exemption from corporate-level income taxes.
- High dividend yield.
- Low income volatility.
- Frequent secondary equity offerings.

The most risky types of REIT property sectors are those in which significant mismatches between supply and demand are likely to happen (particularly health care, hotel, and office REITs), as well as those sectors where the occupancy rates are most likely to vary over a short period of time (especially hotels).

REIT due diligence considerations:

- Remaining lease terms.
- Inflation protection.
- Occupancy rates and leasing activity.
- In-place rents versus market rents.
- Costs to re-lease space.
- Tenant concentration in the portfolio.
- Tenants' financial health.
- New supply versus demand.
- Balance sheet analysis.
- Quality of management.

LOS 44.d

Types of REITs include:

- Retail REITs, which own properties used as shopping centers.
- Office REITs, which provide space to multiple business tenants.
- Residential ("multi-family") REITs, which invest in rental apartments.
- Health care REITs, which lease properties to hospitals and nursing homes.
- Industrial REITs, which own properties used in manufacturing, warehousing, and distribution.
- Hotel REITs, which receive passive rental income from hotel management companies.
- Storage REITs, which rent self-storage lockers to individuals and small businesses.
- Diversified REITs, which own multiple types of real estate.

LOS 44.e

Net asset value per share (NAVPS) is the (per-share) amount by which a REIT's assets exceed its liabilities, using current market value rather than accounting or book values. The REIT or REOC portfolio of operating real estate investments can be valued by capitalizing net operating income:

$$\text{property value} = \frac{\text{net operating income}}{\text{capitalization rate}}$$

	Estimated cash NOI
÷	Assumed cap rate
=	Estimated value of operating real estate
+	Cash and accounts receivable
−	Debt and other liabilities
=	Net asset value
÷	Shares outstanding
=	NAV / share

LOS 44.f

	Accounting net earnings
(+)	Depreciation expense
(+)	Deferred tax expenses
(−)	Gains (losses) from sales of property and debt restructuring
=	Funds from operations

depreciation / deferred tax, Gain / loss of Sales of Profits

FFO

	FFO (funds from operations)
(−)	Non-cash (straight-line) rent adjustment
(−)	Recurring maintenance-type capital expenditures and leasing commissions
=	AFFO (adjusted funds from operations)

AFFO

القوائم المكتشفة انظر الى مسار

FFO   *(FO) AFFO*

LOS 44.g

Approaches to REIT valuation:

- Net asset value per share: NAVPS is based on market values and is considered to be the fundamental measure of value for REITs and REOCs.
- Relative value: Market-based-multiple approaches including price-to-FFO and price-to-AFFO can be used to value REITs and REOCs.
- Discounted cash flow: Dividend discount models typically include two or three stages, based on near- and long-term growth forecasts. Discounted cash flow models use intermediate-term cash flow projections, plus a terminal value based on historical cash flow multiples.

LOS 44.h

Price-to-FFO approach:

(handwritten left margin: FFO Per share ← Then × Sector Average Multiple)

	Funds from operations (FFO)
÷	Shares outstanding
=	FFO / share
×	Sector average P/FFO multiple
=	NAV / share

(handwritten: NAVPS)

Price-to-AFFO approach:

	Funds from operations (FFO)
−	Non-cash rents
−	Recurring maintenance-type capital expenditures
=	AFFO
÷	Shares outstanding
=	AFFO / share
×	Property subsector average P/AFFO multiple
=	NAV / share

(handwritten left margin: AFFO Per share)

(handwritten: NAVPS)

Discounted cash flow approach:

Value of a REIT share
= PV(dividends for years 1 through n) + PV(terminal value at the end of year n)

(handwritten Arabic/notes: Terminal … $\frac{DVD_1}{r-g}$ …)

(handwritten: 14 / 4 / 2018   19 : 02   Costa, Hammersmith)

©2017 Kaplan, Inc.

CONCEPT CHECKERS

1. Which of the following *least accurately* identifies one of the principal types of publicly traded real estate securities?
   A. Commingled real estate fund (CREF).
   B. Shares of real estate operating companies (REOC).
   C. Residential and commercial mortgage-backed securities (MBS).

2. Which of the following statements *most accurately* describes one of the advantages of investing in REITs? REITs:
   A. can pass on tax losses to their investors as deductions from their taxable income.
   B. have lower price and return volatility than a comparable direct investment in properties.
   C. limit investor liability to only the amount of the investor's original capital investment.

3. From the choices given, choose the *most accurate* to complete the following sentence. After overall growth in the economy, the *most* important economic factor affecting a(n):
   A. hotel REIT is job creation.
   B. storage REIT is retail sales growth.
   C. office REIT is population growth.

4. Compared with other publicly traded shares, REITs are *most likely* to offer relatively low:
   A. yields.
   B. stability of income and returns.
   C. growth from reinvested operating cash flows.

5. Which of the following statements *least accurately* describes a feature of the DOWNREIT structure? A DOWNREIT:
   A. is the most common REIT structure in the United States.
   B. may own properties at both the REIT level and the partnership level.
   C. can form partnerships for each property acquisition it undertakes.

6. Which of the following statements about the use of net asset value per share (NAVPS) in REIT valuation is *most accurate*? NAVPS is:
   A. the difference between the accounting book values of a real estate company's assets and its liabilities, divided by shares outstanding.
   B. considered to be a superior measure of the net worth of a REIT's shares, compared with book value per share.
   C. exactly equal to the intrinsic value of REIT shares.

7. In the process of calculating adjusted funds from operations (AFFO) from funds from operations (FFO), an analyst is *most likely* to:
   A. add depreciation and amortization.
   B. subtract non-cash rent.
   C. add recurring maintenance-type capital expenditures and leasing commissions.

8. Which statement regarding approaches to REIT valuation is *least accurate*?
    A. AFFO includes a number of adjustments to FFO that result in AFFO approximating continuing cash earnings.
    B. P/AFFO is the most frequently used multiple in analyzing the REIT sector.
    C. Dividend discount models are appropriate for valuing REITs because REITs return most of their income to investors.

Use the following information for Questions 9 through 12.

Anna Ginzburg, CFA, is using the following information to analyze a potential investment in an industrial building.

Selected REIT Financial Information

	All amounts in $million
Estimated 12 months cash net operating income (NOI)	$40
Funds from operations (FFO)	$30
Cash and equivalents	$30
Accounts receivable	$20
Debt and other liabilities	$250
Non-cash rents	$5
Recurring maintenance-type capital expenditures	$10
Shares outstanding	10 million shares
Expected annual dividend next year (2014)	$3.00
Dividend growth rate in 2015 and 2016	4%
Dividend growth rate (from 2017 into perpetuity)	3%
Assumed cap rate	8%
Office subsector average P/FFO multiple	12×
Office subsector average P/AFFO multiple	20×
Ginzburg's cost of equity capital	11%
Risk-free rate	2%

9. The value of Ginzburg's potential investment using a net asset value (NAV) approach is *closest* to:
    A. $30.
    B. $35.
    C. $40.

10. The value of Ginzburg's potential investment using a price-to-FFO approach is *closest* to:
    A. $30.
    B. $35.
    C. $40.

11. The value of Ginzburg's potential investment using a price-to-AFFO approach is *closest* to:
    A. $30.
    B. $35.
    C. $40.

12. The value of Ginzburg's potential investment using a discounted cash flow approach is *closest* to:
    A. $30.
    B. $35.
    C. $40.

To access other content related to this topic review that may be included in the Schweser package you purchased, log in to your Schweser.com online dashboard. Schweser's OnDemand Video Lectures deliver streaming instruction covering every LOS in this topic review, while SchweserPro™ QBank provides additional quiz questions to help you practice and recall what you've learned.

ANSWERS – CONCEPT CHECKERS

1. **A** A commingled real estate fund (CREF) is an example of a private real estate investment, not a publicly traded security. The three principal types of publicly traded real estate securities available globally are real estate investment trusts (REITs), real estate operating companies (REOCs), and residential and commercial mortgage-backed securities (MBS).

2. **C** REIT investors have no liability for the REITs in which they invest beyond the original amount invested. REITs and REOCs usually cannot pass on tax losses to their investors as deductions from taxable income. Because REIT prices and returns are determined by the stock market, the value of a REIT is more volatile that its appraised net asset value.

3. **A** After growth in the GDP, the most important factor driving demand for hotel rooms is job creation, because business and leisure travel are closely tied to the size of the workforce. More important to the value of a storage REIT than retail sales growth is population growth. More important to the value of an office REIT than population growth is job creation.

4. **C** When we compare REITs to other kinds of publicly traded shares, REITs offer above-average yields and stable income and returns. Due to their high income-to-payout ratios, REITs have relatively low potential to grow by reinvesting operating cash flows.

5. **A** Most REITs in the United States are structured as UPREITs, not DOWNREITs. The other two statements are true: a DOWNREIT may own properties at both the REIT level and at the partnership level, and may form partnerships for each property acquisition it undertakes.

6. **B** NAVPS is the difference between a REIT's assets and its liabilities, using current market values instead of accounting book values and dividing by the number of shares outstanding. NAVPS is a superior measure of the net worth of a REIT, compared to book value per share which is based on historical cost values. NAV is the largest component of the intrinsic value of a REIT; however, other factors, such as the value of non-asset-based income streams, the value added by management, and the value of any contingent liabilities, also contribute to intrinsic value.

7. **B** To calculate AFFO, we begin with FFO and then deduct non-cash rent, maintenance-type capital expenditures, and leasing commissions.

8. **B** FFO has some shortcomings, but because it is the most standardized method of measuring a REIT's earnings, P/FFO is the most commonly used multiple in analyzing REITs. AFFO is used as a convenient proxy for a "cash flow" multiple because AFFO is an approximation of cash earnings. Dividend discount models are appropriate methods for valuing REITs because REITs return a significant portion of their income to their investors and tend to be high-dividend payers.

©2017 Kaplan, Inc.

9. **A** The value per share for this REIT using net asset value valuation is computed as follows:

Estimated cash NOI	40
Assumed cap rate	8%
Estimated value of operating real estate (40 / .08)	500
Plus: cash + accounts receivable	50
Less: debt and other liabilities	250
Net asset value	300
Shares outstanding	10
NAV / share	$30.00

The REIT share value using the net asset value approach is $30.

10. **B** The value per share for this REIT using price-to-FFO valuation is computed as follows:

Funds from operations (FFO)	$30
Shares outstanding (millions)	10
FFO / share = $30 million / 10 million shares	$3.00

Applying the office subsector average P/FFO multiple of 12× yields a value per share of:

$3.00 × 12 = $36.00

The REIT share value using the price-to-FFO approach is $36.

11. **A** The value per share for this REIT using a price-to-AFFO valuation is computed as follows:

Funds from operations (FFO)	$30
Subtract: non-cash rents	$5
Subtract: recurring maintenance-type capital expenditures	$10
Equals: AFFO	$15
Shares outstanding	10 million
AFFO / share = $15 million / 10 million shares	$1.50
Property subsector average P/AFFO multiple	20×

Applying the office subsector average P/AFFO multiple of 20× yields a value per share of $1.50 × 20 = $30.

The REIT share value using the price-to-AFFO approach is $30.

12. **C** The value per share for this REIT using a discounted cash flow valuation is computed as follows:

	2014	*2015*	*2016*	*2017*
Dividends per share:	$3.00	$3.12	$3.24	$3.34

Present value in 2016 of dividends stream beginning in 2017 = $3.34 / (0.11 − 0.03) = $41.78

Present value of all dividends, when discounted at a rate of 11%

$$= PV_{2014 \text{ dividend}} \quad + PV_{2015 \text{ dividend}} \quad + PV_{2016 \text{ dividend}} \quad + PV_{\text{(terminal value)}}$$

$$= \$3.00/(1.11) \quad + \$3.12/(1.11)^2 \quad + \$3.24/(1.11)^3 \quad + \$41.78/(1.11)^3$$

$$= \$38.15$$

The REIT share value using the discounted cash flow approach is $38.15.

PRIVATE EQUITY VALUATION

Study Session 15

EXAM FOCUS

This topic has a great deal of testable material, both conceptual and quantitative. For the exam, know the three sources of value creation in private equity. Know that, relative to buyouts, venture capital concerns companies that are immature and generally more risky. Understand that the drivers of return for buyouts are earnings growth, the increase in multiple upon exit, and the reduction in the debt; whereas for venture capital, it is the pre-money valuation, the investment, and potential subsequent equity dilution.

Be familiar with risks, costs, structure, and terms that are unique to private equity funds. Know how to calculate management fees, carried interest, NAV, DPI, RVPI, and TVPI of a private equity fund. Using both the NPV and IRR venture capital methods, be able to calculate ownership fraction, number of new shares issued, and the price per share for the new investment.

BACKGROUND: PRIVATE EQUITY

Private equity is of increasing importance in the global economy. Private equity firms make investments ranging from investments in early stage companies (called a venture capital investment) to investments in mature companies (generally in a buyout transaction).

The following diagram may help you understand the private equity investment process.

Figure 1: The Typical Private Equity Investment Transaction

We will use the term *portfolio company* to denote the companies that private equity firms invest in. Portfolio companies are sometimes referred to as investee companies.

We will use the term *private equity firm* (PE firm) to denote the intermediary in the illustrated transaction.

We will use the term *private equity investor* to denote the outside investor who makes an investment in a fund offered by the PE firm.

In this review, we examine the perspective of both private equity firms evaluating investments in portfolio companies and the perspective of an outside investor who is evaluating an investment in a private equity firm.

LOS 45.a: Explain sources of value creation in private equity.

CFA® Program Curriculum, Volume 6, page 141

It is commonly believed that PE firms have the ability to add greater value to their portfolio companies than do publicly governed firms. The sources of this increased value are thought to come from the following:

1. The ability to re-engineer the porfolio company and operate it more efficiently.

2. The ability to obtain debt financing on more advantageous terms.

3. Superior alignment of interests between management and private equity ownership.

Re-engineering the Portfolio Company

In order to re-engineer their portfolio companies, many private equity firms have an in-house staff of experienced industry CEOs, CFOs, and other former senior executives. These executives can share their expertise and contacts with portfolio company management.

Obtaining Favorable Debt Financing

A second source of added value is from more favorable terms on debt financing. During 2006 and the first half of 2007, the availability of cheap credit with few covenants led many private equity firms to use debt for buyout transactions. In PE firms, debt is more heavily utilized and is quoted as a multiple of EBITDA (earnings before interest, taxes, depreciation, and amortization) as opposed to a multiple of equity, as for public firms.

The central proposition of the Modigliani-Miller theorems is that the use of debt versus equity is inconsequential for firm value. However, once the assumption of no taxes is removed from their model, the tax savings from the use of debt (i.e., the interest tax shield) increases firm value. The use of greater amounts of financial leverage may increase firm value in the case of private equity firms. Because these firms have a reputation for efficient management and timely payment of debt interest, this helps to allay concerns over their highly leveraged positions and helps maintain their access to the debt markets.

> *Professor's Note: The Modigliani-Miller theorems are discussed in detail in the corporate finance portion of the curriculum. In that corporate finance material, they are referred to as propositions.*

The use of debt is thought to make private equity portfolio companies more efficient. According to this view, the requirement to make interest payments forces the portfolio companies to use free cash flow more efficiently because interest payments must be made on the debt.

Much of the debt financing for private equity firms comes from the syndicated loan market, but the debt is often repackaged and sold as collateralized loan obligations (CLOs). Private equity firms may also issue high-yield bonds which are repackaged as collateralized debt obligations (CDOs). These transactions have resulted in a large transfer of risk. However, the markets slowed beginning in 2007, creating less availability of financing for large buyouts.

A third source of value added for PE firms is the alignment of interests between private equity owners and the managers of the portfolio companies they own, as discussed in the next LOS.

LOS 45.b: Explain how private equity firms align their interests with those of the managers of portfolio companies.

CFA® Program Curriculum, Volume 6, page 142

In many private equity transactions, ownership and control are concentrated in the same hands. In buyout transactions, management often has a substantial stake in the company's equity. In many venture capital investments, the private equity firm offers advice and management expertise. The private equity firm can also gain increased control if the venture capital investee company does not meet specified targets.

In private equity firms, managers are able to focus more on long-term performance because, unlike public companies, private companies do not face the scrutiny of analysts, shareholders, and the broader market. This also allows the private equity firms to hire managers that are capable of substantial restructuring efforts.

Control Mechanisms

Private equity firms use a variety of mechanisms to align the interests of the managers of portfolio companies with the private equity firm's interests. The following contract terms are contained in the **term sheet** that specifies the terms of the private equity firm's investment.

Compensation: Managers of the portfolio companies receive compensation that is closely linked to the company's performance, and the compensation contract contains clauses that promote the achievement of the firm's goals.

Tag-along, drag-along clauses: Anytime an acquirer acquires control of the company, they must extend the acquisition offer to all shareholders, including firm management.

Board representation: The private equity firm is ensured control through board representation if the portfolio company experiences a major event such as a takeover, restructuring, initial public offering (IPO), bankruptcy, or liquidation.

Noncompete clauses: Company founders must agree to clauses that prevent them from competing against the firm within a prespecified period of time.

Priority in claims: Private equity firms receive their distributions before other owners, often in the form of preferred dividends and sometimes specified as a multiple of their original investment. They also have priority on the company's assets if the portfolio company is liquidated.

Required approvals: Changes of strategic importance (e.g., acquisitions, divestitures, and changes in the business plan) must be approved by the private equity firm.

Earn-outs: These are used predominantly in venture capital investments. Earn-outs tie the acquisition price paid by the private equity firm to the portfolio company's future performance over a specified time period.

By specifying the appropriate control mechanisms in the investment contract, private equity firms can make investments in companies of considerable risk.

LOS 45.c: Distinguish between the characteristics of buyout and venture capital investments.

CFA® Program Curriculum, Volume 6, page 145

Valuation Characteristics of Venture Capital vs. Buyout Investments

Venture capital and buyout are the two main forms of private equity investments. As previously noted, companies financed with venture capital are usually less mature than buyout targets. Venture capital firms usually have a specific industry focus, such as biotechnology, and emphasize revenue growth. When private equity firms make buyout purchases, the emphasis is on EBIT or EBITDA growth, and typically a portfolio of companies with stable earnings growth is purchased.

The following chart summarizes the key differences between venture capital and buyout investments.

Figure 2: Key Differences Between Venture Capital and Buyout Investments

Characteristic	Venture Capital Investments	Buyout Investments
Cash Flows	Low predictability with potentially unrealistic projections	Stable and predictable cash flows
Product Market	New product market with uncertain future	Strong market position with a possible niche position
Products	Product is based on new technology with uncertain prospects	Established products
Asset Base	Weak	Substantial base that can serve as collateral
Management Team	New team although individual members typically have a strong entrepreneurial record	Strong and experienced
Financial Leverage	Low debt use with a majority of equity financing	High amounts of debt with a large percentage of senior debt and substantial amounts of junior and mezzanine debt
Risk Assessment	Risk is difficult to estimate due to new technologies, markets, and company history	Risk can be estimated due to industry and company maturity
Exit	Exit via IPO or company sale is difficult to forecast	Exit is predictable
Operations	High cash burn rate required due to company and product immaturity	Potential exists for reduction in inefficiencies
Working Capital Required	Increasing requirements due to growth	Low requirements
Due Diligence Performed by Private Equity Firms	Private equity firms investigate technological and commercial prospects; investigation of financials is limited due to short history	Private equity firms perform extensive due diligence
Goal Setting	Goals are milestones set in business plan and growth strategy	Goals reference cash flows, strategic plan, and business plan
Private Equity Investment Returns	High returns come from a few highly successful investments with writeoffs from less successful investments	Low variability in the success of investments with failures being rare
Capital Market Presence	Generally not active in capital markets	Active in capital markets
Sales Transactions	Most companies are sold as a result of the relationship between venture capital firm and entrepreneurs	Companies are typically sold in an auction-type process
Ability to Grow Through Subsequent Funding	Companies are less scalable as subsequent funding is typically smaller	Strong performers can increase subsequent funding amounts
Source of General Partner's Variable Revenue	Carried interest is most common, transaction and monitoring fees are less common	Carried interest, transaction fees, and monitoring fees

Terms related to private equity, such as carried interest, and revenue of private equity general partners are discussed in greater detail in an upcoming LOS.

Professor's Note: Many of these characteristics can be more easily remembered if you keep in mind that, relative to companies acquired through buyout, venture capital portfolio companies are immature companies with risky prospects and cash flows. They require a great deal of funding but may have limited access to financing, especially debt. The returns on venture capital come from a small number of highly successful investments.

GENERAL VALUATION ISSUES FOR PRIVATE EQUITY

Public companies are bought and sold on regulated exchanges daily. Private companies, however, are bought by buyers with specific interests at specific points in time, with each potential buyer possibly having a different valuation for the company. Furthermore, valuing a private company is more difficult than valuing public companies because, as discussed previously, PE firms often transform and reengineer the portfolio company such that future cash flow estimates are difficult to obtain.

Private Equity Valuation Methodologies

There are six methodologies used to value private equity portfolio companies.

- **Discounted cash flow (DCF) analysis** is most appropriate for companies with a significant operating history because it requires an estimate of cash flows.
- A **relative value** or **market approach** applies a price multiple, such as the price-earnings ratio, against the company's earnings to get an estimate of the company's valuation. This approach requires predictable cash flows and a significant history.
- A third approach uses **real option analysis** and is applicable for immature companies with flexibility in their future strategies.

Professor's Note: Real options are covered in more detail in the topic review on capital budgeting in Corporate Finance.

- The fourth approach uses the **replacement cost** of the business. It is generally not applicable to mature companies whose historical value added would be hard to estimate.
- The last two approaches, the **venture capital method** and the **leveraged buyout method**, are discussed at the end of this review.

Other Considerations

Other considerations for valuing private equity portfolio companies are control premiums, country risk, and marketability and illiquidity discounts. In buyouts, the private equity investors typically have complete control. In venture capital investments, however, these investors usually have a minority position, and their control of the companies depends on the alignment of their interests with that of controlling shareholders. When valuing companies in emerging markets, country risk premiums may be added, thereby increasing the discount rate applied to the company's cash flows. Illiquidity and marketability discounts refer to the ability and right to sell the company's shares, respectively.

©2017 Kaplan, Inc.

Price Multiples

To value private equity portfolio companies, many investors use market data from similar publicly traded companies, most commonly the price multiples from comparable public companies. However, it is often difficult to find public companies at the same stage of development, same line of business, same capital structure, and same risk. A decision must also be made as to whether trailing or future earnings are used. For these reasons, a relative value or market approach should be used carefully.

Discounted Cash Flow Analysis

Market data is also used with discounted cash flow (DCF) analysis, with beta and the cost of capital estimated from public companies while adjusting for differences in operating and financial leverage between the private and public comparables. In DCF analysis, an assumption must be made regarding the company's future value. Typically a terminal value (i.e., an exit value) is calculated using a price multiple of the company's EBITDA.

> *Professor's Note: Adjusting beta for differences in operating and financial leverage between comparables is covered in more detail in the topic review on return concepts in the equity section of the curriculum.*

Given the uncertainty associated with private companies, a variety of valuation techniques is typically applied to a range of different potential scenarios.

BUYOUT VALUATION ISSUES

Types of Buyouts

In a buyout transaction, the buyer acquires a controlling equity position in a target company. Buyouts include takeovers, management buyouts (MBOs), and leveraged buyouts (LBOs). This review focuses on LBOs, in which a high amount of debt is used to finance a substantial portion of the acquisition. The financing of a LBO typically involves senior debt, junk bonds, equity, and mezzanine finance. Mezzanine finance is a hybrid between debt and equity and can be structured to suit each particular transaction.

Leveraged Buyout (LBO)

The view of an LBO transaction, referred to as the LBO model, is not a form of valuation but rather a method of factoring in the company's capital structure and other parameters to determine the return the private equity firm should expect from the transaction. The objective is not to value the company but to determine the maximum price in negotiation that the private equity firm should pay for its stake.

LBO Model

The LBO model has three main inputs:

1. The target company's forecasted cash flows.

2. The expected returns to the providers of the financing.

3. The total amount of financing.

The cash flow forecasts are provided by the target's management but scrutinized by the private equity firm. The exit date (when the target company is sold) is evaluated at different dates to determine its influence on the projected returns. The value of the company at that time is forecast using a relative value or market approach.

LOS 45.d: Describe valuation issues in buyout and venture capital transactions.

CFA® Program Curriculum, Volume 6, page 146

Exit Value

The exit value can be viewed as:

$$\underset{\text{cost}}{\text{investment}} + \underset{\text{growth}}{\text{earnings}} + \underset{\text{price multiple}}{\text{increase in}} + \underset{\text{in debt}}{\text{reduction}} = \text{exit value}$$

As previously mentioned, private equity firms are known for their reengineering and improved corporate governance of target companies, which should result in operational efficiencies and higher earnings growth. As a result, the target company should see an increase in price multiples and increased ability to pay down its debt. Each of the three variables should be examined using scenario analysis to determine the plausibility of their forecasted values and the forecasted exit value. One purpose for calculating the exit value is to determine the investment's internal rate of return sensitivity in the exit year.

Example: Calculating payoff multiples and IRRs for equity investors

Suppose an LBO transaction is valued at $1,000 million and has the following characteristics (amounts are in millions of dollars):

- Exit occurs in five years at a projected multiple of 1.80 of the company's initial cost.
- It is financed with 60% debt and 40% equity.
- The $400 equity investment is composed of:
    - $310 in preference shares held by the private equity firm.
    - $80 in equity held by the private equity firm.
    - $10 in equity held by management equity participation (MEP).
- Preference shares are guaranteed a 14% compound annual return payable at exit.
- The equity of the private equity firm is promised 90% of the company's residual value at exit after creditors and preference shares are paid.
- Management equity receives the other 10% residual value.
- By exit, the company will have paid off $350 of the initial $600 in debt using operating cash flow.

Calculate the payoff for the company's claimants and the internal rate of return (IRR) and payoff multiple for the equity claimants.

Answer:

First calculate the exit value as: $1,000 × 1.8 = $1,800.

Next calculate the claimants' payoffs:

- *Debt:* The claim of debtholders is their initial investment minus the amount that has been paid down: $600 – $350 = $250.   *250 Left*
- *Preference shares:* Earn a return of 14% so their claim is: $310 × (1.14)^5 = $596.88. ✓
- *Private equity firm:* Receives 90% of the residual exit value: 0.90(1,800 – $250 – $596.88) = $857.81. ✓
- *Management:* Receives 10% of the residual exit value: 0.10(1,800 – $250 – $596.88) = $95.31. ✓

Exit Value = 1800 - 250 - 596.88
2561 debt   DVD distribution

The total investment by the private equity firm is $310 + $80 = $390.

DVD + End Value

The total payoff is $596.88 + $857.81 = $1454.69.

Value Equity   Return on Equity

The payoff multiple for the private equity firm is: 1454.69 / 390 = 3.7.

Using your TI BA II Plus, the IRR is calculated as: PV = –$390; FV = $1454.69; N = 5; CPT I/Y ⇒ 30.1%.   *ignore Dividends*

For the management equity, the IRR is: PV = –$10; FV = $95.31; N = 5; CPT I/Y ⇒ 57.0%.

The payoff multiple for the management equity program (MEP) is: 95.31 / 10 = 9.5.

In the example, the equity held by the private equity firm and management experiences a significant increase in value. The IRR for each is attractive at 30.1% and 57.0%, respectively.

The components of the return are:

- The return on the preference shares for the private equity firm.
- The increased multiple upon exit.
- The reduction in the debt claim.

In most LBOs, most of the debt is senior debt that will amortize over time. In the preceding example, the debtholders' claim on assets was reduced from $600 to $250. The use of debt in this example is advantageous and magnifies the returns to the equityholders. However, the use of debt also increases risk to the equityholders. Use of debt becomes disadvantageous if a company experiences difficulties and cannot make the payments on the debt. In this case, the equityholders could lose control of the company if it is forced into bankruptcy.

VALUATION ISSUES IN VENTURE CAPITAL INVESTMENTS

Pre- and Post-Money Valuation

The two fundamental concepts in venture capital investments are pre-money (PRE) valuation and post-money (POST) valuation. A private equity firm makes an investment (INV) in an early-stage start-up company.

The post-money valuation of the investee company is:

$$PRE + INV = POST$$

The ownership proportion of the venture capital (VC) investor is:

$$= INV / POST$$

> **Example: Calculating post-money valuation and proportional ownership**
>
> A company is valued at $3,000,000 prior to a capital infusion of $1,000,000 by a VC investor.
>
> Calculate the post-money valuation and the VC investor's proportional ownership.
>
> **Answer:**
>
> The post-money valuation is:
>
> $3,000,000 + $1,000,000 = $4,000,000
>
> The ownership proportion of the VC investor is:
>
> = $1,000,000 / $4,000,000 = 25%

Appropriate Methods for Venture Capital Valuation

The pre-money valuation and investment will be negotiated between the investee company and the VC investor. Additionally, the VC investor should keep in mind that his ownership could be diluted in the future due to future financing, conversion of convertible debt into equity, and the issuance of stock options to management.

As discussed previously, it is difficult to forecast the cash flows for a VC portfolio company. Therefore, discounted cash flow analysis (the income approach) is not usually used as the primary valuation method for VC companies. It is also difficult to use a relative value or market approach. This is because a VC company is often unique, and there may be no comparable companies to estimate a benchmark price multiple from. A replacement cost approach may also be difficult to apply. Alternative methodologies include real option analysis and the venture capital method, which will be addressed later in this review.

To estimate the pre-money valuation, the VC investor typically examines the company's intellectual property and capital, the potential for the company's products, and its intangible assets. Sometimes a cap (e.g., $3,000,000) is placed on the pre-money valuation due to its uncertain value.

VALUATION ISSUES: BUYOUT VS. VENTURE CAPITAL

The following table highlights the different issues when valuing buyouts versus venture capital.

Figure 3: Valuation Issues for Buyouts vs. Venture Capital Investments

Valuation Issue	Buyout	Venture Capital
Applicability of DCF Method	Frequently used to estimate value of equity	Less frequently used as cash flows are uncertain
Applicability of Relative Value Approach	Used to check the value from DCF analysis	Difficult to use because there may be no truly comparable companies
Use of Debt	High	Low as equity is dominant form of financing
Key Drivers of Equity Return	Earnings growth, increase in multiple upon exit, and reduction in the debt	Pre-money valuation, investment, and subsequent dilution

Professor's Note: Valuation methodologies for buyouts need to factor in the level and pattern of leverage over the investment term. Initially, debt levels are high but are expected to decrease to "normal" levels by the time of exit. We address this issue near the end of this topic review.

LOS 45.e: Explain alternative exit routes in private equity and their impact on value.

CFA® Program Curriculum, Volume 6, page 149

Types of Exit Routes

The exit value is a critical element in the return for the private equity firm and is considered carefully before the investment is undertaken. The means and timing of the exit strongly influence the exit value. There are four exit routes that private equity firms typically use: (1) an initial public offering (IPO), (2) secondary market sale, (3) management buyout (MBO), and (4) liquidation.

Initial Public Offering (IPO)

In an IPO, a company's equity is offered for public sale. An IPO usually results in the highest exit value due to increased liquidity, greater access to capital, and the potential to hire better quality managers. However, an IPO is less flexible, more costly, and a more cumbersome process than the other alternatives.

IPOs are most appropriate for companies with strong growth prospects and a significant operating history and size. The timing of an IPO is key. After the bursting of the U.S. tech bubble in 2000, the IPO market withered and venture capital firms had to find other means of exit.

Secondary Market Sale

In a secondary market sale, the company is sold to another investor or to another company interested in the purchase for strategic reasons (e.g., a company in the same industry wishes to expand its market share). Secondary market sales from one investor to another are quite frequent, especially in the case of buyouts. VC portfolio companies are sometimes exited via a buyout to another firm, but VC companies are usually too immature to support a large amount of debt. Secondary market sales result in the second highest company valuations after IPOs.

Management Buyout (MBO)

In an MBO, the company is sold to management, who utilize a large amount of leverage. Although management will have a strong interest in the subsequent success of the company, the resulting high leverage may limit management's flexibility.

Liquidation

Liquidation, the outright sale of the company's assets, is pursued when the company is deemed no longer viable and usually results in a low value. There is potential for negative publicity as a result of displaced employees and from the obvious implications of the company's failure to reach its objectives.

Exit Timing

The timing of the exit is also very important for company value, and the private equity firm should be flexible in this regard. For example, if a portfolio company cannot be sold due to weak capital markets, the private equity firm may want to consider buying another portfolio company at depressed prices, merging the two companies, and waiting until capital market conditions improve to sell both portfolio companies as one.

When an exit is anticipated in the next year or two, the exit valuation multiple can be forecasted without too much error. Beyond this time horizon, however, exit multiples become much more uncertain and stress testing should be performed on a wide range of possible values.

Professor's Note: Don't lose sight of the purpose of valuation: (1) to assess the ability of the portfolio company to generate cash flow and (2) to represent a benchmark for negotiations.

LOS 45.f: Explain private equity fund structures, terms, valuation, and due diligence in the context of an analysis of private equity fund returns.

CFA® Program Curriculum, Volume 6, page 151

Limited Partnership

The most common form of ownership structure for private equity funds is the limited partnership. In a limited partnership, the limited partners (LPs) provide funding and do not have an active role in the management of the investments. Their liability is limited to what they have invested (i.e., they cannot be held liable for any amount beyond their investment in the fund). The general partner (GP) in a limited partnership is liable for all the firm's debts and, thus, has unlimited liability. The GP is the manager of the fund.

Another form of private equity fund structure is the company limited by shares. It offers better legal protection to the partners, depending on the jurisdiction. Most fund structures are closed end, meaning that investors can only redeem the investment at specified time periods.

Private equity firms must both raise funds and manage the investment of those funds. The private equity firm usually spends a year or two raising funds. Funds are then drawn down for investment, after which returns are realized. Most private equity funds last 10 to 12 years but can have their life extended another 2 to 3 years.

Private Equity Fund Terms

As mentioned previously, private equity investments are often only available to qualified investors, the definition of which depends on the jurisdiction. In the United States, the individual must have at least $1 million in assets.

The terms in a fund prospectus are a result of negotiation between the GP and the LPs. If the fund is oversubscribed (i.e., has more prospective investors than needed), the GP has greater negotiating power.

The terms of the fund should be focused towards aligning the interests of the GP and LPs and specifying the compensation of the GP. The most important terms can be categorized into economic and corporate governance terms.

Economic Terms of a Private Equity Fund

Management fees: These are fees paid to the GP on an annual basis as a percent of committed capital and are commonly 2%. Management fees could instead be based on NAV or paid-in capital.

Transaction fees: These are paid by third parties to the GP in their advisory capacity (e.g., for investment banking services, such as arranging a merger). These fees are usually split evenly with the LPs and, when received, are deducted from management fees.

Carried interest/performance fees: This is the GP's share of the fund profits and is usually 20% of profits (after management fees).

Ratchet: This specifies the allocation of equity between stockholders and management of the portfolio company and allows management to increase their allocation, depending on company performance.

Hurdle rate: This is the IRR that the fund must meet before the GP can receive carried interest. It usually varies from 7% to 10% and incentivizes the GP.

Target fund size: The stated total maximum size of the PE fund, specified as an absolute figure. It signals the GP's ability to manage and raise capital for a fund. It is a negative signal if actual funds ultimately raised are significantly lower than targeted.

Vintage: This is the year the fund was started and facilitates performance comparisons with other funds.

Term of the fund: As discussed previously, this is the life of the firm and is usually ten years.

> *Professor's Note: There are several "capital" terms used throughout this reading. Committed capital is the amount of funds promised by investors to private equity funds. Paid-in capital is the amount of funds actually received from investors (also referred to as invested capital in this reading).*

Example: Calculating carried interest with a hurdle rate

Performance ↓

Suppose a fund has committed capital of $100 million, carried interest of 20%, and a hurdle rate of 9%. The firm called 80% of its commitments in the beginning of Year 1. Of this, $50 million was invested in Company A and $30 million in Company B.

At the end of Year 2, a $7 million profit is realized on the exit from Company A. The investment in Company B is unchanged. The carried interest is calculated on a deal-by-deal basis (i.e., the IRR for determining carried interest is calculated for each deal upon exit).

Determine the theoretical carried interest and the actual carried interest.

Answer:

The theoretical carried interest is: 20% × $7,000,000 = $1,400,000.

The IRR for Company A is: PV = –$50; FV = $57; N = 2; CPT I/Y ⇒ 6.8%.

Because the 6.8% IRR is less than the hurdle rate of 9%, no carried interest is actually paid.

Corporate Governance Terms of a Private Equity Fund

The corporate governance terms in the prospectus provide the legal arrangements for the control of the fund and include the following:

Key man clause: If a key named executive leaves the fund or does not spend a sufficient amount of time at the fund, the GP may be prohibited from making additional investments until another key executive is selected.

Performance disclosure and confidentiality: This specifies the fund performance information that can be disclosed. Note that the performance information for underlying portfolio companies is typically not disclosed.

Clawback: If a fund is profitable early in its life, the GP receives compensation from the GP's contractually defined share of profits. Under a clawback provision, if the fund subsequently underperforms, the GP is required to pay back a portion of the early profits to the LPs. The clawback provision is usually settled at termination of the fund but can also be settled annually (also known as true-up).

Distribution waterfall: This provision specifies the method in which profits will flow to the LPs and when the GP receives carried interest. Two methods are commonly used. In a deal-by-deal method, carried interest can be distributed after each individual deal. The disadvantage of this method from the LPs' perspective is that one deal could earn $10 million and another could lose $10 million, but the GP will receive carried interest on the first deal, even though the LPs have not earned an overall positive return.

In the total return method, carried interest is calculated on the entire portfolio. There are two variants of the total return method: (1) carried interest can be paid only after the entire *committed* capital is returned to LPs; or (2) carried interest can be paid when the value of the portfolio exceeds *invested* capital by some minimum amount (typically 20%). Notice that the former uses committed capital whereas the latter uses only the capital actually invested.

Tag-along, drag-along clauses: Anytime an acquirer acquires control of the company, they must extend the acquisition offer to all shareholders, including firm management.

No-fault divorce: This clause allows a GP to be fired if a supermajority (usually 75% or more) of the LPs agree to do so.

Removal for cause: This provision allows for the firing of the GP or the termination of a fund given sufficient cause (e.g., a material breach of fund prospectus).

Investment restrictions: These specify leverage limits, a minimum amount of diversification, etc.

Co-investment: This provision allows the LPs to invest in other funds of the GP at low or no management fees. This provides the GP another source of funds. The provision also prevents the GP from using capital from different funds to invest in the same portfolio company. A conflict of interest would arise if the GP takes capital from one fund to invest in a troubled company that had received capital earlier from another fund.

Example: Applying distribution waterfalls methods

Suppose a fund has committed capital of $100 million and carried interest of 20%. An investment of $40 million is made. Later in the year, the fund exits the investment and earns a profit of $22 million.

Determine whether the GP receives any carried interest under the three distribution waterfall methods.

Answer:

In the deal-by-deal method, carried interest can be distributed after each individual deal, so carried interest of 20% × $22,000,000 = $4,400,000 is paid to the GP.

In the total return method #1, carried interest can be paid only after the portfolio value exceeds *committed* capital. Committed capital is $100 million and total proceeds from the exit are only $62 million, so no carried interest is paid.

In the total return method #2, carried interest can be paid when the value of the portfolio exceeds *invested* capital by some minimum amount (typically 20%).

Invested capital plus the 20% threshold is: $40,000,000 × 1.20 = $48 million.

The total proceeds from the exit are $62 million, so carried interest of $4,400,000 is paid to the GP.

Example: Applying clawback provision methods

Continuing with the previous example, suppose that in the second year, another investment of $25 million is exited and results in a loss of $4 million. Assume the deal-by-deal method and a clawback with annual true-up apply.

Determine whether the GP must return any former profits to the LPs.

Answer:

In the deal-by-deal method, the GP had received carried interest of $4,400,000.

With a subsequent loss of $4 million, the GP owes the LPs 20% of the loss:

$20\% \times \$4,000,000 = \$800,000$

Net Asset Value (NAV)

Because there is no ready secondary market for private equity investments, they are difficult to value. In a prospectus, however, the valuation is related to the fund's net asset value (NAV), which is the value of fund assets minus liabilities.

Ways to Determine NAV

The assets are valued by the GP in one of six ways:

1. At cost, adjusting for subsequent financing and devaluation.

2. At the minimum of cost or market value.

3. By revaluing a portfolio company anytime there is new financing.

4. At cost, with no adjustment until exit.

5. By using a discount factor for restricted securities (e.g., those that can only be sold to qualified investors).

6. Less frequently, by applying illiquidity discounts to values based on those of comparable publicly traded companies.

Issues in Calculating NAV

There are several issues with calculating NAV for a private equity fund:

- First, if the NAV is only adjusted when there are subsequent rounds of financing, then the NAV will be more stale when financings are infrequent.
- Second, there is no definitive method for calculating NAV for a private equity fund because the market value of portfolio companies is usually not certain until exit.

only Invested

- Third, undrawn LP capital commitments are not included in the NAV calculation but are essentially liabilities for the LP. The value of the commitments depends on the cash flows generated from them, but these are quite uncertain. When a GP has trouble raising funds, this implies that the value of these commitments is low.
- Fourth, the investor should be aware that funds with different strategies and maturities may use different valuation methodologies. In the early stages, a venture capital investment is typically valued at cost. In the later stages, a method based on comparables may be used. Mature funds may use market comparables for their investments that are near exit. Asset price bubbles would inflate the value of these companies.
- Finally, it is usually the GP who values the fund. LPs are increasingly using third parties to value private equity funds.

Due Diligence of Private Equity Fund Investments

Before investing, outside investors should conduct a thorough due diligence of a private equity fund due to the following characteristics:

- First, private equity funds have returns that tend to persist. Hence, a fund's past performance is useful information. In other words, outperformers tend to keep outperforming and underperformers tend to keep underperforming or go out of business.
- Second, the return discrepancy between outperformers and underperformers is very large and can be as much as 20%.
- Third, private equity investments are usually illiquid, long-term investments. The duration of a private equity investment, however, is usually shorter than expected because when a portfolio company is exited, the funds are immediately returned to the fund investors.

LOS 45.g: Explain risks and costs of investing in private equity.

CFA® Program Curriculum, Volume 6, page 156

Post-Investment Investor Expectations

Once an investment is made by a private equity firm, the outside investors in the private equity fund expect to be apprised of the firm's performance. The following material now takes the perspective of this outside investor.

There are two important differences between investing in public equity and in a private equity fund. First, funds are committed in the private investments and later drawn down as capital is invested in portfolio companies. In a public firm, the committed capital is usually immediately deployed. Second, the returns on a private equity investment typically follow a J-Curve pattern through time. Initially, returns are negative but then turn positive as portfolio companies are sold at exit.

Private equity investments are usually regulated such that they are only available to "qualified" investors, usually defined as institutions and wealthy individuals. These regulations exist because of the high risks associated with private equity investing, which are disclosed in the private equity prospectus.

Risks of Investing in Private Equity

Classifying private equity risks broadly, the categories of private equity risk are general private equity risk (discussed in the following), risks specific to the investment strategy, industry risks, risks specific to the investment vehicle, and any regional or country risk.

General Risk Factors

The general private equity risk factors are as follows:

Liquidity risk: Because private equity investments are not publicly traded, it may be difficult to liquidate a position.

Unquoted investments risk: Because private equity investments do not have a publicly quoted price, they may be riskier than publicly traded securities.

Competitive environment risk: The competition for finding reasonably-priced private equity investments may be high.

Agency risk: The managers of private equity portfolio companies may not act in the best interests of the private equity firm and investors.

Capital risk: Increases in business and financial risks may result in a withdrawal of capital. Additionally, portfolio companies may find that subsequent rounds of financing are difficult to obtain.

Regulatory risk: The portfolio companies' products and services may be adversely affected by government regulation.

Tax risk: The tax treatment of investment returns may change over time.

Valuation risk: The valuation of private equity investments reflects subjective, not independent, judgment.

Diversification risk: Private equity investments may be poorly diversified, so investors should diversify across investment development stage, vintage, and strategy of private equity funds.

Market risk: Private equity is subject to long-term changes in interest rates, exchange rates, and other market risks. Short-term changes are usually not significant risk factors.

Costs of Private Equity Investing

The costs of investing in private equity are significantly higher than that with publicly traded securities and include the following:

Transaction costs: These costs include those from due diligence, bank financing, legal fees from acquisitions, and sales transactions in portfolio companies.

Investment vehicle fund setup costs: The legal and other costs of setting up the fund are usually amortized over the life of the fund.

Administrative costs: These are charged on a yearly basis and include custodian, transfer agent, and accounting costs.

Audit costs: These are fixed and charged annually.

Management and performance costs: These are typically higher than that for other investments and are commonly 2% for the management fee and a 20% fee for performance.

Dilution costs: As discussed previously, additional rounds of financing and stock options granted to portfolio company management will result in dilution. This is also true for options issued to the private equity firm.

Placement fees: Placement agents who raise funds for private equity firms may charge up-front fees as much as 2% or annual trailer fees as a percent of funds raised through limited partners.

 Professor's Note: A *trailer fee* is the compensation paid by the fund manager to the person selling the fund to investors.

LOS 45.h: Interpret and compare financial performance of private equity funds from the perspective of an investor.

CFA® Program Curriculum, Volume 6, page 159

Internal Rate of Return (IRR)

The return metric recommended for private equity by the Global Investment Performance Standards (GIPS) is the IRR. The IRR is a cash-weighted (money-weighted) return measure. Although the private equity fund portfolio companies are actually illiquid, IRR assumes intermediate cash flows are reinvested at the IRR. Therefore, the IRR calculation should be interpreted cautiously.

Gross IRR

The IRR can be calculated gross or net of fees. Gross IRR reflects the fund's ability to generate a return from portfolio companies and is the relevant measure for the cash flows between the fund and portfolio companies.

Net IRR

Net IRR can differ substantially from Gross IRR because it is net of management fees, carried interest, and other compensation to the GP. Net IRR is the relevant measure for the cash flows between the fund and LPs and is therefore the relevant return metric for the LPs.

©2017 Kaplan, Inc.

MULTIPLES

Multiples are also used to evaluate fund performance. Multiples are a popular tool of LPs due to their simplicity, ease of use, and ability to differentiate between realized and unrealized returns. Multiples, however, ignore the time value of money.

Quantitative Measures

The more popular multiples and those specified by GIPS include the following:

PIC (paid-in capital). This is the capital utilized by the GP. It can be specified in percentage terms as the paid-in capital to date divided by the committed capital. Alternatively, it can be specified in absolute terms as the cumulative capital utilized or called down.

DPI (distributed to paid-in capital). This measures the LP's realized return and is the cumulative distributions paid to the LPs divided by the cumulative invested capital. It is net of management fees and carried interest. DPI is also referred to as the cash-on-cash return.

RVPI (residual value to paid-in capital). This measures the LP's unrealized return and is the value of the LP's holdings in the fund divided by the cumulative invested capital. It is net of management fees and carried interest.

TVPI (total value to paid-in capital). This measures the LP's realized and unrealized return and is the sum of DPI and RVPI. It is net of management fees and carried interest.

Qualitative Measures

In addition to quantitative analysis of the fund, the investor should also analyze qualitative aspects of the fund, including the following:

- The realized investments, with an evaluation of successes and failures.
- The unrealized investments, with an evaluation of exit horizons and potential problems.
- Cash flow projections at the fund and portfolio company level.
- Fund valuation, NAV, and financial statements.

As an example, consider a fund that was started before the financial market collapse of 2007. If the RVPI is large relative to the DPI, this indicates that the firm has not successfully harvested many of its investments and that the fund may have an extended J-curve (it is taking longer than realized to earn a positive return on its investments). The investor should carefully examine the GP's valuations of the remaining portfolio companies, potential write-offs, and whether the routes for future exit have dried up.

Benchmarks

especially for IRR

The benchmarking of private equity investments can be challenging. Private equity funds vary substantially from one to another; so before performance evaluation is performed, the investor should have a good understanding of the fund's structures, terms, valuation, and the results of due diligence. Because there are cyclical trends in IRR returns, the Net IRR should be benchmarked against a peer group of comparable private equity funds of the same vintage and strategy.

Professor's Note: The vintage refers to the year the fund was set up.

Note also that the private equity IRR is cash flow weighted whereas most other asset class index returns are time weighted. One solution to this problem has been to convert publicly traded equity benchmark returns to cash weighted returns using the cash flow patterns of private equity funds. This method, however, has some significant limitations.

Be careful Cash weighted vs Time weighted

IRR

Example: Comparing the financial performance of private equity funds

Two private equity funds, Fund A and Fund B, are being considered by an investor.

Financial Performance of Private Equity Fund A and Fund B

	Fund A	Fund B
Gross IRR	22.1%	2.4%
Net IRR	17.6%	−0.3%
Performance quartile	1	3
DPI	1.43	0.29
RVPI	1.52	1.03
TVPI	2.95	1.32
Maturity of fund	6 years	4 years

Interpret and compare the financial performance of private equity funds A and B.

Answer:

Examining its DPI, Fund A has distributed $1.43 in return for every dollar invested. Additionally, the RVPI implies that it will return $1.52 as other investments are harvested. Its Gross IRR of 22.1% is attractive, and after fees, the Net IRR is 17.6%. The fund ranks in the first quartile in its peer group of the same strategy and vintage.

At four years, Fund B is a less mature fund than Fund A. Fund B's DPI is 0.29, indicating that the realized returns for the fund are not substantial. Unrealized returns (RVPI) indicate that its investments not yet harvested should provide an additional return. The low Gross and Net IRRs indicate that the firm may still be affected by the J-curve, where a fund experiences initial losses before experiencing later profits. Currently, the firm is lagging its peers, as it ranks in the third quartile.

Note that in this illustrative example, we compared two funds of different maturities. As noted, a fund should be benchmarked against peers of the same vintage.

Must

we have to compare against same vintage.

LOS 45.i: Calculate management fees, carried interest, net asset value, distributed to paid in (DPI), residual value to paid in (RVPI), and total value to paid in (TVPI) of a private equity fund.

CFA® Program Curriculum, Volume 6, page 161

In this section, we calculate the quantitative measures previously discussed using an example.

Example: Calculating performance measures

The GP for private equity Fund C charges a management fee of 2% of paid-in-capital and carried interest of 20%, using the first total return method (i.e., carried interest is paid only when the value of the investment portfolio exceeds committed capital). The total committed capital for the fund was $150 million. The statistics for years 2011–2016 are shown in the following table (in millions).

Cash Flows for Private Equity Fund C

	Capital Called Down	Paid-in Capital	Management Fees	Operating Results	NAV before Distributions	Carried Interest	Distributions	NAV after Distributions
2011	50	50	1.0	–10	39.0			39.0
2012	20	70	1.4	–25	32.6			32.6
2013	30	100	2.0	25	85.6			85.6
2014	20	120	2.4	50	153.2	0.6	20	132.6
2015	10	130	2.6	60	200.0	9.4	40	150.6
2016	10	140	2.8	110	267.8	13.6	80	174.2

Handwritten annotations: "J curve", "Net of 2 fees", "50 × 2% = 1.0", "in loss", "20 < 25", "153.2 > 150", "132.6 + 10 + 60 – 2.6 = 200", "140"

Professor's Note: In the table, assume the capital called down, operating results, and distributions were given. The other statistics can be calculated.

Calculate the management fees, carried interest, NAV before distributions, NAV after distributions, distributed to paid in (DPI), residual value to paid in (RVPI), and total value to paid in (TVPI) of private equity Fund C.

Answer:

Paid-in capital: This is just the cumulative sum of the capital called down. For example, in 2012, it is the sum of the capital called down in 2011 and 2012: $50 + $20 = $70.

Management fees: In each year, these are calculated as the percentage fee (here 2%) multiplied by the paid-in capital. For example, in 2012, it is 2% × $70 = $1.4.

Carried interest: Carried interest is not paid until the GP generates realized and unrealized returns (as reflected in the NAV before distributions) greater than the committed capital of $150.

In 2014, the NAV before distributions exceeded the committed capital for the first time. In this first year, the carried interest is 20% multiplied by the NAV before distributions minus the committed capital: 20% × ($153.2 − $150) = $0.6.

In subsequent years, it is calculated using the increase in the NAV before distributions. For example, in 2015, it is: 20% × ($200 − $153.2) = $9.4.

NAV before distributions: These are calculated as:

$$= \frac{\text{NAV after}}{\text{distributions in}} + \frac{\text{capital called}}{\text{down}} - \frac{\text{management}}{\text{fees}} + \frac{\text{operating}}{\text{results}}$$
$$\text{prior year}$$

For example in 2015, NAV before distributions is: $132.6 + $10 − $2.6 + $60 = $200.

NAV after distributions: These are calculated as:

$$= \frac{\text{NAV before}}{\text{distributions}} - \frac{\text{carried}}{\text{interest}} - \text{distributions}$$

For example in 2015, NAV after distributions is: $200 − $9.40 − $40 = $150.60.

For DPI, RVPI, and TVPI, we will calculate these as of the most recent year (2016):

DPI: The DPI multiple is calculated as the cumulative distributions divided by the paid-in capital: ($20 + $40 + $80) / $140 = 1.0. This indicates that, in terms of distributed returns, the fund has returned every dollar invested.

RVPI: The RVPI multiple is calculated as the NAV after distributions (i.e., the net non-distributed value of the fund) divided by the paid-in capital: $174.2 / $140 = 1.24. This indicates that, although the distributed returns are not impressive for this fund, the fund has unrealized profits that should accrue to the LPs as investments are harvested.

TVPI: The TVPI multiple is the sum of the DPI and RVPI: 1.0 + 1.24 = 2.24. This indicates that on a realized and unrealized basis, the GP has more than doubled the investment of the LPs.

LOS 45.j: Calculate pre-money valuation, post-money valuation, ownership fraction, and price per share applying the venture capital method 1) with single and multiple financing rounds and 2) in terms of IRR.

CFA® Program Curriculum, Volume 6, page 166

Here, we describe the valuation of an investment in an existing company using the **venture capital (VC) method**.

At the time of a new investment in the company, the discounted present value of the estimated exit value, PV(exit value), is called the **post-money value** (after the investment is made). The value before the investment is made can be calculated as the post-money value minus the investment amount and is called the **pre-money value**.

POST = PV(exit value)

PRE = POST – INV

In order to determine the number of new shares issued to the venture capital firm (shares$_{VC}$) for an investment in an existing company, we need to determine the fraction of the company value (after the investment is made) that the investment represents. Based on the expected future value of the company (exit value) and the expected or required rate of return on the investment, we can do this in either of two ways with the same result.

The fraction of VC ownership (f) for the VC investment can be computed as:

The first method (**NPV method**):

$$f = \frac{INV}{POST}$$

where:

INV = amount of new investment for the venture capital investment.

POST = post-money value after the investment.

$$POST = \frac{exit\ value}{(1+r)^n}$$

The second method (**IRR method**):

$$f = \frac{FV(INV)}{exit\ value}$$

where:

FV(INV) = future value of the investment in round 1 at the expected exit date.

exit value = value of the company upon exit.

As long as the same compound rate is used to calculate the present value of the exit value and to calculate the future value of the VC investment, the fractional ownership required (f) is the same under either method.

Once we have calculated f, we can calculate the number of shares issued to the VC (shares$_{VC}$) based on the number of existing shares owned by the company founders prior to investment (shares$_{Founders}$).

$$shares_{VC} = shares_{Founders}\left(\frac{f}{1-f}\right)$$

The price per share at the time of the investment (price) is then simply the amount of the investment divided by the number of new shares issued.

$$price = \frac{INV}{shares_{VC}}$$

Example: Calculations using the NPV venture capital method and a single financing round

Ponder Technologies is a biotech company. Ponder's entrepreneur founders believe they can sell the company for $40 million in five years. They need $5 million in capital now, and the entrepreneurs currently hold 1 million shares.

The venture capital firm, VC Investors, decides that given the high risk of this company, a discount rate of 40% is appropriate.

Calculate the pre-money valuation, post-money valuation, ownership fraction, and price per share applying the NPV venture capital method with a single financing round.

Answer:

Step 1: The post-money (POST) valuation is the present value of the expected exit value (this assumes the investment was made in the company):

$$POST = \frac{40,000,000}{(1+0.40)^5} = 7,437,377$$ ✓

Step 2: The pre-money (PRE) valuation is what the company would hypothetically be worth without the investment:

PRE = 7,437,377 – 5,000,000 = 2,437,377

Step 3: To put $5 million in a company worth $7.4 million, the private equity firm must own 67.23% of the company:

$$f = \frac{5,000,000}{7,437,377} = 67.23\%$$

Note that under the IRR method, f is the same:

$$f = \frac{5 \text{ million}(1.40^5)}{40 \text{ million}} = 67.23\%$$

Step 4: If the entrepreneurs want 1 million shares, the private equity firm must get 2.05 million shares to get 67.23% ownership:

$$S_{VC} = 1,000,000\left[\frac{0.6723}{(1-0.6723)}\right] = 2,051,572$$ ✓

Step 5: Given a $5 million investment and 2.05 million shares, the stock price per share (P) must be:

$$P = \frac{5,000,000}{2,051,572} = \$2.44 \text{ per share}$$ ✓

Professor's Note: For the purpose of differentiating terms between multiple rounds of venture capital investment, we are using subscripts 1 and 2 in this section to denote first and second round, respectively. For multiple rounds of VC financing, we work backwards (from last round to first).

If there is a second round of VC financing (INV_2), we can calculate the new fractional ownership from the new investment (f_2) and the number of new shares required ($shares_{VC2}$) using the NPV method, as:

$$f_2 = \frac{INV_2}{POST_2}$$

$$f = \frac{INV}{POST} \; (NPV)$$

Where $POST_2$ is the discounted present value of the company as of the time of the second financing round, its post-money value after the second round investment.

$$POST_2 = \frac{exit\ value}{(1+r_2)^{n2}}$$

$$PV\ of\ (Exit\ Value)$$

and

Premoney

$$PRE_2 = POST_2 - INV_2$$

$POST_1$ is the discounted present value of the company as of the time of the first financing round, its post-money value after the first round investment.

$$POST_1 = \frac{PRE_2}{(1+r_1)^{n1}}$$

$$POST_{①} = PV\ of\ Exit\ Value = \frac{PRE_2}{(1+r_{①})^{n_{①}}} \longrightarrow Pre\ Investment\ of\ Time\ 2$$

As before, we can calculate the fractional ownership from the first round investment (f_1) using the NPV method, as:

$$f_1 = \frac{INV_1}{POST_1}$$

The new shares required to be issued to the VC in return for the first round financing amount (INV_1) and the price per share can then be calculated as:

$$shares_{VC1} = shares_{Founders}\left(\frac{f_1}{1-f_1}\right)$$

$$price_1 = \frac{INV_1}{shares_{VC1}}$$

$$\#_2 = \left(shares_1 + so\ pany\right) \times \frac{f_2}{1-f_2}$$

The new shares required to be issued to the VC in return for the second round financing amount (INV_2) and the price per share can also be calculated as:

$$shares_{VC2} = \left(shares_{VC1} + shares_{Founders}\right)\left(\frac{f_2}{1-f_2}\right)$$

$$price_2 = \frac{INV_2}{shares_{VC2}}$$

If the second round of financing is considered less risky than the first round (since the company has survived longer), a different, lower discount rate may be used in calculating the PV of the exit value at the time of the second round of financing. In the following example, we use a discount rate of 30% in calculating the company's value to reflect this fact.

Example: Calculating shares issued and share price for a second round financing

Suppose that instead of a single round of financing of $5 million, the company will need $3 million in the first round and a second round of financing (three years later) of $2 million to finance company expansion to the size expected at exit.

Use a discount rate of 40% for the first three years and 30% for the last two years. The company is still expected to be worth $40 million after five years, and founders will hold 1 million shares.

The value of the company at the time of the second round of financing (two years remaining to exit) is:

$$POST_2 = \frac{\text{exit value}}{(1+r_2)^{n2}} = \frac{40,000,000}{(1.30)^2} = 23,668,639$$

The fractional VC ownership required for the second round investment of $2 million is:

$$f_2 = \frac{INV_2}{POST_2} = \frac{2,000,000}{23,668,639} = 0.0845 \text{ or } 8.45\%$$

The value of the company before the second round financing would then be:

$$PRE_2 = POST_2 - INV_2 = 23,668,639 - 2,000,000 = 21,668,639$$

Value of the company at the first round of financing is:

$$POST_1 = \frac{PRE_2}{(1+r_1)^{n1}} = \frac{21,668,639}{(1.40)^3} = 7,896,734$$

The fractional VC ownership required for the first round investment of $3 million is:

$$f_1 = \frac{INV_1}{POST_1} = \frac{3,000,000}{7,896,734} = 0.38 \text{ or } 38\%$$

Number of shares issued at the time of first round of financing is:

$$\text{shares}_{VC1} = \text{shares}_{Founders}\left(\frac{f_1}{1-f_1}\right) = 1,000,000\left(\frac{0.38}{1-0.38}\right) = 612,903$$

The price per share at the time of first round of financing is:

$$\text{price}_1 = \frac{INV_1}{\text{shares}_{VC1}} = \frac{3,000,000}{612,903} = \$4.89$$

Number of shares issued to the VC firm at the time of the second round of financing is:

$$\text{shares}_{VC2} = \left(\text{shares}_{VC1} + \text{shares}_{Founders}\right)\left(\frac{f_2}{1-f_2}\right)$$

$$= (612{,}903 + 1{,}000{,}000)\left(\frac{0.0845}{1-0.0845}\right) = 148{,}870 \quad \text{✓}$$

The price per share at the time of second round of financing is:

$f = \dfrac{\text{Inv}}{\text{Post}}$

$$\text{price}_2 = \frac{\text{INV}_2}{\text{shares}_{VC2}} = \frac{2{,}000{,}000}{148{,}870} = \$13.43$$

$f_1 \times (1 - f_2)$

After the second round, the first round investor's share dilutes from f_1 to $f_1(1 - f_2)$.

In this example, the dilution takes the investor's share from 38% to $0.38(1 - 0.0845) =$ 0.3479 or 34.79%.

$f_1 = 38\%$ $f_1 = 38 \times (1 - 0.08) = 35$

LOS 45.k: Demonstrate alternative methods to account for risk in venture capital.

CFA® Program Curriculum, Volume 6, page 171

Our previous discussions have been highly dependent on the assumptions, and sensitivity analysis should be used to determine how changes in the input variables will affect company valuation. The discount rate used and the estimate of terminal value will strongly influence the current valuation.

Projections by entrepreneurs are typically overly optimistic and based on an assumption that the company will not fail. Instead of arguing over the validity of the projections with the entrepreneurs, most investors simply apply a high discount rate that reflects both the probability of failure and lack of diversification available in these investments.

Adjusting the Discount Rate

One approach to arriving at a more realistic valuation is to adjust the discount rate to reflect the risk that the company may fail in any given year. In the following formula, r^* is adjusted for the probability of failure, q: Probability of failure

$$r^* = \frac{1+r}{(1-q)} - 1$$

where:
r = discount rate unadjusted for probability of failure

Survival probability

Example: Adjusting the discount rate for the probability of failure

Suppose that a private equity investor has a discount rate of 30%. The investor believes, however, that the entrepreneur's projection of the company's success is overly optimistic and that the chance of the company failing in a given year is 25%.

Calculate a discount rate that factors in the company's probability of failure.

Answer:

$$r^* = \frac{1 + 0.30}{1 - 0.25} - 1 = 73.33\%$$

[handwritten annotations: q = failure probability; $\frac{1+r}{1-q}$ = survival probability]

Alternatively, the investor could have deflated each future cash flow for the cumulative probability that the company will fail. The adjusted discount rate approach is more straightforward.

Adjusting the Terminal Value Using Scenario Analysis

A second approach to generating a realistic valuation is to adjust the terminal value for the probability of failure or poor results. Typically to obtain the terminal value, the future earnings are estimated and multiplied by an industry multiple. The problem is that almost by definition, early-stage companies are innovative with few true comparables. Price multiples also fluctuate a great deal so that the current multiple may not be indicative of what can be obtained in the future. We should therefore use scenario analysis to calculate an expected terminal value, reflecting the probability of different terminal values under different assumptions.

In theory, we should just determine the present value of future cash flows to get the current value. But estimating future cash flows is subject to error, and this method may not be any better than a price multiple approach.

Example: Using scenario analysis to arrive at an expected terminal value

In the previous valuation example, we were given a terminal value of $40 million. Assume that the scenario analysis is performed and examines three possible scenarios:

1. The expected earnings are $4 million and the expected price-earnings multiple is 10, resulting in the $40 million (as before).

2. The company is not as successful, and earnings are only $2 million. Growth is slower, so the expected price-earnings multiple is 5. The expected terminal value is $10 million.

3. The company fails, and its terminal value is $0.

If each scenario is equally likely, each possible value is weighted by one-third, and the expected terminal value is:

$$= \frac{1}{3}(\$40) + \frac{1}{3}(\$10) + \frac{1}{3}(\$0) = \$16.7 \text{ million}$$

The terminal value of $16.7 million is then used instead of the $40 million in the valuation analysis above. This is an alternative to adjusting the discount rate for the probability of failure.

In summary, VC valuation is highly dependent on the assumptions used and how risk is accounted for. Additionally, scenario and sensitivity analysis should be used to determine how changes in the input variables will affect the valuation of the company.

Note that the purpose of the valuation procedures discussed here is not to ascertain the exact value of the company. Rather, the purpose is to place some bounds on the value of the company before negotiations begin between the startup (investee) company and the private equity firm. The final price paid for the investee company will also be affected by the bargaining power of the respective parties.

KEY CONCEPTS

LOS 45.a

The sources of value creation in private equity are: (1) the ability to reengineer the company, (2) the ability to obtain debt financing on more favorable terms, and (3) superior alignment of interests between management and private equity ownership.

LOS 45.b

Private equity firms use the following mechanisms to align their interests with those of the managers of portfolio companies:

- Manager's *compensation* tied to the company's performance.
- *Tag-along, drag-along* clauses ensure that anytime an acquirer acquires control of the company, they must extend the acquisition offer to all shareholders, including firm management.
- *Board representation* by private equity firm.
- *Noncompete clauses* required for company founders.
- *Priority in claims.* PE firms have priority if the portfolio company is liquidated.
- *Required approval* by PE firm for changes of strategic importance.
- *Earn-outs.* Acquisition price paid is tied to portfolio company's future performance.

LOS 45.c

Relative to buyouts, venture capital portfolio companies are characterized by: unpredictable cash flows and product demand; weak asset base and newer management teams; less debt; unclear risk and exit; high demand for cash and working capital; less opportunity to perform due diligence; higher returns from a few highly successful companies; limited capital market presence; company sales that take place due to relationships; smaller subsequent funding; and general partner revenue primarily in the form of carried interest.

LOS 45.d

Valuation Issue	Buyout	Venture Capital
Applicability of DCF Method	Frequently used to estimate value of equity	Less frequently used as cash flows are uncertain
Applicability of Relative Value Approach	Used to check the value from DCF analysis	Difficult to use because there may be no true comparable companies
Use of Debt	High	Low as equity is dominant form of financing
Key Drivers of Equity Return	Earnings growth, increase in multiple upon exit, and reduction in the debt	Pre-money valuation, investment, and subsequent equity dilution

LOS 45.e
The means and timing of the exit strongly influence the exit value.

The four typical exit routes:
- Initial public offerings usually result in the highest exit value due to increased liquidity, greater access to capital, and the potential to hire better quality managers.
- Secondary market sales to other investors or firms result in the second highest company valuations after IPOs.
- In an MBO, the company is sold to management, who utilize a large amount of leverage.
- A liquidation is pursued when the company is deemed no longer viable and usually results in a low exit value.

LOS 45.f
The most common form of ownership structure for private equity funds is the limited partnership where limited partners (LPs) provide funding and have limited liability. The general partner (GP) manages the investment fund.

The economic terms in a private equity prospectus address the following issues: management fees; transaction fees; carried interest (the GP's share of the fund profits); ratchet (the allocation of equity between stockholders and management of the portfolio company); hurdle rate (the IRR that the GP must meet before receiving carried interest); target fund size; vintage year; and term of the fund.

The corporate governance terms in the prospectus address the following issues: key man clause (the provisions for the absence of a key named executive); performance disclosure and confidentiality (specifies the fund performance information that can be disclosed); clawback (the provision for when the GP must return profits); distribution waterfall (the method in which profits will flow to the LPs before the GP receives carried interest); tag-along, drag-along clauses (give management the right to sell their equity stake if the private equity firm sells its stake); no-fault divorce (specify when a GP can be fired); removal for cause (provisions for the firing of the GP or the termination of a fund); investment restrictions; and co-investment (allows the LPs to invest in other funds of the GP at low or no management fees).

Valuations are difficult for private equity funds because there is no ready secondary market for their investments. Additional issues with NAV calculations include the following: (1) the NAV will be stale if it is only adjusted when there are subsequent rounds of financing; (2) there is no definitive method for calculating NAV; (3) undrawn LP capital commitments are not included in the NAV calculation but are essentially liabilities for the LP; (4) different strategies and maturities may use different valuation methodologies; and (5) it is the GP who usually values the fund.

Investors should conduct due diligence before investing in a private equity fund due to the persistence in returns in private equity fund returns, the return discrepancies between outperformers and underperformers, and their illiquidity.

LOS 45.g

The general private equity risk factors are liquidity risk, unquoted investments risk, competitive environment risk, agency risk, capital risk, regulatory risk, tax risk, valuation risk, diversification risk, and market risk.

The costs of investing in private equity are significantly higher than those associated with publicly traded securities and include transactions costs, investment vehicle fund setup costs, administrative costs, audit costs, management and performance fee costs, dilution costs, and placement fees.

LOS 45.h

The Gross IRR reflects the fund's ability to generate a return from portfolio companies. The Net IRR is the relevant return metric for the LPs and is net of management fees, carried interest, and other compensation to the GP. The Net IRR should be benchmarked against a peer group of comparable private equity funds of the same vintage and strategy.

LOS 45.i

The following statistics are important for evaluating the performance of a PE fund:

- Management fees are calculated as the percentage fee multiplied by the total paid-in capital.
- The carried interest is calculated as the percentage carried interest multiplied by the increase in the NAV before distributions.
    - The NAV before distributions is calculated as:

$$= \begin{matrix} \text{NAV after} \\ \text{distributions in} \\ \text{prior year} \end{matrix} \; (+) \; \begin{matrix} \text{capital called} \\ \text{down} \end{matrix} \; (-) \; \begin{matrix} \text{management} \\ \text{fees} \end{matrix} \; (+) \; \begin{matrix} \text{operating} \\ \text{results} \end{matrix}$$

    - The NAV after distributions is calculated as:

$$= \begin{matrix} \text{NAV before} \\ \text{distributions} \end{matrix} \; (-) \; \begin{matrix} \text{carried} \\ \text{interest} \end{matrix} \; (-) \; \text{distributions}$$

- The DPI multiple is the cumulative distributions divided by the paid-in capital.
- The RVPI multiple is the NAV after distributions divided by the paid-in capital.
- The TVPI multiple is the sum of the DPI and RVPI.

LOS 45.j

Under the NPV method, the proportion of the company (f) received for an investment in the company is calculated as the investment amount (INV) divided by the post-money (post-investment) value of the company. The post-money value of the company is calculated by discounting the estimated exit value for the company to its present value PV(exit value), as of the time the investment is made.

$$f = \frac{\text{INV}}{\text{POST}}$$

Alternatively, under the <u>IRR method,</u> we can calculate the fraction, f, as the future value of the VC investment at the time of exit (using the discount rate as a compound rate of return), divided by the value of the company at exit:

$$f = \frac{FV(INV)}{\text{exit value}}$$

Once we have calculated this post-money ownership share, we can calculate the number of shares issued to the venture capital investor for the investment (shares$_{VC}$) and the price per share as:

$$\text{shares}_{VC} = \text{shares}_{\text{Founders}}\left(\frac{f}{1-f}\right)$$

$$\text{price} = \frac{INV}{\text{shares}_{VC}}$$

If there is a second round of financing, we first calculate the fraction of the company (f_2) purchased for the second round of financing as:

$$f_2 = \frac{INV_2}{POST_2}$$

where:

$$POST_2 = \frac{\text{exit value}}{(1+r_2)^{n2}}$$

and

$$PRE_2 = POST_2 - INV_2$$

We then compute the fractional ownership from the first round of financing as:

$$f_1 = \frac{INV_1}{POST_1}$$

where:

$$POST_1 = \frac{PRE_2}{(1+r_1)^{n1}}$$

We can finally compute the number of shares issued and price per share in each round as:

$$\text{shares}_{VC1} = \text{shares}_{\text{Founders}}\left(\frac{f_1}{1-f_1}\right)$$

$$\text{price}_1 = \frac{INV_1}{\text{shares}_{VC1}}$$

$$\text{shares}_{VC2} = \left(\text{shares}_{VC1} + \text{shares}_{\text{Founders}}\right)\left(\frac{f_2}{1-f_2}\right)$$

$$\text{price}_2 = \frac{INV_2}{\text{shares}_{VC2}}$$

LOS 45.k

The valuation of a venture capital investment is highly dependent on the assumptions used. The risk of the investment can be assessed using two methods.

- In the first approach, the discount rate is adjusted to reflect the risk that the company may fail in any given year:

$$r^* = \frac{1+r}{1-q} - 1$$

adjusting (IRR)   discount factor

where:

r^* = discount rate adjusted for probability of failure

r = discount rate unadjusted for probability of failure

q = probability of failure in a year

- In the second approach, scenario analysis is used to calculate an expected terminal value, reflecting different values under different assumptions.

08:22 PM
17/04/2018
Beauclerc Advisory Services
London

CONCEPT CHECKERS

1. Which of the following is *least likely* a source of value creation in private equity firms?
   A. The use of debt with few covenants.
   B. The overutilization of cheap equity financing in private equity firms.
   C. The ability to reengineer companies through the use of an experienced staff of former senior managers.

2. Which of the following is *least likely* to be contained in a private equity term sheet?
   A. Tag-along, drag-along clauses.
   B. Earn-outs that ensure portfolio company manager compensation.
   C. A clause that ensures private equity firm representation on the portfolio company board.

3. Which of the following is *more likely* to be associated with a venture capital investment as compared to a buyout investment?
   A. Valuation using a discounted cash flow model.
   B. High cash burn rate.
   C. Due diligence covering all aspects of the business.

4. Which of the following is *most likely* to be a key driver for the equity return in a buyout opportunity?
   A. The pre-money valuation.
   B. The reduction in debt's claim on assets.
   C. The potential subsequent equity dilution.

5. Which of the following exit routes typically results in the highest exit valuation?
   A. An initial public offering.
   B. A management buyout.
   C. A secondary market sale.

6. Which of the following *best* describes the competitive environment risk of investing in private equity?
   A. The competition for finding reasonably priced private equity investments may be high.
   B. The competition for funds from private equity investors has increased as financial markets have fallen in activity.
   C. The competitive environment in the product markets for portfolio companies has increased due to the economic slowdown.

7. Which of the following *best* describes the placement fee cost of investing in private equity?
   A. The general partner may charge the fund fees for finding prospective portfolio companies.
   B. Investment banking fees are paid when exiting a private equity portfolio company via an IPO.
   C. Placement agents who raise funds for private equity firms may charge up-front or annual trailer fees.

8. What is the most typical organizational structure of a private equity investment?
   A. An S-corporation.
   B. A limited partnership.
   C. A sole proprietorship.

9. A private equity general partner has invested in portfolio Company A that has been funded by private equity Fund A. Portfolio Company A is experiencing financial difficulty, so the general partner uses funds from a newly formed private equity fund, Fund B, to assist the company. Which of the following terms in the private equity prospectus has the general partner *most likely* violated?
   A. The co-investment clause.
   B. The no-fault divorce clause.
   C. The tag-along, drag-along clause.

10. Using the information in the table below, which of the following firms *likely* has the best corporate governance system?
    A. Firm A.
    B. Firm B.
    C. Firm C.

	Firm A	*Firm B*	*Firm C*
Key Man Clause	Yes	Yes	No
Management Fees	1.5%	2.0%	2.3%
Transaction Fees	The split between LPs and GP is 50/50	The split between LPs and GP is 50/50	GP share is 100%
Carried Interest	25%	20%	22%
Hurdle Rate	10%	8%	9%
Clawback Provision	Yes	Yes	No
Distribution Waterfall	Total return	Total return	Deal-by-deal
Removal for Cause Clause	Yes	No	No

11. Which of the following *best* describes the method that most private equity funds use to incorporate undrawn capital commitments into NAV calculations?
    A. The GP uses public comparables to determine their value.
    B. There is no straightforward method for calculating the value of the commitments.
    C. The GP estimates the net present value of the capital commitments using the historical record of previous allocations to the portfolio companies.

12. Which of the following measures the limited partner's unrealized return in a private equity fund?
    A. The DPI.
    B. The RVPI.
    C. The TVPI.

Professor's Note: From this point on, this set of Concept Checkers contains several multi-part questions where questions "nest" on each other—meaning that you need the answer to one question to complete the next. It is unlikely you will encounter this situation on the exam. We recommend that after you complete a question, you check your answer to ensure that you begin the next question with the correct information.

Use the following information to answer Questions 13 through 21.

The GP for the private equity fund charges a management fee of 2% and carried interest of 20%, using the first total return method. The total committed capital for the fund was $200 million. The figures in the table are in millions.

	Capital Called Down	Paid-in Capital	Management Fees	Operating Results	NAV Before Distributions	Carried Interest	Distributions	NAV After Distributions
2011	60	60	1.2	–15	43.8	?		43.8
2012	20	80	1.6	–20	42.2	?		42.2
2013	10	90	1.8	30	80.4	?		80.4
2014	20	110	2.2	50	148.2	?	30	118.2
2015	25	135	2.7	70	210.5	?	50	158.4
2016	10	?	?	120	?	?	90	?

13. What is the paid-in capital for 2016?
    A. $125.
    B. $142.
    C. $145.

14. What are the management fees for 2016?
    A. $2.7.
    B. $2.9.
    C. $15.4.

15. In what year is carried interest first paid?
    A. 2014.
    B. 2015.
    C. 2016.

16. What is the NAV before distributions for 2016?
    A. $275.50.
    B. $285.50.
    C. $288.40.

17. What is the carried interest for 2016?
    A. $2.9.
    B. $15.0.
    C. $17.9.

18. What is the NAV after distributions for 2016?
    A. $180.50.
    B. $195.50.
    C. $270.50.

19. What is the DPI after 2016?
    A. 0.62.
    B. 0.83.
    C. 1.17.

20. What is the RVPI after 2016?
    A. 1.24.
    B. 1.35.
    C. 1.97.

21. What is the TVPI after 2016?
    A. 1.76.
    B. 2.41.
    C. 3.14.

Use the following information to answer Questions 22 through 26.

ScaleIt is a startup specializing in mobile applications. The company's founders believe they can sell the company for $50 million in four years. They need $7 million in capital now, and the founders wish to hold 1 million shares. The venture capital investor firm decides that, given the high risk of this company, a discount rate of 45% is appropriate. Use the NPV venture capital method, assuming a single financing round.

22. What is the post-money valuation?
    A. $4,310,922.
    B. $11,310,922.
    C. $50,000,000.

23. What is the pre-money valuation?
    A. $4,310,922.
    B. $7,310,922.
    C. $43,000,000.

24. What is the ownership fraction for the venture capital firm?
    A. 14.00%.
    B. 38.11%.
    C. 61.89%.

25. What is the number of shares for the venture capital firm?
    A. 615,846.
    B. 1,623,983.
    C. 2,603,078.

26. What is the stock price per share?
    A. $2.69.
    B. $4.31.
    C. $11.37.

Use the following information to answer Questions 27 through 32.

A company's founders believe that their company can be sold for $60 million in four years. The company needs $6 million in capital now and $3 million in three years. The entrepreneurs want to hold 1 million shares. The venture capital firm uses a discount rate of 50% over all four years.

27.   What is the post-money valuation at the time of second-round financing?
        A. $17,777,778.
        B. $40,000,000.
        C. $57,000,000.

28.   What is the post-money valuation at the time of first-round financing?
        A. $4,962,963.
        B. $9,851,259.
        C. $10,962,963.

29.   What is the required fractional ownership for the second-round investors?
        A. 5.00%.
        B. 7.50%.
        C. 16.88%.

30.   What is the fractional ownership for the first-round investors, after dilution by the second-round investors?
        A. 50.63%.
        B. 54.73%.
        C. 92.50%.

31.   What is the stock price per share after the first round of financing?
        A. $4.96.
        B. $5.85.
        C. $6.00.

32.   What is the stock price per share after the second round of financing?
        A. $5.77.
        B. $16.75.
        C. $37.00.

Use the following information to answer Questions 33 through 36.

The venture capital company's founders believe they can sell the company for $70 million in five years. They need $9 million in capital now, and the entrepreneurs wish to hold 1 million shares. The venture capital investor requires a return of 35%. Use the IRR venture capital method, assuming a single financing round.

33.   What is the investor's ownership fraction?
        A. 12.86%.
        B. 42.35%.
        C. 57.65%.

34.   What is the stock price per share?
        A. $2.39.
        B. $6.61.
        C. $12.25.

35.   What is the post-money valuation?
        A. $6.61 million.
        B. $15.61 million.
        C. $70.00 million.

36.   What is the pre-money valuation?
        A. $6.61 million.
        B. $9.00 million.
        C. $61.00 million.

37.   A private equity investor has a discount rate of 30%. The investor believes,
        however, that the entrepreneur's projection of the company's success is overly
        optimistic and that the chance of the company failing in a given year is 20%.
        What is the discount rate that factors in the company's probability of failure?
        A. 50.0%.
        B. 62.5%.
        C. 71.4%.

*To access other content related to this topic review that may be included in the Schweser
package you purchased, log in to your Schweser.com online dashboard. Schweser's OnDemand
Video Lectures deliver streaming instruction covering every LOS in this topic review, while
SchweserPro™ QBank provides additional quiz questions to help you practice and recall
what you've learned.*

ANSWERS – CONCEPT CHECKERS

1. **B** It is actually the overutilization of cheap *debt* financing in private equity firms that leads to value creation. Private equity firms carry more debt than public firms but have a reputation for paying it back.

2. **B** Earn-outs do not ensure portfolio company manager compensation. Earn-outs tie the acquisition price paid by private equity firms to the portfolio company's future performance. These are used predominantly in venture capital investments.

3. **B** Venture capital investments typically have significant cash burn rates. Discounted cash flow analysis is typically used for companies with substantial operating history and is, therefore, more likely to be associated with a buyout investment rather than a venture capital investment. Full due diligence is conducted for a buyout investment. Due diligence for typical venture capital investment is limited to technological feasibility and commercial potential due to limited operating results history.

4. **B** The pre-money valuation, investment, and potential subsequent equity dilution are issues for venture capital equity return. The key drivers of equity return for buyouts are earnings growth, the increase in multiple upon exit, and the reduction in the debt.

5. **A** Initial public offerings usually result in the highest exit value due to increased liquidity, greater access to capital, and the potential to hire better-quality managers.

6. **A** Competitive environment risk examines risk from the perspective of an investor who is considering an investment in private equity. It refers to the fact that the competition for finding reasonably priced private equity investments may be high.

7. **C** Placement fees are those charged by placement agents who raise funds for private equity firms. They may charge up-front fees as much as 2% or annual trailer fees as a percent of funds raised from limited partners.

8. **B** The most typical organizational structure of a private equity investment is a limited partnership. In a limited partnership, the limited partners provide funding and have limited liability. The general partner manages the investment fund.

9. **A** The clause in the private equity prospectus that the general partner has likely violated is the co-investment clause. The co-investment clause prevents the GP from using capital from different funds to invest in the same portfolio company. A conflict of interest arises here because portfolio Company A may be a poor use of the funds from Fund B investors.

10. **A** Firm A likely has the best corporate governance system. A large amount of the GP's compensation comes in the form of incentive-based compensation as the carried interest and hurdle rate necessary to obtain carried interest is the highest, but the compensation unrelated to performance (the management and transactions fees are the lowest). The clawback provision also incentivizes the GP because they have to return previously received profits.

Furthermore, the key man clause and the removal for cause clause give the LPs the right to dismiss an underperforming GP. The total return distribution waterfall method is used instead of the deal-by-deal method, in which the GP can receive carried interest even in cases when the LPs have not earned a net positive return.

11. **B**   There is no straightforward method for calculating the value of the commitments, which are essentially liabilities for the LP. The value of the commitments depends on the cash flows generated from them, but these are quite uncertain.

12. **B**   The RVPI (residual value to paid-in capital) measures the limited partner's unrealized return in a private equity fund. It is the value of the LP's holdings in the fund divided by the cumulative invested capital. It is net of management fees and carried interest. The DPI (distributed to paid-in capital) measures the LP's realized return, and the TVPI (total value to paid-in capital) measures both the LP's realized and unrealized return.

13. **C**   This is the cumulative sum of the capital called down, and in 2016 is:
$135 + $10 = $145.

14. **B**   These are calculated as the percentage fee of 2% times the paid-in capital:
2% × $145 = $2.9.

15. **B**   Carried interest is not paid until the NAV before distributions exceeds the committed capital of $200 million, which is the year 2015.

16. **B**   NAV before distributions is calculated as:

$$= \text{NAV after distributions in prior year} + \text{capital called down} - \text{management fees} + \text{operating results}$$

For 2016, NAV before distributions is: $158.4 + $10 − $2.9 + $120 = $285.50.

17. **B**   It is calculated as the percentage carried interest times the increase in the NAV before distributions. In 2016, it is: 20% × ($285.50 − $210.50) = $15.00.

18. **A**   NAV after distributions is calculated as:

$$= \text{NAV before distributions} - \text{carried interest} - \text{distributions}$$

In 2016, NAV after distributions is: $285.50 − $15.00 − $90 = $180.50.

19. **C**   The DPI multiple is calculated as the cumulative distributions divided by the paid-in capital: ($30 + $50 + $90) / $145 = 1.17. The GP has distributed more than the paid-in capital.

20. **A**   The RVPI multiple is calculated as the NAV after distributions divided by the paid-in capital: ($180.50) / $145 = 1.24. The net unrealized returns are more than the paid-in capital.

21. **B**   The TVPI multiple is the sum of the DPI and RVPI: 1.17 + 1.24 = 2.41.

22. **B**   The post-money valuation is the present value of the expected exit value:

$$\text{POST} = \frac{50,000,000}{(1+0.45)^4} = 11,310,922$$

23. **A**   The pre-money valuation is what the company is worth before the investment:

PRE = 11,310,922 − 7,000,000 = 4,310,922

24. **C** To put up $7 million in a company worth $11.3 million, the venture capital firm must own 61.89% of the company:

$$f = \frac{7,000,000}{11,310,922} = 61.89\%$$

25. **B** If the entrepreneurs want 1 million shares, the venture capital firm must receive 1.6 million shares to get 61.89% ownership:

$$\text{Shares}_{VC} = 1,000,000 \left[\frac{0.6189}{(1-0.6189)} \right] = 1,623,983$$

26. **B** Given a $7 million investment and 1.6 million shares, the stock price per share must be:

$$P = \frac{7,000,000}{1,623,983} = \$4.31 \text{ per share}$$

27. **B** Discount the terminal value of the company at exit back to the time of second round financing to obtain the post-money ($POST_2$) valuation:

$$POST_2 = \frac{60,000,000}{(1+0.5000)} = \$40,000,000$$

28. **C** First, calculate the second-round pre-money (PRE_2) valuation by netting the second-round investment (INV_2) from the post-money ($POST_2$) valuation:

$$PRE_2 = 40,000,000 - 3,000,000 = \$37,000,000$$

Next, discount the second-round pre-money valuation back to the time of the first-round financing to obtain the post-money ($POST_1$) valuation:

$$POST_1 = \frac{37,000,000}{(1+0.50)^3} = \$10,962,963$$

29. **B** The required fractional ownership for the second-round investors is:

$$f_2 = \frac{3,000,000}{40,000,000} = 7.50\%$$

30. **A** The required fractional ownership for the first-round investors is:

$$f_1 = \frac{6,000,000}{10,962,963} = 54.73\%$$

The first round investors will be later diluted by the second round investors to an ownership of: $54.73\% \times (1 - 0.0750) = 50.63\%$.

©2017 Kaplan, Inc.

31. **A** First determine the number of shares the first-round venture capital investors ($Shares_{VC1}$) need to obtain their fractional ownership:

$$Share_{VC1} = 1,000,000 \left[\frac{0.5473}{(1-0.5473)} \right] = 1,208,968$$

To obtain a 54.73% share of the company, the first-round investors must receive 1,208,968 shares.

Next, determine the stock price per share after the first round of financing (P_1):

$$P_1 = \frac{6,000,000}{1,208,968} = \$4.96$$

32. **B** First determine the number of shares the second-round venture capital investors ($Shares_{VC2}$) need to obtain their fractional ownership:

$$Shares_{VC2} = (1,000,000 + 1,208,968) \left[\frac{0.0750}{(1-0.0750)} \right] = 179,106$$

To obtain a 7.50% share of the company, the second-round investors must receive 179,106 shares.

Next, determine the stock price per share after the second round of financing (P_2):

$$P_2 = \frac{3,000,000}{179,106} = \$16.75$$

33. **C** First, calculate the investor's expected future wealth (W):

$$W = 9,000,000 \times (1 + 0.35)^5 = 40,356,301$$

Given this expected wealth, we determine the required fractional ownership (f) by calculating how much of the terminal value should be the investor's:

$$f = \frac{40,356,301}{70,000,000} = 57.65\%$$

34. **B** First, determine the number of shares the venture capital firm ($Shares_{VC}$) requires for its fractional ownership:

$$Shares_{VC} = 1,000,000 \left[\frac{0.5765}{(1-0.5765)} \right] = 1,361,275$$

Next, determine the stock price per share (P):

$$P = \frac{9,000,000}{1,361,275} = \$6.61$$

35. **B** Divide the investment by the fractional ownership to obtain the post-money (POST) valuation:

$$POST = \frac{9,000,000}{0.5765} = 15.61 \text{ million}$$

36. **A** Determine the pre-money (PRE) valuation by netting the investment (INV) from the post-money (POST) valuation:

PRE = 15.61 million − 9 million = 6.61 million

37. **B** The discount rate that factors in the company's probability of failure is calculated as:

$$r^* = \frac{1+r}{1-q} - 1$$

$$r^* = \frac{1+0.30}{1-0.20} - 1 = 62.5\%$$

COMMODITIES AND COMMODITY DERIVATIVES: AN INTRODUCTION

Study Session 15

EXAM FOCUS

This topic review will help you understand different commodity sectors and key factors influencing prices in those sectors. Pay special attention to what backwardation and contango mean in terms of spot and futures prices. You should understand the different components of returns to commodity futures and what determines whether roll return is positive or negative. Finally, familiarize yourself with the Insurance Theory, the Hedging Pressure Hypothesis, and the Theory of Storage and what they say about futures prices.

LOS 46.a: Compare characteristics of commodity sectors.

CFA® Program Curriculum, Volume 6, page 187

Commodities can be classified by their characteristics into sectors, including:

- Energy—crude oil, natural gas, and refined petroleum products.
- Industrial metals—aluminum, nickel, zinc, lead, tin, iron, and copper.
- Grains—wheat, corn, soybeans, and rice.
- Livestock—hogs, sheep, cattle, and poultry.
- Precious metals—gold, silver, and platinum.
- Softs (cash crops)—coffee, sugar, cocoa, and cotton.

The factors that influence supply and demand and the nature of production differ for these sectors. A summary of these differences can help explain the differences in price dynamics among the sectors.

The **energy sector** comprises crude oil, natural gas, and refined products. It is the sector with the greatest market value and is a very important source of revenue to many countries and regions.

Crude oil from different regions has different characteristics. Light oil (low viscosity) and sweet oil (low sulfur content) are less costly to refine and, therefore, sell at a premium relative to heavier or higher sulfur crude oils. Crude oil can be stored indefinitely by keeping it in the ground and is also stored in tanks and aboard tanker ships. Many countries store large amounts of crude oil as strategic reserves.

The supply of crude oil has been augmented by advances in drilling and extraction technology, especially in the 21st century. While global economic growth is an important driver of worldwide demand for oil, other factors have slowed this growth in demand. Improvements in refining technology have tended to increase the output

Study Session 15
Cross-Reference to CFA Institute Assigned Reading #46 – Commodities and Commodity Derivatives: An Introduction

Study Session 15

of petroleum distillates from each barrel of crude oil, and improved engines are able to produce more work from each gallon of these distillates.

Economic cycles also affect the demand for oil, which is higher during expansions when credit is widely available and can decrease sharply when contractions lead to reductions in the availability of credit.

Improvements in the efficiency of alternative sources of energy production have also reduced the overall growth in the demand for oil. Increasingly stringent restrictions on oil exploration and production in response to environmental concerns have tended to increase the cost of oil production and decrease supply.

Political risk is an important factor in oil supply. Over half the crude oil supply comes from countries in the Middle East, and conflict there can reduce supply dramatically.

Refined products, such as gasoline, heating oil, and jet fuel, are only stored for short periods. Refinery output is the relevant supply consideration. The geographic concentration of refinery capacity means that extreme weather in some coastal regions can significantly affect the supply of refined products.

Seasonal factors affect the demand for refined products in that greater vacation travel in the summer months increases gasoline demand, and colder weather in the winter increases the demand for heating oil.

Unlike crude oil, **natural gas** can be used just as it comes out of the ground with very little processing. Transportation costs play an important role in energy pricing. Crude oil can be transported at a relatively low cost on ships, while natural gas must be cooled to its liquid state to be transported by ship, significantly increasing the cost of transport.

The supply of *associated gas*—gas produced in conjunction with the extraction of crude oil—is tied to the production of crude oil. *Unassociated gas* is produced from formations where oil is not present so that its supply is not tied to the demand for and production of crude oil.

Worldwide demand and supply for gas depends on many of the same factors as supply and demand for crude oil, but seasonality due to weather is more pronounced. Cold winters increase the demand for gas for heating fuel. Hot summers increase the demand for gas as well (for cooling) because gas is a primary source of fuel for electrical power generation.

Demand for **industrial metals** is primarily tied to GDP growth and business cycles because these metals are used extensively in construction and manufacturing. Storage of metals is not costly.

Political factors, especially union strikes and restrictive environmental regulations, can have a significant effect on the supply of an industrial metal. Industrial metals must be smelted from mined ore. Both mines and smelters are large-scale operations with high development costs and high fixed costs.

Grains are grown over an annual cycle and stored, although multiple crops in a single year are possible in some areas. The risks to grain supply are the usual: droughts, hail, floods, pests, diseases, changes in climate, and so on. It would be difficult to overstate the importance of grains in feeding the world's population, especially given the potential for political instability when grain stocks are insufficient.

Precious metals are used in electronics and for jewelry and can be stored indefinitely. Gold has long been used as a store of value and has provided a hedge against the inflation risk of holding currency. Jewelry demand is high where wealth is being accumulated. Industrial demand for precious metals is sensitive to business cycles.

Livestock supply depends on the price of grain, which is the primary input in its production. When increasing grain prices increase the cost of feeding livestock, the rate of slaughter also increases, which leads to a decrease in price. Such a drawdown in population can result in subsequent increases in price over time.

Weather can affect the production of some animals. Disease is a source of significant risk to livestock producers, and some diseases have had a large impact on market prices.

Income growth in developing economies is an important source of growth in demand for livestock. Freezing allows the storage of meat products for a limited amount of time.

Softs refers to cotton, coffee, sugar, and cocoa, which are all grown in the warmer climates of the lower latitudes. Just as with grains, weather is the primary factor in determining production and price, but disease is a significant risk as well. Demand increases with increases in incomes in developing economies but is dependent on consumer tastes as well.

LOS 46.b: Compare the life cycle of commodity sectors from production through trading or consumption.

CFA® Program Curriculum, Volume 6, page 192

The life cycle of crude oil begins with the time it takes to drill a well and extract the crude. After being transported, crude oil is typically stored for no more than a few months. The next step is refining the crude oil into various fuels such as gasoline, heating oil, diesel oil, and jet fuel. These fuels must then be transported to the consumer.

Natural gas requires minimal processing after it is extracted. While natural gas often reaches the consumer through a pipeline, it can be cooled to liquid form and transported on specially constructed ships. Energy commodities are delivered year-round, but demand is seasonal to some extent.

The life cycle of industrial metals is straightforward: the extracted ore is smelted into the quality of metal that end users need. Industrial metals can be stored indefinitely in most cases, and the regular flow of output means that end users can meet their needs with monthly deliverable futures contracts.

A key characteristic of industrial metals production is economies of scale due to large, efficient mining and smelting operations. The large size projects required for efficient operation cost billions of dollars and take significant time to construct. Construction of new capacity or facilities when capacity utilization and earnings are high can result in the additional capacity coming online at or past the peak of the economic cycle. Mining and smelting operations are most efficient running near their capacity, so individual producers are hesitant to decrease production when prices fall because the peak of the economic cycle has passed or because facilities growth has created excess capacity in the industry.

Livestock production times vary with animal size, with chickens ready for slaughter after only weeks, hogs in about six months, and cattle after a few years. Freezing allows storage for some period after slaughter and allows international trade in livestock. Livestock production has a significant seasonal component.

Grain production is seasonal, so deliverable futures contracts are available on dates to coincide with the harvest. Because planting occurs five months or more before harvest, quantities harvested are set largely by expectations for demand when crops are planted. Grains can be stored for significant time periods after harvest. The six-month offset to harvest times in the northern and southern hemispheres brings crops to markets more frequently.

Production cycles and storage options for softs vary by product. Among softs, coffee offers an example of an agricultural commodity that is harvested somewhere around the world in almost every month. Coffee is stored in warehouses after transport by ship. Local coffee roasters then roast the beans and deliver to end users or to retail sales outlets. Coffee plants can take up to four years to produce the fruit that will become coffee beans, so there is a significant lag between investment in new capacity and increases in supply.

To hedge their price risk, coffee producers can sell in the futures market for delivery to a warehouse, and consumer companies can buy in the futures market and take delivery at the warehouse. Two different types of coffee beans are traded, robusta and arabica, with arabica being the premium product.

LOS 46.c: Contrast the valuation of commodities with the valuation of equities and bonds.

CFA® Program Curriculum, Volume 6, page 199

Unlike stocks and bonds, commodities are physical assets, have no cash flows, and may incur storage and transportation costs.

Stocks and bonds (financial assets) can be valued by calculating the present value of their expected future cash flows (e.g., dividends, interest, etc.). Commodities produce no earnings or cash flows; however, the current (spot) price of a commodity can be viewed as the discounted value of the expected selling price at some future date. Storage costs for commodities can lead to forward prices that are higher the further the forward settlement date is in the future.

LOS 46.d: Describe types of participants in commodity futures markets.

CFA® Program Curriculum, Volume 6, page 201

Participants in commodity futures markets can be categorized as hedgers, traders and investors, exchanges, analysts, and regulators.

Traders and investors in the commodities market can be classified as informed investors—those who provide liquidity to the markets—and arbitrageurs. **Hedgers** are considered informed investors because they either produce or use the commodity. Hedgers reduce their risk by buying (going long) or selling (going short) futures contracts. A corn farmer can reduce the uncertainty about the price she will receive for her corn by selling corn futures. A cattle producer, however, would hedge his price risk by buying corn futures to reduce his uncertainty about the cost of feed for the cattle.

> *Professor's Note: Hedgers are said to "do in the futures market what they must do in the future." A wheat farmer will need to sell wheat in the future (i.e., after the harvest) and can hedge price risk by selling futures contracts. A grain miller will need to buy wheat in the future and can hedge price risk by buying futures contracts.*

Speculators take on commodity risk in futures markets and may act as informed investors, seeking to exploit an information or information processing advantage to profit from trading with hedgers. Speculators can also earn profits by providing liquidity to markets: buying futures when short hedgers (commodity producers) are selling and selling futures when long hedgers (commodity users) are buying.

Arbitrageurs in the commodity markets are often those in the business of buying, selling, and storing the physical commodities when the difference between spot and futures prices is too large or too small based on the actual cost of storing the commodity. When the difference is too large, an arbitrageur can buy and store the commodity and sell it at its (too high) futures price. When the difference is too small, an arbitrageur can effectively "not store" the commodity by selling from his own inventory and going long futures, replacing the inventory at the future date.

Commodity exchanges operate in many of the world's financial centers to reflect the worldwide production and consumption of commodities as well as the globalization of financial markets in general. Investors can trade commodity futures on a smart phone or via a Bloomberg terminal.

Commodity market analysts, considered non-market participants, use market information to perform analytical work for various entities including governments, universities, economic forecasters, and commercial data analysis firms.

Various **commodity regulators** are responsible for the regulation of commodities markets around the world. In the U.S., the Commodities Futures Trading Commission (CFTC) is responsible for market regulation.

LOS 46.e: Analyze the relationship between spot prices and expected future prices in markets in contango and markets in backwardation.

CFA® Program Curriculum, Volume 6, page 205

The difference between the spot (cash) market price and the futures price for a date in the future is referred to as the **basis** of that particular contract. The basis is calculated as the spot price minus the futures price and can be positive or negative. The difference between the futures price of a more distant maturity and the futures price of a nearer maturity is known as the **calendar spread**.

When futures prices are higher at dates further in the future, the futures market (or futures curve) is said to be in **contango**. In a contango market, the calendar spread and basis are negative. Conversely, if futures prices are lower at dates further in the future, the market is said to be in **backwardation**, and the basis and calendar spread are positive.

When a futures market is in backwardation, long futures positions have a positive returns component (the "roll return," which we will describe later in this topic review). With a futures curve in backwardation, futures prices are lower than spot prices for the commodity. Since futures prices converge to spot prices over the term of a futures contract, there is a positive returns component from the passage of time.

When a futures market is in contango, so that futures prices are greater than spot prices, there is a negative returns component for long futures positions. As time passes, convergence of futures prices to spot prices (or longer-dated futures prices to nearer-term futures prices) results in a decrease in the value of a long futures position.

LOS 46.f: Compare theories of commodity futures returns.

CFA® Program Curriculum, Volume 6, page 209

Three theories of the determinants of returns on commodities, based on the shape of the futures curve, have been expounded: the Insurance Theory, the Hedging Pressure Hypothesis, and the Theory of Storage.

Economist John Maynard Keynes put forward the **Insurance Theory** of futures returns, which states that the desire of commodity producers to reduce their price risk drives commodity futures returns. Producers face uncertainty about the price they will receive for their output and reduce this uncertainty by selling futures contracts. This selling drives down futures prices. The Insurance Theory states that the futures prices will be less than current spot prices to provide a return to those buying futures from producers (i.e., speculators). In this view, the resulting positive return to the buyers of futures contracts is their return for providing insurance against price uncertainty to producers. Keynes contended that this results in backwardation "normally," and the situation was termed "normal backwardation" based on this theory.

The Insurance Theory was found to be lacking based on two empirical findings. The first finding is that for markets in backwardation, buying futures has not resulted in the extra returns the theory says buyers should receive for providing "insurance." The second finding is that many markets are not in backwardation but are in contango (future prices higher than spot prices), which would imply a negative return for providing insurance to producers.

The **Hedging Pressure Hypothesis** added the hedging behavior of commodity consumers to the Insurance Theory in an attempt to better explain observed futures returns. Just as a wheat farmer faces uncertainty about the price at which he will sell his wheat in the future, a baking company faces uncertainty about the price it will pay for flour in the future. To hedge its price risk, the baking company will go long wheat futures. The more commodity users hedge with long positions (buying futures), the more upward price pressure there is on the futures price. Under the Hedging Pressure Theory, when producers' hedging behavior dominates, the market will be in backwardation, and when users' hedging behavior dominates, the market will be in contango.

Despite the intuitive appeal of the Hedging Pressure Hypothesis, it has some shortcomings. Producers typically face more concentrated price risk than consumers. Individual consumers will spend only a small portion of their income on a single commodity, and for commercial users of the commodity, the actual cost of the commodity may represent only a small portion of the total cost of the production.

Additionally, both producers and consumers may be speculators in the market, not just hedgers. Another problem with the Hedging Pressure Hypothesis is that hedging pressure is not observable, so we cannot directly test the hypothesis that relative hedging pressure is the cause of backwardation and contango.

The **Theory of Storage** is based on the idea that whether a futures market is in backwardation or contango depends on the relationship between the costs of storing the commodity for future use and the benefits of holding physical inventory of the commodity. When the costs of storage outweigh the benefits of holding physical inventory, futures are more attractive than current inventory, futures will trade at a higher price than spot, and the market will be in contango. Conversely, when the benefits of holding physical inventory outweigh the costs of storage, current possession is more attractive than future possession, spot prices are higher than futures prices, and the market will be in backwardation.

The benefits of having physical inventory available are referred to as a commodity's **convenience yield**. When physical stocks are low and there is a high probability that the commodity will be in short supply, the benefits of holding physical stock (and the convenience yield) are higher.

The Theory of Storage takes both the costs and benefits of holding a commodity into account in the following relation:

futures price = spot price + storage costs – convenience yield

Relative to spot prices, futures prices are higher when storage costs are higher, and futures prices are lower when the convenience yield is higher. Further, we can say that the shape of the futures price curve depends on available supply (i.e., current inventory of the commodity) along with expected future supply and demand.

Even with these three theories, we are left without a complete theory of commodity futures returns. "Hedging pressure" and "convenience yield" are not observable, and storage costs are not readily disclosed by participant firms.

LOS 46.g: Describe, calculate, and interpret the components of total return for a fully collateralized commodity futures contract.

CFA® Program Curriculum, Volume 6, page 215

An investor who desires long exposure to a commodity price will typically achieve this exposure through a derivative investment in forwards or futures. Some physical commodities cannot be effectively purchased and stored long term, and for others, such as precious metals, derivative positions may be a more efficient means of gaining long exposure than purchasing the commodities outright and storing them long term.

The return on a derivatives position is not the same as the return on a commodity itself. The total return on a fully collateralized long futures position has three components: collateral return, price return, and roll return.

To take a position in futures, an investor must post collateral. When a futures portfolio is *fully collateralized*, the investor has posted cash or acceptable securities with a value equal to the notional value (price multiplied by contract size) of the futures contracts in the portfolio. If U.S. Treasury bills are deposited as collateral, the **collateral return** or **collateral yield** is simply the holding period yield on the T-bills.

The **price return** or **spot yield** on an investment in commodity futures is the change in spot prices (which can be proxied by futures prices on near-month contracts).

$$\text{price return} = (\text{current price} - \text{previous price}) \, / \, \text{previous price}$$

Since commodity derivative contracts expire, an investor who wants to maintain a position over time must close out the expiring futures position and reestablish a new position with a settlement date further in the future. This process is referred to as *rolling over* the position and leads to gains or losses which are termed the **roll return** or **roll yield**. The roll return can be positive if the futures price curve is in backwardation or negative if the futures price curve is in contango.

To hold the value of a long position constant, an investor must buy more contracts if the new longer-dated futures are trading at a lower price (market in backwardation) and buy fewer contracts if the new longer-dated futures are trading at a higher price (market in contango). In any event, the roll return on the contracts traded can be calculated as:

$$\text{roll return} = \frac{\text{price of expiring futures contract} - \text{price of new futures contract}}{\text{price of expiring futures contract}}$$

Roll return has a relatively small impact on overall returns on commodity futures over the short term but can have a meaningful impact over longer periods.

LOS 46.h: Contrast roll return in markets in contango and markets in backwardation.

CFA® Program Curriculum, Volume 6, page 219

Consider a situation where the manager of a portfolio of commodity futures contracts is rolling over July corn futures trading at 397 (cents per bushel) into November corn futures trading at 406. The roll return is:

[handwritten: Contango   Spot < Future   395 < 406]

$$\frac{397 - 406}{397} = -2.27\%$$

With the corn futures market in contango, the roll return is negative.

Now consider a situation where the manager is rolling over July natural gas futures trading at 2.35 (dollars per million cubic feet) into August futures trading at 2.22. In this case the roll return is:

[handwritten: Backwardation ⇒ Positive Roll return]

$$\frac{2.35 - 2.22}{2.35} = 5.53\%$$

Suppose we wanted a specific dollar exposure to natural gas, say $10,000. We would have originally gone long 10,000 / 2.35, or approximately 4,255 contracts. To maintain the dollar exposure upon rolling over into new contracts, we would have gone long 10,000 / 2.22, or approximately 4,504 contracts. Hence, when the contract is in backwardation, the roll return is positive and results in a larger number of long contracts upon rolling over.

[handwritten: To keep it constant P. 116]

If natural gas exposure is 8.5% of the manager's portfolio, we can calculate the **net roll return** for the portfolio as 0.085 × 5.53% = 0.47%. *[handwritten: in Portfolio weighted]*

LOS 46.i: Describe how commodity swaps are used to obtain or modify exposure to commodities.

[handwritten: increases or decrease Risk in . . .]

CFA® Program Curriculum, Volume 6, page 222

Swaps can be used to increase or decrease exposure to commodities risk. Swaps are customized instruments created and sold by dealers, who may take on the risk of their swap exposure or hedge their exposure by entering into an offsetting swap contract (in which they have the opposite exposure to the risk factor) or by holding the physical commodity.

Swaps are created for which the payments between the two parties are based on various risk factors such as the excess returns on a commodity, the total return on the commodity, or a measure of price volatility.

In a **total return swap**, the swap buyer (the long) will receive periodic payments based on the change in the price of a commodity, in return for a series of fixed payments. Each period, the long will receive the total return on holding the commodity times a notional principal amount, net of the payment promised to the short. If the total return is negative, the long makes the promised fixed payment percentage *plus* the negative return percentage on the commodity over the period, times the notional amount.

For example, consider a total return swap on oil with a notional value of $10 million, in which for two years the long must pay 25 basis points monthly and will receive the total return on West Texas Intermediate (WTI) crude oil. If over the first month the price of WTI increases from 41.50 bbl to 42.10 bbl (+1.45%), the long will receive a net payment of (0.0145 − 0.0025) × $10 million = $120,000.

If over the second month the price of WTI decreases from 42.10 to 41.20 (−2.14%), the long must make a payment of (−0.0214 − 0.0025) × $10 million = $239,000 to the short.

Total return swaps are often used by institutions to gain exposure to the price risk of the underlying commodity, avoiding either holding the commodity or managing a long position in futures contracts over time.

Professor's Note: Some of the swaps described here are not constructed with two periodic payment streams and net payments based on the difference between the two payments each period, as we have seen with interest rate, currency, and equity swaps. The swap buyer instead may make a single payment at the initiation of the swap and then receive periodic payments based on the total returns, excess returns, or price volatility of a commodity, essentially "buying" exposure to the underlying risk factor.

In an **excess return swap**, a party may make a single payment at the initiation of the swap and then receive periodic payments of any percentage by which the commodity price exceeds some fixed or benchmark value, times the notional value of the swap. In months in which the commodity price does not exceed the fixed value, no payments are made.

In a **basis swap**, the variable payments are based on the difference between the prices of two commodities. Often the two commodities are one that has liquid traded futures available for hedging and the other (the one the swap buyer actually uses in production) with no liquid futures contracts available. Because the price changes of the two commodities are less than perfectly correlated, the difference between them (the basis) changes over time. By combining a hedge using the liquid futures with a basis swap, the swap buyer can hedge the price risk he faces from the input that does not have a liquid futures market.

In a **commodity volatility swap**, the underlying factor is the volatility of the commodity's price. If the volatility of the commodity's price is higher than the expected level of volatility specified in the swap, the volatility buyer receives a payment. When actual volatility is lower than the specified level, the volatility seller receives a payment. A similar swap settles based on variance in price levels of a commodity, with a swap buyer receiving a payment if the actual variance exceeds the fixed variance established at the onset of the swap. If the actual variance is lower, the variance seller receives a payment.

LOS 46.j: Describe how the construction of commodity indexes affects index returns.

CFA® Program Curriculum, Volume 6, page 226

There are several published commodity indexes. To be most useful, an index should be investable, in that an investor should be able to replicate the index with available liquid futures contracts.

The available commodity indexes differ in the following dimensions:

- Which commodities are included
- The weighting of the commodities in the index
- The method of rolling contracts over as they near expiration
- The method of rebalancing portfolio weights

While no index methodology will consistently outperform another index methodology, differences in methodology do result in returns differences, at least over shorter periods. Over long periods, differences between the mix and weights of constituent commodities in individual indexes will result in differences between returns, as some commodities outperform others.

Indexes may be equal weighted or weighted on some factor, such as the value of global production of an individual commodity or commodity sector. A production value weighted index will have more exposure to energy than to livestock or softs, for example.

With regard to roll methodology, a passive strategy may be to simply roll the expiring futures contracts into the near-month contract each month. A more active strategy would be to maximize roll return by selecting the further-out contracts with the greatest backwardation or smallest contango.

The frequency of rebalancing will also affect commodity index returns. Rebalancing portfolio weights will decrease returns when prices are trending but increase returns when price changes are choppy and mean-reverting. For this reason, price behavior across rebalancing periods will influence returns. If the prices of a commodity are choppy over short horizons but trending on a longer-term basis, frequent rebalancing may capture gains from mean reversion over the shorter periods but give up some of the gains from the trend of the commodity's price over the longer term.

While differences in index construction methodology will lead to differences among index returns over relatively shorter periods, no one methodology is necessarily superior over longer periods. Correlations between returns on different indexes have been relatively high, while correlations between commodity indexes and returns on stocks and bonds have been low.

Study Session 15
Cross-Reference to CFA Institute Assigned Reading #46 – Commodities and Commodity Derivatives: An Introduction

Study Session 15

KEY CONCEPTS

LOS 46.a

Commodity sectors include energy (crude oil, natural gas, and refined petroleum products); industrial metals (aluminum, nickel, zinc, lead, tin, iron, and copper); grains (wheat, corn, soybeans, and rice); livestock (hogs, sheep, cattle, and poultry); precious metals (gold , silver, and platinum); and softs or cash crops (coffee, sugar, cocoa, and cotton).

Crude oil must be refined into usable products but may be shipped and stored in its natural form. Natural gas may be used in its natural form but must be liquefied to be shipped overseas.

Industrial and precious metals have demand that is sensitive to business cycles and typically can be stored for long periods.

Production of grains and softs is sensitive to weather. Livestock supply is sensitive to the price of feed grains.

LOS 46.b

The life cycle of commodity sectors includes the time it takes to produce, transport, store, and process the commodities.
- Crude oil production involves drilling a well and extracting and transporting the oil. Oil is typically stored for only a short period before being refined into products that will be transported to consumers.
- Natural gas requires little processing and may be transported to consumers by pipeline.
- Metals are produced by mining and smelting ore, which requires producers to construct large-scale fixed plants and purchase equipment. Most metals can be stored long term.
- Livestock production cycles vary with the size of the animal. Meat can be frozen for shipment and storage.
- Grain production is seasonal, but grains can be stored after harvest. Growing seasons are opposite in the northern and southern hemispheres.
- Softs are produced in warm climates and have production cycles and storage needs that vary by product.

LOS 46.c

In contrast to equities and bonds, which are valued by estimating the present value of their future cash flows, commodities do not produce periodic cash inflows. While the spot price of a commodity may be viewed as the estimated present value of its future selling price, storage costs (i.e., cash outflows) may result in forward prices that are higher than spot prices.

LOS 46.d

Participants in commodity futures markets include hedgers, speculators, arbitrageurs, exchanges, analysts, and regulators.

Informed investors are those who have information about the commodity they trade. Hedgers are informed investors because they produce or use the commodity. Some speculators act as informed investors and attempt to profit from having better information or a better ability to process information. Other speculators profit from providing liquidity to the futures markets.

LOS 46.e

Basis is the difference between the spot price and a futures price for a commodity. Calendar spread is the difference between futures prices for contracts with different expiration dates. _short – long Maturity Prices_

A market is in contango if futures prices are greater than spot prices, or in backwardation if futures prices are less than spot prices. Calendar spreads and basis are negative in contango and positive in backwardation.

LOS 46.f

Insurance Theory states that futures returns compensate contract buyers for providing _Consumer_ protection against price risk to futures contract sellers (i.e., the producers). This theory implies that backwardation is a normal condition. → _Producers_

The Hedging Pressure Hypothesis expands on Insurance Theory by including long hedgers as well as short hedgers. This theory suggests futures markets will be in backwardation when short hedgers dominate and in contango when long hedgers dominate.

The Theory of Storage states that spot and futures prices are related through storage costs and convenience yield.

LOS 46.g

The total return on a fully collateralized long futures position consists of collateral return, price return, and roll return. Collateral return is the yield on securities the investor deposits as collateral for the futures position. Price return or spot yield is produced by a change in spot prices. Roll return results from closing out expiring contracts and reestablishing the position in longer-dated contracts.

LOS 46.h

Roll return is positive when a futures market is in backwardation because a long position holder will be buying longer-dated contracts that are priced lower than the expiring contracts. Roll return is negative when a futures market is in contango because the longer-dated contracts are priced higher than the expiring contracts.

LOS 46.i

Investors can use swaps to increase or decrease exposure to commodities. In a total return swap, the variable payments are based on the change in price of a commodity. In an excess return swap, the variable payments are based on the difference between a commodity price and a benchmark value. In a basis swap, the variable payments are based on the difference in prices of two commodities. In a commodity volatility swap, the variable payments are based on the volatility of a commodity price.

LOS 46.j

Returns on a commodity index are affected by how the index is constructed. The index components and weighting method affect which commodities have the greatest influence on the index return. The methodology for rolling over expiring contracts may be passive or active. Frequent rebalancing of portfolio weights may decrease index returns in trending markets or increase index returns in choppy or mean-reverting markets.

CONCEPT CHECKERS

1. The commodity sector that is *least affected* by weather risk is:
    A. grains.
    B. precious metals.
    C. refined energy products.

2. For which of the following commodities is the production and consumption cycle *least affected* by seasonality?
    A. Hogs.
    B. Coffee.
    C. Natural gas.

3. Which of the following factors is *most likely* to distinguish the valuation of a commodity from the valuation of an equity that pays no dividends?
    A. Holding costs.
    B. Discount rate.
    C. Timing of the future sale.

4. A commodity is *most likely* to be physically stored by a(n):
    A. exchange.
    B. speculator.
    C. arbitrageur.

5. A futures market in backwardation will exhibit:
    A. positive basis and positive calendar spreads.
    B. negative basis and positive calendar spreads.
    C. negative basis and negative calendar spreads.

6. Which theory of commodity futures returns is *least likely* to explain why futures markets can be in contango?
    A. Insurance Theory.
    B. Theory of Storage.
    C. Hedging Pressure Hypothesis.

7. Suppose that a commodity market exhibits the following futures curve on July 1, 20X1:
    *   Spot price: 42.0
    *   August futures price: 41.5
    *   October futures price: 40.8
    *   December futures price: 39.7

    An investor establishes a fully collateralized long position on July 1, 20X1, and maintains the position for one year. The futures curve on July 1, 20X2, is identical to the futures curve on July 1, 20X1, and calendar spreads did not change significantly during the year. The investor's total return on the position is *most likely*:
    A. equal to the collateral return.
    B. less than the collateral return.
    C. greater than the collateral return.

8. An investor enters into a swap contract under which the net payment will vary directly with the price of a commodity. This contract is *most accurately* described as a(n):
   A. basis swap.
   B. total return swap.
   C. excess return swap.

To access other content related to this topic review that may be included in the Schweser package you purchased, log in to your Schweser.com online dashboard. Schweser's OnDemand Video Lectures deliver streaming instruction covering every LOS in this topic review, while SchweserPro™ QBank provides additional quiz questions to help you practice and recall what you've learned.

ANSWERS – CONCEPT CHECKERS

1. **B** Precious metals mining and smelting are less susceptible to changing weather. Weather is an important factor in grain production with both droughts and flooding affecting crop yields. Oil refineries are concentrated in coastal areas where hurricanes and other extreme weather cause periodic refinery shutdowns.

2. **B** Coffee has a long production cycle but is grown at warm latitudes and harvested throughout the year. Livestock production is strongly influenced by seasonality. Natural gas demand has a seasonal component due to its uses for heating and electricity generation for cooling.

3. **A** While a commodity or a nondividend-paying equity security can be valued in terms of the present value of its future sale price, a commodity may have holding costs, such as storage, that can result in a forward price that is higher than the spot price.

4. **C** Arbitrageurs may store a physical inventory of a commodity to exploit differences between spot and futures prices relative to the costs of storing the commodity.

5. **A** In backwardation, longer-dated futures contracts are priced lower than shorter-dated contracts or spot prices, resulting in positive basis and calendar spreads.

6. **A** According to Insurance Theory, backwardation is normal because futures contract buyers should earn a positive return for protecting commodity producers (short hedgers) from price risk. The Hedging Pressure Hypothesis and the Theory of Storage can explain either backwardation or contango.

7. **C** The price return is zero because the spot price is unchanged over the life of the position. The roll return is positive because the market is in backwardation. Therefore the total return (price return + roll return + collateral return) is greater than the collateral return.

8. **B** In a total return swap, the variable payment is based on the price of a commodity. In an excess return swap, the variable payment is based on the amount by which a commodity price is greater than a benchmark, and the payment is zero if the price is less than the benchmark. The variable payment of a basis swap depends on the difference between two commodity prices.

You have now finished the Alternative Investments topic section. The following self-test will provide immediate feedback on how effective your study of this material has been. The test is best taken timed; allow 3 minutes per subquestion (18 minutes per item set). This self-test is more exam-like than typical Concept Checkers or QBank questions. A score less than 70% suggests that additional review of this topic is needed.

Use the following information for Questions 1 through 6.

Eva Williams is an investment manager for Straughn Capital Management (SCM). Williams believes that it would be beneficial to add some alternative investments to SCM's existing portfolio. She has asked Steven Riley, an analyst with the firm, to present some investment ideas to her. Riley is not certain which type of alternative investment might be most suitable for SCM, so he has prepared information regarding three different types of investments. The first investment is a hedge fund. The second investment is an office building in the downtown district of a major city. The third investment is a venture capital fund.

While describing each of the properties, Riley makes the following observations:

Observation 1: Commodity investments, such as an investment in precious metals, are a good inflation hedge. Commodities as an asset class are receiving a lot of attention from hedge funds.

Observation 2: The value of an office building is heavily influenced by its location. Demand for office space is positively correlated with job growth. Also, the average length of lease terms varies globally. Furthermore, leases can be gross or net leases. In a net lease, the owner is responsible for the operating expense of a real estate property.

Observation 3: Similar to hedge funds, venture capital funds tend to be very illiquid. In evaluating venture capital funds, one needs to be careful about the economic terms. For example, the ratchet arrangement specifies the allocation of equity between the general partner and limited partners of the fund. Additionally, carried interest specifies the general partner's share of the fund profits. One should also consider the general partner's ability to raise capital as indicated by the difference between target fund size and funds actually raised.

Riley also provides information for the office building. The building under consideration is 200,000 square feet and has several structural issues that cannot be repaired. The effective age of the building is 12 years. The economic life of the building is 50 years. The elevators in the property need to be replaced at a cost of $1,200,000, but this replacement will increase the value of the building by $1,400,000. The design of the building is inferior to that of newer buildings and hence the rental income is lower by $375,000 per year. Cost of new construction including builder profit is $400 per square foot and the value of the land is estimated at $6,000,000. The applicable cap rate is 7.5%.

Finally, Riley provides information on a specific venture capital deal under consideration by Greenleaf Partners, a venture capital fund. Greenleaf is considering investing $2 million in a startup that is expected to be worth $40 million in seven years. Greenleaf considers 30% an appropriate rate of return given the risk of this investment.

1. Compared to an investment in REOCs, one disadvantage of investing in REITs is:
    A. limited potential for income growth.
    B. greater taxation.
    C. lack of control.

2. Hedge fund managers who believe in the Insurance Theory are *most likely* to take what kind of positions in commodity futures contracts?
    A. Long only.
    B. Short only.
    C. Long or short positions.

3. With respect to observation 2, Riley's assertions regarding office buildings, which statement would be *least accurate*? The statement about:
    A. the length of the lease.
    B. correlation with job growth.
    C. net lease characteristics.

4. With respect to observation 3, Riley's assertions regarding venture capital funds, which statement is *least accurate*? The statement about:
    A. the liquidity of venture capital funds.
    B. ratchet.
    C. the general partner's ability to raise capital.

5. Using the cost approach, the value of the office building is *closest* to:
    A. $54 million.
    B. $55 million.
    C. $61 million.

6. Based on the information provided, the maximum fractional equity ownership allocated to the founders after Greenleaf's $2 million investment is *closest* to:
    A. 30%.
    B. 46%.
    C. 69%.

1. **A** Due to high dividend payout (and low retention rates), REITs have limited potential for income growth. Exemption from taxation is an advantage that REITs enjoy compared to REOCs. Investors in both REITs and REOCs suffer from lack of control.

2. **A** The insurance perspective holds that commodity producers will hedge their commodity price risk. Under the insurance perspective, the cost of this risk reduction is a premium paid to speculators to entice them to take the long position in futures contracts. Consequently, futures prices should be less than expected spot prices, and a long-only position should result in positive excess returns.

3. **C** Net lease entails that the tenant (and not the owner) incurs the operating expense for the property.

4. **B** Ratchet determines the allocation of equity between management of the investee company and the stockholders and not the allocation between the general and limited partners of the private equity fund.

5. **C**

Replacement cost (200,000 sq. ft. @ $400)	$80 million
(–) Curable depreciation [elevators]	$1.2 million
Replacement cost after curable dep.	$78.8 million
(–) Incurable physical deterioration [structural issues]	$18.9 million
(12 / 50 × 78.8 million)	
(–) Incurable functional obsolescence (design)	$5 million
(375,000 lower rent/0.075 cap rate)	
(+) Market value of land	$6 million
(=) Value of property	$60.9 million

6. **C** POST = 6.375 (PV of $40 million in 7 years @ 30%)

Greenleaf's fractional equity ownership = 2 / 6.375 = 31.37%.

Maximum equity allocated to founders = 100 – 31.37 = 68.63%.

The following is a review of the Portfolio Management principles designed to address the learning outcome statements set forth by CFA Institute. Cross-Reference to CFA Institute Assigned Reading #47.

THE PORTFOLIO MANAGEMENT PROCESS AND THE INVESTMENT POLICY STATEMENT

Study Session 16

EXAM FOCUS

This qualitative material on portfolio management revisits concepts first introduced at Level I and provides an introduction to the extensive treatment of the topic you'll see in Level III. Keep the following points in mind: (1) the investment environment is ever-changing, so investment decision making must recognize the potential for shifts in a variety of factors, and (2) every investment decision should be framed within a portfolio perspective—it is not enough to know the characteristics of a potential investment itself, you must be aware of how an investment affects the risk and return characteristics of your overall portfolio.

ELEMENTS OF PORTFOLIO MANAGEMENT

Although specifying objectives and constraints and evaluating relevant economic and market conditions represent the beginning of the process, these decisions are also linked to the measurement, monitoring, and evaluation steps of the process. The integrative nature of portfolio management involves numerous feedback loops and allows managers to be as rigid or flexible (or as quantitative or qualitative) as they desire. There is no end point to the process, only evaluation of performance that may indicate a need for rebalancing. The following represents the elements of the portfolio management process.

Evaluating investor and market characteristics. The first step is to determine the objectives and constraints of the investor. Objectives are related to the risk and return expectations of the investor. Constraints are those factors that limit or restrict certain decisions or investment choices. The second step is to evaluate the economic environment. The factors relevant to an economic evaluation are mostly *macro* issues dealing with the overall state of the economy (growth prospects, inflation expectations, unemployment, and other considerations). An economic evaluation can also work down to *micro* issues, such as those related to sector-, industry-, and security-specific considerations.

Developing an investment policy statement. This next portion of the investment management process formalizes objectives and constraints into an investment policy statement (IPS), which will guide investment decisions and formalize the investment strategy (e.g., whether the portfolio will be actively managed or follow a more passive approach). Capital market expectations that take into account the economic evaluation conducted previously are also formalized in this step.

Determining an asset allocation strategy. After the formal documentation of the IPS is completed, decisions on how and where funds will be invested are completed, and a strategic asset allocation is created. Securities are evaluated as to how they might fit into a portfolio that meets the objectives and constraints of the investor. Portfolio decisions are implemented and then executed in a timely fashion so that the investor's funds can be put to use in attaining goals and objectives.

Measuring and evaluating performance. After a stated time period, which will be specified in the IPS, portfolio performance will be measured and an evaluation as to whether the portfolio attained investor objectives and followed the IPS will be prepared. Portfolio rebalancing may be indicated by the results of the evaluation. Connecting the evaluation step to the beginning of the process must occur to ensure portfolio decisions parallel investor needs and desires.

Monitoring dynamic investor objectives and capital market conditions. Continuous monitoring of both investor and marketplace characteristics takes place throughout the entire process. Multiple feedback mechanisms throughout the entire portfolio management process indicate where significant changes in either investor factors or marketplace prospects require adjustments to the portfolio. Remember, this is a dynamic, ongoing process. There are no end points, only continuous connections between objectives and constraints to portfolio monitoring and evaluation.

LOS 47.a: Explain the importance of the portfolio perspective.

CFA® Program Curriculum, Volume 6, page 246

The portfolio perspective is a key underlying principle of the entire CFA curriculum. The equity pricing models in the Level II curriculum are all based on the principle that only systematic risk is priced. Furthermore, one of the basic principles of the New Prudent Investor Rule is that diversification is expected of portfolio managers as a method of reducing risk.

Investors, analysts, and portfolio managers should analyze the **risk-return tradeoff** of the portfolio as a whole, not the risk-return tradeoff of the individual investments in the portfolio, because unsystematic risk can be diversified away by combining the investments into a portfolio. The systematic risk that remains in the portfolio is the result of the economic fundamentals that have a general influence on the security returns, such as GDP growth, unexpected inflation, consumer confidence, unanticipated changes in credit spreads, and business cycle.

LOS 47.b: Describe the steps of the portfolio management process and the components of those steps.

CFA® Program Curriculum, Volume 6, page 247

The ongoing portfolio management process can be detailed within the integrative steps described by **planning**, **execution**, and **feedback**. Each general step contains numerous components. The planning phase consists of analyzing objectives and constraints,

Study Session 16

Cross-Reference to CFA Institute Assigned Reading #47 – The Portfolio Management Process and the Investment Policy Statement

developing an IPS, determining the appropriate investment strategy, and selecting an appropriate asset allocation. The focus of this topic review at Level II is the first step: planning.

LOS 47.c: Explain the role of the investment policy statement in the portfolio management process and describe the elements of an investment policy statement.

CFA® Program Curriculum, Volume 6, page 247

The investment policy statement (IPS) is a formal document that governs investment decision making, taking into account objectives and constraints. The main roles of the IPS are to:

- Be readily implemented by current or future investment advisers (i.e., it is easily transportable).
- Promote long-term discipline for portfolio decisions.
- Help protect against short-term shifts in strategy when either market environments or portfolio performance cause panic or overconfidence.

There are numerous elements to an IPS. Some elements that are typically included are:

- A client description that provides enough background so any competent investment adviser can gain a common understanding of the client's situation.
- The purpose of the IPS with respect to policies, objectives, goals, restrictions, and portfolio limitations.
- Identification of duties and responsibilities of parties involved.
- The formal statement of objectives and constraints.
- A calendar schedule for both portfolio performance and IPS review.
- Asset allocation ranges and statements regarding flexibility and rigidity when formulating or modifying the strategic asset allocation.
- Guidelines for portfolio adjustments and rebalancing.

LOS 47.d: Explain how capital market expectations and the investment policy statement help influence the strategic asset allocation decision and how an investor's investment time horizon may influence the investor's strategic asset allocation.

CFA® Program Curriculum, Volume 6, page 250

The final step in the planning stage is creation of a **strategic asset allocation**. This step combines the IPS and capital market expectations to formulate long-term target weightings for the asset classes to be included in the portfolio. The need for flexibility in the asset allocation to allow for temporary shifts (called tactical asset allocations) in response to alterations in short-term capital market expectations should also be considered.

There are three common approaches used to implement the strategic asset allocation:

- *Passive investment strategies* represent those strategies that are not responsive to changes in expectations. Indexing and buy-and-hold investment strategies are examples of passive investment strategies.
- *Active investment strategies* are much more responsive to changing expectations. These strategies attempt to capitalize on differences between a portfolio manager's beliefs concerning security valuations and those in the marketplace. Generating alpha and investing according to a particular investment style fall into the active investment strategy category.
- *Semi-active, risk-controlled active,* or *enhanced index strategies* are hybrids of passive and active strategies. Index tilting, where portfolio managers attempt to match the risk characteristics of a benchmark portfolio, but also deviate from the exact benchmark portfolio weights in order to earn higher returns, is one example of this approach to strategic asset allocation.

Forecasts of risk-return characteristics are required for asset classes that are included in the investor's portfolio so that the portfolio's expected risk-return profile is well understood. The role played by this step is to connect realistic market expectations to the objectives and constraints of the investor. Should the portfolio's risk-return profile diverge significantly from the investor's objectives, the strategic asset allocation may need to be reviewed.

The length of the time horizon may also influence the investor's asset allocation. An investor with a shorter investment time horizon will often choose a strategic asset allocation that is relatively less risky, with a smaller allocation to equities, for example.

LOS 47.e: Define investment objectives and constraints and explain and distinguish among the types of investment objectives and constraints.

CFA® Program Curriculum, Volume 6, page 253

Investment objectives relate to what the investor wants to accomplish with the portfolio. Objectives are mainly concerned with risk and return considerations.

Risk objectives are those factors associated with an investor's willingness and ability to take risk. Combining willingness and ability to accept risk is termed *risk tolerance*. *Risk aversion* indicates an investor's inability and unwillingness to take risk.

For an individual, willingness and ability to take risk may be determined by behavioral or psychological factors, whereas for an institution, these factors are determined primarily by portfolio constraints. Some specific factors that affect ability to accept risk are as follows:

- *Required spending needs:* How much variation in portfolio value can the investor tolerate before being inconvenienced in the short term?
- *Long-term wealth target:* How much variation in portfolio value can the investor tolerate before it jeopardizes meeting long-term wealth goals?

Study Session 16

Cross-Reference to CFA Institute Assigned Reading #47 – The Portfolio Management Process and the Investment Policy Statement

- *Financial strength:* Can the investor increase savings (or decrease expenditures) if the portfolio is insufficient to meet spending needs?
- *Liabilities:* Is the investor legally obligated to make future payments to beneficiaries, or does the investor have certain set spending requirements in retirement (i.e., pseudo liabilities)?

If the investor's portfolio is large relative to spending and obligations, a greater ability to take risk is apparent. Appropriately connecting willingness to ability may require educating the client in risk-return principles, as shown in Figure 1.

Figure 1: Investor's Risk Tolerance

Willingness to Take Risk	Ability to Take Risk	
	Below Average	Above Average
Below Average	Below-average risk tolerance	Education/resolution required
Above Average	Below-average risk tolerance	Above-average risk tolerance

Professor's Note: When the investor's ability and willingness to assume risk are in conflict, resolution is required. If ability exceeds willingness, the investor should be counseled that the assumption of more risk may be appropriate, with the ultimate decision left up to the investor. If willingness exceeds ability, ability should define the maximum risk tolerance.

There are two classes of risk objective measurements: absolute risk objectives and relative risk objectives. Standard deviation of total return represents an example of an absolute risk objective, whereas deviations from an underlying index, or *tracking risk*, represent an example of a relative risk objective. Relative risk measures are often easier to quantify from an individual investor's perspective, but absolute risk objectives are also referred to, even if only stated in qualitative forms.

Individuals often state their willingness to assume risk in broad terms; for example, "I have a moderate level of risk tolerance." Although institutions may state specific quantitative risk measures, such as "The level of portfolio volatility should not exceed 25% in any given year," their risk objectives can also be ranked along a qualitative risk objective spectrum. It is important to incorporate whatever level of specificity is mentioned when analyzing the risk objective.

Return objectives can be classified as either a *desired* or a *required* return. A desired return is that level of return stated by the client, indicating how much the investor wishes to receive from the portfolio. A required return represents some level of return that must be achieved by the portfolio, at least on an average basis to meet the target financial obligations. As such, required returns serve as a much stricter benchmark than desired returns.

In either case, the level of return needs to be consistent with the risk objective. Desired or required returns might be unrealistic, given available market conditions or risk objectives. Educating the investor as to disconnections between return and risk may be required. Some additional considerations in calculating return levels are differentiating between *real* and *nominal* returns, and distinguishing *pretax* and *after-tax* returns.

Whatever the return level generated, one factor to remember is that the return objective should be considered from a *total return* perspective. Even if a substantial income (or spending) component is required from the portfolio, the return objective should be evaluated by the total return, the return from both income and capital gains, and the characteristics of the portfolio. The assumption is that spending needs can be met through both investment income and capital appreciation.

INVESTMENT CONSTRAINTS

Investment constraints are those factors restricting or limiting the universe of available investment choices. Constraints can be generated either internally (those determined by the investor) or externally (those determined by some outside entity, such as a governmental agency). The five main classes of constraints relate to liquidity, time horizon, legal and regulatory concerns, tax considerations, and unique circumstances.

Liquidity constraints relate to expected cash outflows that will be needed at some specified time and are in excess of available income. In addition, it is ordinarily prudent to set aside some amount (e.g., three months living expenses) to meet unexpected cash needs. Often, liquidity is required over multiple time periods. A down payment for a home, funding for children's education, and providing for special needs during retirement are all liquidity concerns. The reason liquidity constraints are important to consider is that, depending on marketability, certain assets may generate only a portion of their fair value if they must be sold quickly. Attention must be paid to an asset's ability to be turned into cash without significant impact on portfolio value or asset allocation.

Linkages between liquidity and risk objectives are also apparent. Higher liquidity requirements usually indicate a lower tolerance for risk taking. Sensitivity to liquidity is a factor potentially affecting the willingness to take risk.

Time horizon constraints are associated with the time period(s) over which a portfolio is expected to generate returns to meet specific future needs (e.g., paying for retirement or children's college education).

Tax constraints depend on how, when, and if portfolio returns of various types are taxed. Some institutional investors (e.g., pension funds and endowments) have tax-exempt status. However, income and realized gains generated by personal portfolios are taxable and attention must be paid to the taxing environment when formulating the IPS. Often, differential tax treatments are applied to investment income and capital gains, which may be taxed at a lower rate. On the other hand, returns on certain types of retirement accounts are tax deferred until withdrawals are made.

Study Session 16

Cross-Reference to CFA Institute Assigned Reading #47 – The Portfolio Management Process and the Investment Policy Statement

Depending on which investment vehicle is chosen for the portfolio, tax consequences may adversely impact the after-tax returns. Estate taxes can also affect portfolio decisions. As a result, investment choices must be made with careful consideration of how a portfolio's returns will be taxed.

Legal and regulatory factors are externally generated constraints that mainly affect institutional investors. These constraints are usually associated with specifying which investment classes are not allowed or dictating any limitations placed on allocations to particular investment classes. Trust portfolios for individual investors may also be subject to substantial legal and regulatory oversight, which must be considered when establishing the IPS. Otherwise, this constraint does not usually affect individual investors. An example of a legal constraint that affects the management of trust assets for an individual is the New Prudent Investor Rule.

Unique circumstances are internally generated and represent special concerns of the investor. University endowments and philanthropic organizations, for example, might not allow investments in companies selling tobacco, alcohol, or defense products. Individuals might wish to have their portfolios fund specific activities (e.g., grandchildren's education, cancer research, or support for the arts), or they might be unfamiliar or inexperienced with certain investments. These, as well as any special investor circumstance restricting investment activities, must be considered in the formulation of the IPS.

> *Professor's Note: A helpful way to remember the IPS objectives and constraints is to use the acronym RRTTLLU for Risk, Return, Time horizon, Taxes, Liquidity needs, Legal/regulatory, and Unique circumstances.*

A brief summary of return objectives and risk tolerance for individual and various institutional investors is shown in Figure 2.

Risk Return Time Tax Liquidity Legal Unique

Figure 2: Investment Objectives of Individual and Institutional Investors

Investor	Return Requirement	Risk Tolerance
Individual investor	Depends on life-cycle stage and financial position	Depends on life-cycle stage and financial position
Defined benefit pension plan	Sufficient to fund pension liability while accounting for inflation	Depends on plan features, age of workforce, and funding status of plan
Defined contribution pension plan	Depends on life-cycle stage of beneficiaries	Depends on risk tolerance of beneficiaries
Endowments and foundations	Sufficient to cover spending needs, expenses, and inflation	Generally average or above average
Life insurance company	Function of policyholder reserve rates	Below average because of significant regulatory constraints
Non-life insurance company	Function of policy pricing and financial strength	Below average because of significant regulatory constraints
Bank	Function of cost of funds	Depends on business model and financial strength

LOS 47.f: Contrast the types of investment time horizons, determine the time horizon for a particular investor, and evaluate the effects of this time horizon on portfolio choice.

CFA® Program Curriculum, Volume 6, page 258

The time horizon for an investment portfolio may be short, as with a couple saving to purchase a home in two years, or long, as in the case of a couple in their 30s saving for retirement. Investors may also have a combination of short and long investment time horizons, as in the case of a couple who are saving both to fund their children's educations in five years and for retirement in 30 years.

The importance of the time horizon as an investment constraint is based on the idea that the longer the investment time horizon, the more risk an investor can take on. For time horizons of ten years or more, the fact that returns will average over economic and market cycles is generally believed to justify a greater allocation to equities and perhaps to riskier equities. The uncertainty about returns and the inability to make up for poor results over a short investment horizon leads many short-term investors to select relatively low-risk (predictable) securities. For a specific investor, however, a low *willingness* to take risk may constrain portfolio risk because of sensitivity to interim results, even when the investment horizon is relatively long and the *ability* to take on risk is greater.

Study Session 16

Cross-Reference to CFA Institute Assigned Reading #47 – The Portfolio Management Process and the Investment Policy Statement

LOS 47.g: Justify ethical conduct as a requirement for managing investment portfolios.

CFA® Program Curriculum, Volume 6, page 261

The investment professional who manages client portfolios well meets standards of competence and standards of conduct. It is important to recognize that the portfolio manager, who is an expert in the field with presumably more knowledge of investment principles than the client, is in a position of trust and so must meet the highest standards of ethical conduct in order to truly serve clients. The appropriate standard of conduct is embodied by the CFA Institute Code and Standards of Practice.

KEY CONCEPTS

LOS 47.a

Because different economic factors influence the returns of various assets differently, the risk of one asset is only somewhat correlated with the risk of other assets. If we evaluate the risk of each asset in isolation and ignore these interrelationships, we will misunderstand the risk and return potential of the investor's total investment position. The portfolio perspective tells us that our fundamental concern is to understand the risk and return in a portfolio context.

LOS 47.b

The three phases of the portfolio management process are planning, execution, and feedback; the Level II curriculum focuses on the planning phase.

- The planning phase consists of analyzing objectives and constraints, developing an IPS, determining the appropriate investment strategy, and selecting an appropriate asset allocation.
- The execution process relates to portfolio construction and revision.
- The feedback process consists of monitoring, rebalancing, and performance evaluation.

LOS 47.c

The IPS is a written document providing guidelines for portfolio investment decision making. The IPS does the following:

- Provides guidance for current and subsequent investment adviser decisions.
- Promotes long-term discipline in investment decision making.
- Protects against short-term shifts in strategy when either market conditions or portfolio performance cause panic or overconfidence.

There are several elements to a suitable IPS: (1) a description of the client's situation, (2) the purpose, as well as identification, of responsibilities, (3) formal statements of objectives and constraints, (4) a schedule for portfolio performance and IPS review, (5) asset allocation ranges, and (6) guidance for rebalancing and adjustment activities.

LOS 47.d

While the investment policy statement will outline the appropriate risk-return characteristics for an investment portfolio, the strategic asset allocation to provide these characteristics will depend on capital markets expectations (risk, returns, and correlations) for the various asset classes. Typically, a longer investment time horizon will lead investors to tolerate more portfolio risk and employ strategic asset allocations more heavily weighted toward asset classes with greater risk and greater expected returns, such as equities.

Study Session 16

Cross-Reference to CFA Institute Assigned Reading #47 – The Portfolio Management Process and the Investment Policy Statement

LOS 47.e

The two investment objectives to consider are:
- Return objectives.
- Risk objectives.

The five common constraints are:
- Liquidity.
- Time horizon.
- Legal and regulatory concerns.
- Tax considerations.
- Unique circumstances.

Differences between an investor's willingness and ability to take risk create additional education/resolution responsibilities for the portfolio manager with regard to formulating the risk objectives.

LOS 47.f

Investors may have short or long investment horizons, or some combination of the two when multiple investment goals are identified. Investors with longer horizons (>10 years) have the ability, but not necessarily the willingness, to employ strategic asset allocations with more risk since returns will be averaged over economic and market cycles and investors have more time to recover from periods of relatively poor returns.

LOS 47.g

The investment professional who manages client portfolios well meets standards of competence and standards of conduct. It is important to recognize that the portfolio manager, who is an expert in the field with presumably more knowledge of investment principles than the client, is in a position of trust and so must meet the highest standards of ethical conduct in order to truly serve his clients. The appropriate standard of conduct is embodied by the CFA Institute Code and Standards.

CONCEPT CHECKERS

Use the following information to answer Questions 1 through 3.

Jane Smith has an investment portfolio of $5 million. She is 68 years old, retired, and has no children. After her death, she wishes to leave her portfolio to a local art museum that has given her relatively free access to art exhibits over the past decade. Her health is better than average, and she maintains an active lifestyle consisting of frequent swimming, biking, and playing tennis with friends at her country club. Smith estimates that to maintain her standard of living, she needs approximately $250,000 per year. Expenses are expected to grow at an expected inflation rate of 2%. She states that as a retiree, her tolerance for risk is "below average." Smith has come to you for assistance in investing her assets.

1. Smith's return objective is *closest* to:
    A. 3%.
    B. 5%.
    C. 7%.

2. Smith's ability to take risk is *most appropriately* characterized as:
    A. below average.
    B. average.
    C. significantly above average.

3. In terms of Smith's time horizon and liquidity constraints, Smith *most likely* has:
    A. a short-term time horizon and no significant liquidity constraints.
    B. a short-term time horizon and significant liquidity constraints.
    C. a long-term time horizon and no significant liquidity constraints.

Use the following information to answer Questions 4 and 5.

Joe Farmingham is 38 years old, married, and has two children, ages 12 and 7. He recently received an inheritance of $300,000 and is considering investing "real money" for the first time. Farmingham likes to read the financial press and indicates that if he had money to invest in the past, he could have taken advantage of some undervalued security opportunities. Farmingham believes he has an average tolerance for risk-taking in investment activities, but he also enjoys skydiving every other weekend.

4. Farmingham's ability to take risk is *most appropriately* characterized as:
    A. below average.
    B. average.
    C. above average.

5. The *most appropriate* investment strategy for Farmingham to take advantage of his stated propensity for finding undervalued investments is a(n):
    A. active investment strategy.
    B. risk-controlled active investment strategy.
    C. enhanced index strategy.

CHALLENGE PROBLEMS

6. Lanaster University's endowment fund was recently estimated to be around $200 million. The university's endowment investment committee oversees numerous asset managers and is responsible for creating the investment policy statement (IPS). Ellen Hardinger and Will Smithson have been discussing the many factors that go into an IPS and are somewhat perplexed as to how to state the fund's risk objective. Hardinger and Smithson make three statements regarding the risk objectives of the endowment fund:

    Statement 1: The fund is relatively conservative in its investment approach.
    Statement 2: The fund performance should not exhibit more than a 20% standard deviation in any given year.
    Statement 3: The fund should not exhibit performance differences of more than 5% from the Wilshire 5000 over any 3-year period.

    They need assistance in understanding how to combine those risk statements into a risk objective. How many of the statements represent absolute risk?
    A. One.
    B. Two.
    C. Three.

Use the following information for Questions 7 through 9.

William and Elizabeth Elam recently inherited $500,000 from Elizabeth's father, Abraham, and have come to Alan Schneider, CFA, for assistance in financial planning for their retirement. Both William and Elizabeth are 30 years old. William is employed as a factory worker with a salary of $40,000. Elizabeth is a teacher's aide and has a salary of $18,000. Their four children are ages 6, 5, 4, and 3. They have no other investments and have a current credit card debt of $60,000. When interviewed by Schneider, William made the following statements:

*   I love being on top of the latest trends in investing.
*   My friend Keith told me that the really smart investor holds stocks for no more than a month. After that, if you haven't made a profit, you probably won't.
*   Technology stocks are hot! Everyone has been buying them.
*   Can you believe that my mother still has the same portfolio she had a year ago? How boring!

7. The Elams' ability and willingness to take on risk are *most appropriately* characterized as:
    A. above average willingness and ability.
    B. below average ability and average willingness.
    C. average ability and above average willingness.

8. The Elams' time horizon constraint can be *best* characterized as:
    A. long-term and single stage.
    B. long-term and multistage.
    C. variable term and single stage.

9. The Elams' liquidity and legal/regulatory constraints are *best* characterized as:
    A. significant.
    B. insignificant.
    C. liquidity significant and legal/regulatory insignificant.

Study Session 16

Cross-Reference to CFA Institute Assigned Reading #47 – The Portfolio Management Process and the Investment Policy Statement

ANSWERS – CONCEPT CHECKERS

1. **C** Smith states that she needs $250,000 annually to maintain her standard of living. This amount of annual expenditures represents 5% ($250,000 / $5,000,000) of the current portfolio. Accounting for an expected increase in expenses at the anticipated level of inflation indicates a return objective around 7%.

2. **B** Although her stated willingness to take risk is below average, the size of her portfolio, her good health, and relative long time horizon indicate an ability to take average risk. As a retiree, sensitivity to substantial declines in portfolio value is probably a concern.

3. **C** Barring any unexpected health-related costs, the inflation-adjusted income needed will probably not change dramatically. Smith's concern for liquidity primarily relates to unusual cash outflows (e.g., health care costs, emergency spending) that might take place during her retirement years and hence, she has no significant liquidity constraints. Smith has essentially a long-term time horizon for her portfolio: until the end of her life, which could be another 20 years.

4. **C** Farmingham appears to have the ability and willingness to take risk. He frequently enjoys risk-seeking activities, such as skydiving. His relatively young age indicates a somewhat long time horizon for his investment portfolio. These facts couple ability and willingness to take an above-average level of risk.

5. **A** Farmingham indicates that he follows the financial press and has spotted what he considered to be undervalued securities. This activity indicates that Farmingham pays attention to security valuation issues and that he probably will do so in the future. His portfolio, therefore, should follow an active investment strategy.

To access other content related to this topic review that may be included in the Schweser package you purchased, log in to your Schweser.com online dashboard. Schweser's OnDemand Video Lectures deliver streaming instruction covering every LOS in this topic review, while SchweserPro™ QBank provides additional quiz questions to help you practice and recall what you've learned.

ANSWERS – CHALLENGE PROBLEMS

6. **A**   The statement of "20% standard deviation in any given year" is an absolute risk measure because it quantitatively states a specified level of total risk not to be exceeded. Conversely, the statement "performance differences from the Wilshire 5000 of more than 5% over any 3-year period" is a relative risk measure. Comparing measures of portfolio risk to another investment vehicle is an indication of relative risk.

     Institutional investors tend to be more quantitative in their assessments of risk, but the statement that the fund "is relatively conservative in its investment approach" also specifies a qualitative component to the risk objective.

7. **A**   Because of their long time horizon and their situational profile, the Elams have the ability to tolerate an above-average level of risk. Based on the interview with William, the Elams have stated a willingness to tolerate an above-average level of risk. Therefore, the portfolio can be constructed based on an above-average level of risk.

     Based upon their lack of investing experience and rather aggressive attitude toward portfolio risk management, however, the financial services professional should be certain that the Elam's have a clear understanding of the concepts of risk and return.

8. **B**   The Elams' time horizon is long term and at least two-fold: the time until retirement and their retirement years. It is possible that a third time horizon could develop should the Elams decide to support their children through post-secondary education. Should they decide to retire at age 60, their pre-retirement time horizon would be 30 years.

9. **C**   The main liquidity constraint presented in the case is immediate and significant (the $60,000 in credit card debt). Schneider should recommend that the Elams eliminate this liability with the inheritance funds immediately. No special legal or regulatory problems are apparent. Prudent investor rules apply if William is interested in creating a trust fund.

AN INTRODUCTION TO MULTIFACTOR MODELS

Study Session 16

EXAM FOCUS

Factor models are important in understanding risk exposures and in asset selection. Be able to construct arbitrage portfolios and be familiar with different multifactor models (and their differences), how they can be used, and their advantages over CAPM. Also understand the application of multifactor models to return and risk decomposition and the use of multifactor models in portfolio construction, including the use of factor portfolios in making bets on a specific risk factor.

LOS 48.a: Describe arbitrage pricing theory (APT), including its underlying assumptions and its relation to multifactor models.

CFA® Program Curriculum, Volume 6, page 275

Arbitrage pricing theory (APT) was developed as an alternative to the capital asset pricing model. It is a linear model with multiple systematic risk factors priced by the market. However, unlike CAPM, APT does not identify the specific risk factors (or even the number of factors).

Assumptions of Arbitrage Pricing Theory (APT)

1. *Unsystematic risk can be diversified away in a portfolio.* Investors have the choice of a large number of assets such that unsystematic risk can be diversified by forming portfolios of assets. This is a reasonable assumption and is supported by empirical evidence.

2. *Returns are generated using a factor model.* Unfortunately, the APT provides little practical guidance for the identification of the risk factors. The lack of clarity for the risk factors is a major weakness of the APT.

3. *No arbitrage opportunities exist.* An arbitrage opportunity is defined as an investment opportunity that bears no risk and no cost, but provides a profit. This assumption implies that investors will undertake infinitely large positions (long and short) to exploit any perceived mispricing, causing asset prices to adjust immediately to their equilibrium values.

The asset pricing model developed by the arbitrage pricing theory is called the *arbitrage pricing model.*

The APT Equation

The APT describes the equilibrium relationship between expected returns for well-diversified portfolios and their multiple sources of systematic risk.

[handwritten: Multiple Risk factors (R₇-R_F)]

$$E(R_P) = R_F + \beta_{P,1}(\lambda_1) + \beta_{P,2}(\lambda_2) + \ldots + \beta_{P,k}(\lambda_k)$$

Each λ stands for the expected risk premium associated with each risk factor. λ_j equals the risk premium for a portfolio (called a *pure factor portfolio*) with factor sensitivity of 1 to factor *j* and factor sensitivities equal to zero for the remaining factors. Remember that a risk premium is the difference between the expected return and the risk-free rate (R_F). It is the extra expected return from taking on more risk.

[handwritten margin notes: β = 1 to 5 with only one factor CAPM ... Factor sensitivity = β, risk factor = λ]

Each β represents the factor sensitivity of portfolio P to that risk factor. Each factor in the arbitrage pricing model is "priced," meaning that each risk premium is statistically and economically significant. Unlike the CAPM, the APT does *not* require that one of the risk factors is the market portfolio. This is a major advantage of the arbitrage pricing model.

> *Professor's Note: The CAPM can be considered a special restrictive case of the APT in which there is only one risk factor, and where that one factor is restricted to be the market risk factor.*

LOS 48.b: Define arbitrage opportunity and determine whether an arbitrage opportunity exists.

CFA® Program Curriculum, Volume 6, page 276

The method for exploiting arbitrage opportunities in the APT framework is detailed in the following example.

Example: Exploiting an arbitrage opportunity

Suppose your investment firm uses a single-factor model to evaluate assets. Consider the following data for portfolios A, B, and C:

Portfolio	Expected Return	Factory Sensitivity (beta)
A	10%	1.0
B	20%	2.0
C	13%	1.5

Calculate the arbitrage opportunity from the data provided.

Answer:

By allocating 50% of our funds to portfolio A and 50% to portfolio B, we can obtain a portfolio (D) with beta equal to the portfolio C beta (1.5):

Beta for portfolio D = 0.5(1) + 0.5(2) = 1.5

While the betas for portfolios D and C are identical, the expected returns are different:

Expected return for portfolio D = 0.5(0.10) + 0.5(0.20) = 0.15 = 15%

Therefore, we have created portfolio D that has the same risk as portfolio C (beta = 1.5) but has a higher expected return than portfolio C (15% versus 13%). By purchasing portfolio D and short-selling portfolio C, we expect to earn a 2% return (15% minus 13%).

 Professor's Note: Recall that a portfolio beta equals the weighted average of the individual asset betas, and, likewise, the portfolio expected return equals the weighted average of the individual asset expected returns.

The portfolio that is long portfolio D and short portfolio C is called the arbitrage portfolio. We have invested nothing upfront because we can use the proceeds of the short sale on portfolio C to purchase portfolio D, and we have undertaken no net systematic risk. The overall beta of our investment equals the difference in betas between our long and short positions: 1.5 – 1.5 = 0. As investors exploit the arbitrage opportunity, prices of assets in portfolio C will drop and the (future) expected return for portfolio C will rise to its equilibrium value.

The APT assumes there are no market imperfections preventing investors from exploiting arbitrage opportunities. As a result, extreme long and short positions are permitted and mispricing will disappear immediately. Therefore, all arbitrage opportunities such as the one described in the previous example would be exploited and eliminated immediately.

LOS 48.c: Calculate the expected return on an asset given an asset's factor sensitivities and the factor risk premiums.

CFA® Program Curriculum, Volume 6, page 277

Given a portfolio's factor exposures (betas) and factor risk premiums, we can easily compute the portfolio's expected return as shown in the following example.

Example: Calculating expected returns from the arbitrage pricing model

An investment firm employs a two-factor APT model. The risk-free rate equals 5%. Determine the expected return for the Invest Fund using the following data:

	Factor 1	Factor 2
Invest Fund factor betas	1.50	2.00
Factor risk premiums	0.0300	0.0125

Answer:

Using the two-factor APT model, the expected return for the Invest Fund (IF) equals:

$$E(R_{IF}) = 0.05 + 1.5(0.03) + 2(0.0125) = 0.12 = 12\%$$

We can also use factor models to compute the parameter values given expected returns and factor exposures.

Example: Calculating APT parameters given expected returns

1. Given a one-factor model and the following information, calculate the risk-free rate and the factor risk premium.

Portfolio	Expected Return	Factor Sensitivity
A	7.0%	1.0
B	7.8%	1.2

2. Verify that portfolio C with an expected return of 6.2% and factor sensitivity of 0.8 is priced correctly.

Answer:

1. Expected return = risk-free rate + factor sensitivity × risk premium
    Therefore, given the information for portfolios A and B:

    $$0.07 = R_f + 1.0 \times \lambda; \quad R_f = 0.07 - \lambda$$

    Substituting this information for portfolio B:

    $$0.078 = (0.07 - \lambda) + 1.2\lambda; \quad \lambda = 0.04 \text{ or } 4\%$$
    $$R_f = 0.07 - \lambda = 0.07 - 0.04 = 0.03 \text{ or } 3\%$$

2. Expected return for portfolio C = 0.03 + (0.8 × 0.04) = 6.2%. Hence, portfolio C is correctly priced.

LOS 48.d: Describe and compare macroeconomic factor models, fundamental factor models, and statistical factor models.

CFA® Program Curriculum, Volume 6, page 281

The CAPM could be described as a single-factor model because it assumes asset returns are explained by a single factor: the return on the market portfolio. A *multifactor model* assumes asset returns are driven by more than one factor. There are three general classifications of multifactor models: (1) **macroeconomic factor models**, (2) **fundamental factor models**, and (3) **statistical factor models**:

1. *Macroeconomic factor models* assume that asset returns are explained by surprises (or "shocks") in macroeconomic risk factors (e.g., GDP, interest rates, and inflation). Factor surprises are defined as the difference between the realized value of the factor and its consensus predicted value.

   > *Professor's Note: The key to macroeconomic factor models is that the variables that explain returns reflect not the value of the macroeconomic variable itself, but rather the* unexpected *part (i.e., the surprise), because we assume that the expected value has already been reflected in stock prices. For example, if the government announces that GDP grew at an annual rate of 1.5% and the consensus prediction was 2.5%, the surprise was negative 1%. The 2.5% consensus forecast was already reflected in market prices, so the negative surprise, which was bad news to the market, should cause stock prices to fall (i.e., the expected return will be negative).*

2. *Fundamental factor models* assume asset returns are explained by multiple firm-specific factors (e.g., P/E ratio, market cap, leverage ratio, and earnings growth rate).

3. *Statistical factor models* use statistical methods to explain asset returns. Two primary types of statistical factor models are used: factor analysis and principal component models. In factor analysis, factors are portfolios that explain covariance in asset returns. In principal component models, factors are portfolios that explain the variance in asset returns. The major weakness is that the statistical factors do not lend themselves well to economic interpretation. Therefore, *statistical* factors are *mystery* factors.

Because of the popularity of macroeconomic factor and fundamental factor models, we will provide a more expanded discussion of these models.

explnd by surprise

MACROECONOMIC FACTOR MODELS

The following model is an example of a two-factor macroeconomic model in which stock returns are explained by surprises in GDP growth rates and credit quality spreads:

$$R_i = E(R_i) + b_{i1}F_{GDP} + b_{i2}F_{QS} + \varepsilon_i$$

with No surprise   *b is Sensitivity Factor*

where:

R_i = return for Asset i

$E(R_i)$ = expected return for Asset i (in the absence of any surprises)

F_{GDP} = surprise in the GDP rate

F_{QS} = surprise in the credit quality spread (BB-rated bond yield − Treasury bond yield)

b_{i1} = GDP surprise sensitivity of Asset i

b_{i2} = credit quality spread surprise sensitivity of Asset i

ε_i = firm-specific surprise (unrelated to the two macro factors)

Let's take a closer look at each of the components:

- Each "F" is a factor surprise, the difference between the predicted value of the factor and the realized value.
- Each "b" is the sensitivity of the stock to that surprise. The higher the sensitivity, the larger the change in return for a given factor surprise.
- The firm-specific surprise captures the part of the return that can't be explained by the model. It represents unsystematic risk related to firm-specific events like a strike or a warehouse fire.

Unsystematic Risk

Example: Compute a stock return using a macroeconomic factor model

The following two-factor model is used to explain the returns for Media Tech (MT):

$$R_{MT} = E(R_{MT}) + b_{MT,1}F_{GDP} + b_{MT,2}F_{QS} + \varepsilon_{MT}$$

The expected return for Media Tech equals 10%. Over the past year, GDP grew at a rate that was 2 percentage points higher than originally expected, and the quality spread was 1 percentage point lower than originally expected. Media Tech's sensitivity to the GDP rate factor equaled 2, and its sensitivity to the quality spread factor equaled –0.5. Over the past year, Media Tech also experienced a 2% company-unique surprise return (i.e., unrelated to the two macro factors). Construct the macroeconomic factor model for Media Tech, and calculate its return for the year.

Answer:

The two-factor model for Media Tech is:

$R_{MT} = 0.10 + 2(0.02) - 0.50(-0.01) + 0.02 =$

  0.100 (the expected return)

  + 0.040 (the return from the positive GDP surprise)

  + 0.005 (the return from the positive quality spread surprise)

  + 0.020 (the return from unexpected firm specific events)

  = 0.165, or 16.5%

The Media Tech return was higher than originally expected because MT was positively affected by higher-than-expected economic growth (GDP), lower-than-expected credit quality risk spreads (QS), and positive company-specific surprise events.

> *Professor's Note: Be careful to interpret the signs properly. A decrease in the quality spread (a surprise less than zero) is good news for MT stock because it has a negative sensitivity to the factor. When credit quality spreads increase, MT's return goes down, and when credit quality spreads decrease, MT's return goes up.*

The main features of the macroeconomic factor model include the systematic or priced risk factors and the factor sensitivities.

Priced Risk Factors

A risk that does not affect many assets (i.e., an *unsystematic risk*) can usually be diversified away in a portfolio and will not be priced by the market. "Not priced" means investors cannot expect to be rewarded for being exposed to that type of risk.

The factors in our example model, GDP and credit quality spread shocks, are *systematic* risk factors, meaning that they will affect even well-diversified portfolios. Since they cannot be avoided, systematic factors represent priced risk (i.e., risk for which investors can expect compensation).

Factor Sensitivities

In a macroeconomic multifactor model, asset returns are a function of unexpected surprises to systematic factors, and different assets have different *factor sensitivities*. For example, retail stocks are very sensitive to GDP growth and, hence, have a large sensitivity to the GDP factor. Small, unexpected changes in GDP growth cause large changes in retail stock prices because changes in income affect retail spending. Other stocks are less sensitive to GDP and have smaller GDP factor sensitivities. Retail grocer stocks, for example, do not react as much to changes in GDP because spending on food items is less sensitive to changes in national income. The factor sensitivities of the model can be estimated by regressing historical asset returns on the corresponding historical macroeconomic factors.

FUNDAMENTAL FACTOR MODELS

Consider the following fundamental factor model:

$$R_i = a_i + b_{i1}F_{P/E} + b_{i2}F_{SIZE} + \varepsilon_i$$

[handwritten: → Intercept]

[handwritten right margin: F Regression ...; E → unexplained Return; Gr: unique Return]

where:

R_i = return for stock i

$F_{P/E}$ = return associated with the P/E factor

F_{SIZE} = return associated with the SIZE (market capitalization) factor

a_i = intercept

b_{i1} = standardized sensitivity of stock i to the P/E factor

b_{i2} = standardized sensitivity of stock i to the SIZE factor

ε_i = portion of asset i return not explained by the factor model

Let's take a closer look at each of the components of a fundamental factor model.

Standardized sensitivities (b_{i1} and b_{i2}). Sensitivities in most fundamental factor models are not regression slopes. Instead, the fundamental factor sensitivities are standardized attributes (similar to z-statistics from the standard normal distribution). For example, the standardized P/E sensitivity in a fundamental factor model is calculated as:

[handwritten right margin: Be careful Betas are Not Slope of Regression → They are standardized and had a formula]

[handwritten box: Beta = (P/E - AVG P/E Market) / SD of P/E Market]

$$b_{i1} = \frac{(P/E)_i - \overline{P/E}}{\sigma_{P/E}}$$

[handwritten annotations above equation: stock - Average; P/E Market]

[handwritten: Z table for Beta Normal distribution, with curve sketch labeled -2s -s 0 2s]

where:

$(P/E)_i$ = P/E for stock i

$\overline{P/E}$ = average P/E calculated across all stocks

$\sigma_{P/E}$ = standard deviation of P/E ratios across all stocks

Also note that by standardizing the factor sensitivity, we measure the number of standard deviations that each sensitivity is from the average. For example, a stock with a standardized P/E sensitivity of 2.0 has a P/E that is 2 standard deviations above the mean; a stock with a sensitivity of –1.5 has a P/E that is one and a half standard deviations below the mean. This standardization process allows us to use fundamental factors measured in different units in the same factor model. For example, P/E ratios are usually greater than 1.00, while dividend yields are in percentages (i.e., less than 1.00). The one exception is factors for binary variables (e.g., industry classification).

[handwritten right margin: DIV / Price]

> **Example: Calculating a standardized sensitivity in a fundamental factor model**
>
> The P/E for stock i is 15.20, the average P/E for all stocks is 11.90, and the standard deviation of P/E ratios is 6.30. Calculate the standardized sensitivity of stock i to the P/E factor.

Answer:

The sensitivity of stock i to the P/E factor is:

$$\beta_{i,\frac{P}{E}} = \frac{15.20 - 11.90}{6.30} = 0.52$$

Therefore, the P/E ratio for the stock is 0.52 standard deviations higher than the average stock P/E.

Factor returns ($F_{P/E}$ *and* F_{SIZE}). The fundamental factors are rates of return associated with each factor (e.g., the difference in rate of return between low and high P/E stocks). The return difference between low and high P/E stocks is commonly referred to as the return on a factor mimicking portfolio. In practice, the values of the fundamental factors are estimated as slopes of cross-sectional regressions in which the dependent variable is the set of returns for all stocks and the independent variables are the standardized sensitivities.

Intercept term (a_i). In fundamental factor models, the factors are not return surprises. Hence, the expected factor values are not zero, and the intercept term is no longer interpreted as the expected return.

The Macroeconomic Factor Model vs. the Fundamental Factor Model

The key differences between the macroeconomic factor model and the fundamental factor model can be summarized as follows:

- *Sensitivities.* The standardized sensitivities in the fundamental factor model (b_{i1} and b_{i2}) are calculated directly from the attribute (e.g., P/E) data—they are not estimated. This contrasts with the macroeconomic factor model, in which the sensitivities are regression slope estimates.
- *Interpretation of factors.* The macroeconomic factors (F_{GDP} and F_{QS}) are surprises in the macroeconomic variables (e.g., inflation shock and interest rate shock). In contrast, the fundamental factors ($F_{P/E}$ and F_{SIZE}) are rates of return associated with each factor and are estimated using multiple regression.
- *Intercept term.* The intercept in the macroeconomic factor model equals the stock's expected return (based on market consensus expectations of the macro factors) from an equilibrium pricing model like the APT. In contrast, the intercept of a fundamental factor model with standardized sensitivities has no economic interpretation; it is simply the regression intercept necessary to make the unsystematic risk of the asset equal to zero.

LOS 48.e: Explain sources of active risk and interpret tracking risk and the information ratio.

CFA® Program Curriculum, Volume 6, page 292

Active return equals the differences in returns between a managed portfolio and its benchmark:

$$\text{Active return} = R_P - R_B$$

Active risk (also known as *tracking error* or *tracking risk*) is defined as the standard deviation of the active return:

SD of the difference of Return (Active Return) Return

$$\text{Active risk} = \text{tracking error} = \sigma_{(R_P - R_B)}$$

The Information Ratio

Active return alone is insufficient for measuring an investment manager's performance over a series of measurement periods. For example, imagine that Manager A earned a constant 0.5% (50 bps) active return over each of the last four quarters. Furthermore, suppose Manager B earned active returns of 8%, 5%, –3%, and –8% over the same four quarters. The average active returns for managers A and B are both 0.5%, but Manager B experienced far more volatility (i.e., less consistency) than Manager A.

Information Ratio

To demonstrate a manager's consistency in generating active return, we use the *information ratio,* which standardizes average active return by dividing it by its standard deviation. In other words, the historical or ex-post information ratio equals the portfolio's average active return divided by the portfolio's tracking risk:

5.5% 5% 5×sum 0.5%   *σ of (Active Return) R_P - R_B*

$$IR = \frac{\overline{R_P} - \overline{R_B}}{\sigma_{(R_P - R_B)}}$$

Averages

> **Example: Calculating the information ratio**
>
> Imagine that the portfolio and benchmark returns over the past 12 months have been as shown in the following table.

S.D. $= \dfrac{\Sigma(x-\bar{x})}{n}$

Portfolio and Benchmark Returns for Twelve Months

Active Return

Month	R_p	R_B	$R_p - R_B$
1	0.0101	0.0091	0.0010
2	−0.0013	0.0062	−0.0075
3	0.0110	0.0069	0.0041
4	0.0135	0.0071	0.0064
5	0.0103	0.0067	0.0036
6	0.0093	0.0051	0.0042
7	−0.0011	0.0007	−0.0018
8	0.0085	0.0105	−0.0020
9	0.0091	0.0101	−0.0010
10	−0.0073	−0.0030	−0.0043
11	0.0186	0.0012	0.0174
12	0.0103	0.0097	0.0006
Average	0.0076	0.0059	0.0017
		Sample Std. Dev.	0.0063

Tracking Error   التتبع   ←   *Tracking Error*

Given the data in the table, calculate and interpret the manager's information ratio.

Answer:

$$IR = \frac{(\bar{R}_P - \bar{R}_B)}{\sigma_{(R_P - R_B)}} = \frac{0.0076 - 0.0059}{0.0063} \approx 0.27$$

Average   Average

The higher the IR, the more active return the manager earned per unit of active risk. An information ratio of 0.27 indicates the manager earned about 27 basis points of active return per unit of active risk.

$Sharpe = \dfrac{R_P - R_f}{\sigma_P}$

Professor's Note: The information ratio is similar to the Sharpe ratio, in that their numerators both compare average portfolio return to a benchmark. The difference is that the Sharpe ratio uses the risk-free rate as the benchmark and the IR uses a portfolio benchmark return (one that best matches the investment style of the managed portfolio). In the denominator, the Sharpe ratio uses the standard deviation of portfolio total returns while the information ratio uses the standard deviation of the active (vs. the benchmark) return.

$R_P - R_B$

LOS 48.f: Describe uses of multifactor models and interpret the output of analyses based on multifactor models.

CFA® Program Curriculum, Volume 6, page 289

Multifactor models can be useful for return attribution, risk attribution, and portfolio construction.

Return Attribution

Multifactor models can be used to attribute a manager's active portfolio return to different factors.

Recall that active return = $R_P – R_B$.

We can decompose active return into its two components: (1) factor return (arising from the manager's decision to take on factor exposures that differ from those of the benchmark) and (2) security selection (arising from the manager choosing a different weight for specific securities compared to the weight of those securities in the benchmark). These two differences also contribute to active risk (discussed later).

> Active return = factor return + security selection return

where:

$$\text{factor return} = \sum_{i=1}^{k}(\beta_{pi} - \beta_{bi}) \times (\lambda_i)$$

β_{pi} = factor sensitivity for the *i*th factor in the active portfolio
β_{bi} = factor sensitivity for the *i*th factor in the benchmark portfolio
λ_i = factor risk premium for factor *i*

The security selection return is then the *residual* difference between active return and factor return:

> security selection return = active return – factor return

Example: Return decomposition

Glendale Pure Alpha Fund generated a return of 11.2% over the past 12 months, while the benchmark portfolio returned 11.8%. Attribute the cause of difference in returns using a fundamental factor model with two factors as given below and describe the manager's apparent skill in factor bets as well as in security selection.

Factor	Factor Sensitivity (betas)		Factor
	Portfolio	Benchmark	Risk Premium (λ)
P/E	1.10	1.00	-5.00%
Size	0.69	1.02	2.00%

$(Beta_p - Beta_B) \times$ عوامل

Answer:

Factor	Factor Sensitivity (betas)			Factor Risk Premium (λ)	Contribution to Active Return
	Portfolio	Benchmark	Difference		
	(1)	(2)	(3)	(4)	(5) = (3) × (4)
P/E	1.10	1.00	0.10	-5.00%	–0.50%
Size	0.69	1.02	–0.33	2.00%	–0.66%
				Total	–1.16%

standard

Difference between portfolio return and benchmark return = 11.20% – 11.80% = –0.60%
Return from factor tilts (computed above) = –1.16%
Return from security selection = –0.6% – (–1.16%) = +0.56%

The active manager's regrettable factor bets resulted in a return of –1.16% relative to the benchmark. However, the manager's superior security selection return of +0.56% resulted in a total active return of –0.60% relative to the benchmark.

Risk Attribution

Recall that active risk = tracking error = $\sigma_{(R_P - R_B)}$.

The active risk of a portfolio can be separated into two components:

1. *Active factor risk:* Risk from active factor tilts attributable to deviations of the portfolio's factor sensitivities from the benchmark's sensitivities to the same set of factors.

2. *Active specific risk:* Risk from active asset selection attributable to deviations of the portfolio's individual asset weightings versus the benchmark's individual asset weightings, after controlling for differences in factor sensitivities of the portfolio versus the benchmark.

The sum of active factor risk and active specific risk is equal to active risk squared (which is the variance of active returns):

active risk squared = active factor risk + active specific risk

Both components contribute to deviations of the portfolio's returns from the benchmark's returns. For example, consider a fundamental factor model that includes industry risk factors. In this case, active risk can be described as follows:

- *Active factor risk example*: A portfolio manager may decide to under- or overweight particular industries relative to the portfolio's benchmark. Therefore, the portfolio's industry factor sensitivities will not coincide with those of the benchmark, and, consequently, the portfolio returns may deviate from the benchmark.

Sectors در Factor

- *Active specific risk example*: The active portfolio manager may decide to overweight or underweight individual stocks within specific industries. For example, a stock's market capitalization may comprise 1% of the industry, but the portfolio manager may allocate 2% of industry allocation to the stock, causing the portfolio returns to deviate from the benchmark returns.

Active specific risk can be computed as:

$$\text{active specific risk} = \sum_{i=1}^{n}(W_{pi} - W_{bi})^2\sigma_{\varepsilon i}^2$$

where:

W_{pi} and W_{bi} = weight of ith security in the active and benchmark portfolio, respectively

$\sigma_{\varepsilon i}^2$ = residual (i.e., unsystematic) risk of the ith asset

Active factor risk represents the risk explained by deviation of the portfolio's factor exposures relative to the benchmark and is computed as the residual (plug):

active factor risk = active risk squared – active specific risk

Example: Risk decomposition

Steve Martingale, CFA is analyzing the performance of three actively managed mutual funds using a two-factor model. The results of his risk decomposition are shown below:

Fund	Active Factor		Total Factor	Active Specific	Active Risk Squared
	Size Factor	Style Factor			
Alpha	6.25	12.22	18.47 +	3.22 =	21.69
Beta	3.20	0.80	4.00 +	12.22 =	16.22
Gamma	17.85	0.11	17.96 +	19.7 =	37.66

1. Which fund assumes the highest level of active risk?

2. Which fund assumes the highest level of style factor risk as a proportion of active risk?

3. Which fund assumes the highest level of size factor risk as a proportion of active risk?

4. Which fund assumes the lowest level of active specific risk as a proportion of active risk?

Answer:

The table below shows the proportional contributions of various sources of active risk as a proportion of active risk squared. For example, the proportional contribution of style factor risk for Alpha fund can be calculated as 12.22 / 21.69 = 56%.

| | Active Factor | | | Active | |
Fund	Size Factor	Style Factor	Total Factor	Specific	Active Risk
Alpha	29%	56%	85%	15%	4.7%
Beta	20%	5%	25%	75%	4.0%
Gamma	47%	0%	48%	52%	6.1%

1. The Gamma fund has the highest level of active risk (6.1%). Note that active risk is the square root of active risk squared (as given).

2. The Alpha fund has the highest exposure to style factor risk as seen by 56% of active risk being attributed to differences in style.

3. The Gamma fund has highest exposure to size factor as a proportion of total active risk (47%) compared to the other two funds.

4. The Alpha fund has the lowest exposure to active specific risk (15%) as a proportion of total active risk.

Uses of Multifactor Models

Multifactor models can be useful, for example, to a passive manager who seeks to replicate the factor exposures of a benchmark, or to an active manager who seeks to make directional bets on specific factors. Specific applications of multifactor models include:

1. *Passive management.* Managers seeking to track a benchmark can construct a *tracking portfolio*. Tracking portfolios have a deliberately designed *set* of factor exposures. That is, a tracking portfolio is intentionally constructed to have the same set of factor exposures to match (track) a predetermined benchmark.

2. *Active management.* Active managers use factor models to make specific bets on desired factors while hedging (or remaining neutral) on other factors. A *factor portfolio* is a portfolio that has been constructed to have sensitivity of one to just one risk factor and sensitivities of zero to the remaining factors. Factor portfolios are particularly useful for speculation or hedging purposes. For example, suppose that a portfolio manager believes GDP growth will be stronger than expected but wishes to hedge against all other factor risks. The manager can take a long position in the GDP factor portfolio; the factor portfolio is exposed to the GDP risk factor, but has

zero sensitivity to all other risk factors. This manager is speculating that GDP will rise beyond market expectations.

Alternatively, consider a manager who wishes to hedge his portfolio against GDP factor risk. Imagine that the portfolio's GDP factor sensitivity equals 0.8, and the portfolio's sensitivities to the remaining risk factors are different from zero. Suppose the portfolio manager wishes to hedge against GDP risk but remain exposed to the remaining factors. The manager can hedge against GDP risk by taking an 80% short position in the GDP factor portfolio. The 0.8 GDP sensitivity of the managed portfolio will be offset by the –0.8 GDP sensitivity from the short position in the GDP factor portfolio.

3. *Rules-based or algorithmic active management (alternative indices).* These strategies use rules to mechanically tilt factor exposures when constructing portfolios. These strategies introduce biases in the portfolio relative to value-weighted benchmark indices.

We will use the Carhart model to illustrate the use of factor portfolios.

Carhart Model

The Carhart four-factor model is a multifactor model that extends the Fama and French three-factor model to include not only market risk, size, and value as relevant factors, but also momentum.

$$E(R) = R_F + \beta_1 RMRF + \beta_2 SMB + \beta_3 HML + \beta_4 WML$$

where:

E(R) = expected return
R_F = risk-free rate of return
RMRF = return on value-weighted equity index – the risk-free rate
SMB = average return on small cap stocks – average return on large cap stocks
HML = average return on high book-to-market stocks – average return on low book-to-market stocks
WML = average returns on past winners – average returns on past losers

Example: Factor Portfolios

Sam Porter is evaluating three portfolios based on the Carhart model. The table below provides the factor exposures of each of these portfolios to the four Carhart factors.

	Value weighted Index	Risk Factor		
Portfolio	RMRF	SMB	HML	WML
Eridanus	1.0	0.0	0.0	0.0
Scorpius	0.0	1.0	0.0	0.0
Lyra	1.2	0.0	0.2	0.8

Which strategy would be *most* appropriate if the manager expects that:

    A. RMRF will be higher than expected.
    B. Large cap stocks will outperform small cap stocks. (Small – Large)

Negative

Answer:

A. The manager would go long in the Eridanus portfolio as it is constructed to have exposure only to the RMRF factor. The Lyra portfolio would not be ideal for Porter's purpose because it provides unneeded exposures to the HML and WML factors as well.

B. The manager would go short the Scorpius portfolio, which is constructed to be a pure bet on SMB (i.e., Scorpius is a factor portfolio). We short the portfolio because we are expecting that large cap stocks will outperform small cap stocks.

LOS 48.g: Describe the potential benefits for investors in considering multiple risk dimensions when modeling asset returns.

CFA® Program Curriculum, Volume 6, page 292

Under the CAPM framework, investors choose a combination of the market portfolio and the risk-free asset depending on their risk tolerance. By including more risk factors, multifactor models enable investors to zero in on risks that the investor has a comparative advantage in bearing and avoid the risks that the investor is incapable of absorbing. For example, a pension plan invests for long-term and, hence, would not be averse to holding a security that bears liquidity risk (and that offers a liquidity risk premium).

Also, if the actual asset returns are better described by multifactor models, then using such models can help investors select more efficient portfolios.

KEY CONCEPTS

LOS 48.a

The APT describes the equilibrium relationship between expected returns for well-diversified portfolios and their multiple sources of systematic risk. APT makes only three key assumptions: (1) unsystematic risk can be diversified away in a portfolio, (2) returns are generated using a factor model, and (3) no arbitrage opportunities exist.

LOS 48.b

An arbitrage opportunity is defined as an investment opportunity that bears no risk and has no cost, but provides a profit. Arbitrage is conducted by forming long and short portfolios; the proceeds of the short sale are used to purchase the long portfolio. Additionally, the factor sensitivities (betas) of the long and short portfolios are identical and, hence, our net exposure to systematic risk is zero. The difference in returns on the long and short portfolios is the arbitrage return.

LOS 48.c

$$\text{expected return} = \text{risk-free rate} + \sum(\text{factor sensitivity}) \times (\text{factor risk premium})$$

LOS 48.d

A multifactor model is an extension of the one-factor market model; in a multifactor model, asset returns are a function of more than one factor. There are three types of multifactor models:

- Macroeconomic factor models assume that asset returns are explained by surprises (or shocks) in macroeconomic risk factors (e.g., GDP, interest rates, and inflation). Factor surprises are defined as the difference between the realized value of the factor and its consensus expected value.
- Fundamental factor models assume asset returns are explained by the returns from multiple firm-specific factors (e.g., P/E ratio, market cap, leverage ratio, and earnings growth rate).
- Statistical factor models use multivariate statistics (factor analysis or principal components) to identify statistical factors that explain the covariation among asset returns. The major weakness is that the statistical factors may not lend themselves well to economic interpretation.

LOS 48.e

Active return is the difference between portfolio and benchmark returns $(R_P - R_B)$, and active risk is the standard deviation of active return over time. Active risk is determined by the manager's active factor tilt and active asset selection decisions:

active risk squared = active factor risk + active specific risk.

The information ratio is active return divided by active risk:

$$IR = \frac{\overline{R}_P - \overline{R}_B}{\sigma_{(R_P - R_B)}}$$

LOS 48.f

Mutifactor models can be useful for risk and return attribution and for portfolio composition. In return attribution, the difference between an active portfolio's return and the benchmark return is allocated between factor return and security selection return.

$$\text{factor return} = \sum_{i=1}^{k} (\beta_{pi} - \beta_{bi}) \times (\lambda_i)$$

In risk attribution, the sum of the active factor risk and active specific risk is equal to active risk squared (which is the variance of active returns):

active risk squared = active factor risk + active specific risk

$$\text{active specific risk} = \sum_{i=1}^{n} (W_{pi} - W_{bi})^2 \sigma_{\varepsilon i}^{2}$$

active factor risk = active risk squared – active specific risk

Multifactor models can also be useful for portfolio construction. Passive managers can invest in a tracking portfolio, while active managers can go long or short factor portfolios.

A factor portfolio is a portfolio with a factor sensitivity of 1 to a particular factor and zero to all other factors. It represents a pure bet on a single factor and can be used for speculation or hedging purposes. A tracking portfolio is a portfolio with a specific set of factor sensitivities. Tracking portfolios are often designed to replicate the factor exposures of a benchmark index like the S&P 500.

LOS 48.g

Multifactor models enable investors to take on risks that the investor has a comparative advantage in bearing and avoid the risks that the investor is unable to absorb.

Models that incorporate multiple sources of systematic risk have been found to explain asset returns more effectively than single-factor CAPM.

CONCEPT CHECKERS

1. Which of the following *least accurately* identifies an assumption made by the APT?
    A. Asset returns are described by a factor model.
    B. Unsystematic risk can be diversified away.
    C. Arbitrage will force risk premia on systematic risk to be zero.

2. Eileen Bates, CFA has collected information on the following three portfolios:

Portfolio	Expected Return	Factor Sensitivity
A	10%	1.20
B	20%	2.00
C	13%	1.76

    An arbitrage strategy would *most likely* involve a short position in which portfolio?
    A. Portfolio A
    B. Portfolio B
    C. Portfolio C

3. Catalyst Fund uses a two-factor model to analyze asset returns.

	Factor 1	Factor 2
Stock A factor sensitivities	0.88	1.10
Factor risk premiums	0.03	0.01

    Given that the risk-free rate equals 5%, the expected return for the stock A is *closest* to:
    A. 4.2%.
    B. 8.7%.
    C. 9.2%.

4. A multifactor model to evaluate style and size exposures (e.g., large cap value) of different mutual funds would be *most appropriately* called a:
    A. systematic factor model.
    B. fundamental factor model.
    C. macroeconomic factor model.

5.   Jones Brothers uses a two-factor macroeconomic factor model to evaluate stocks and has derived the following results for the stock of AmGrow (AG):
- Expected return: 10%
- GDP factor sensitivity: 2
- Inflation factor sensitivity: –0.5

Over the past year, GDP grew at a rate that was two percentage points lower than originally expected, and inflation rose two percentage points higher than originally expected. AG also experienced a large unexpected product recall causing a firm-unique surprise of –4% to its stock price. Based on the information provided, the rate of return for AG for the year was *closest* to:

A. 1%.
B. 2%.
C. 3%.

6.   A portfolio that has the same factor sensitivities as the S&P 500, but does not hold all 500 stocks in the index, is *best* described as a:

A. factor portfolio.
B. tracking portfolio.
C. market portfolio.

7.   A portfolio with a factor sensitivity of one to the yield spread factor and a sensitivity of zero to all other macroeconomic factors is *best* described as a:

A. factor portfolio.
B. tracking portfolio.
C. market portfolio.

8.   Factor Investment Services, LLC manages a tracking portfolio that claims to outperform the S&P 500. The active factor risk and active specific risk for the tracking portfolio are *most likely* to be described as:

A. high active factor risk and high active specific risk.
B. high active factor risk and low active specific risk.
C. low active factor risk and high active specific risk.

9.   Relative to the CAPM, the *least likely* advantage of multifactor models is that multifactor models help investors to:

A. target risks that the investor has a comparative advantage in bearing.
B. select an appropriate proportion of the portfolio to allocate to the market portfolio.
C. assemble more efficient and better diversified portfolios.

To access other content related to this topic review that may be included in the Schweser package you purchased, log in to your Schweser.com online dashboard. Schweser's OnDemand Video Lectures deliver streaming instruction covering every LOS in this topic review, while SchweserPro™ QBank provides additional quiz questions to help you practice and recall what you've learned.

ANSWERS – CONCEPT CHECKERS

1. **C** The assumptions of APT include (1) unsystematic risk can be diversified away in a portfolio, (2) returns can be explained by a factor model, and (3) no arbitrage opportunities exist. However, arbitrage does not cause the risk premium for systematic risk to be zero.

2. **C** An arbitrage portfolio comprises long and short positions such that the net return is positive yet the net factor sensitivity is zero. In this question, the low expected return of portfolio C per unit of factor sensitivity indicates that portfolio C should be shorted. Suppose that we arbitrarily assign portfolio C a 100% short weighting and, furthermore, we assign a weighting of w to portfolio A and a weighting of $(1 - w)$ to portfolio B. Because the weighted sum of long and short factor sensitivities must be equal, we develop the following equation: $w \times 1.20 + (1 - w) \times 2.00 = 1.00 \times 1.76$. Solving algebraically for w gives a 30% long weight on portfolio A, a 70% long weight on portfolio B, and a 100% short weight on portfolio C. The factor sensitivity of this portfolio will be $(0.3)(1.20) + (0.7)(2.0) - (1)(1.76) = 0$. The expected return on this zero risk, zero investment portfolio will be $(0.3)(10) + (0.7)(20) - (1)(13) = 4\%$.

3. **B** Using the two-factor APT model, the expected return for stock A equals:

   $E(R_{IF}) = 0.05 + (0.88) \times (0.03) + (1.10) \times (0.01) = 0.0874 = 8.74\%$

4. **B** Style (e.g., value versus growth) can be evaluated based on company-specific fundamental variables such as P/E or P/B ratio. Size is generally proxied by market capitalization. A fundamental factor model is appropriate when the underlying variables are company-specific.

5. **A** The two-factor model for AG is $R_{AG} = 0.10 + 2(-0.02) - 0.50(0.02) - 0.04 = 0.01 = 1\%$

   The AG return was less than originally expected because AG was hurt by lower-than-expected economic growth (GDP), higher-than-expected inflation, and a negative company-specific surprise event.

6. **B** A *tracking portfolio* is a portfolio with a specific set of factor sensitivities. Tracking portfolios are often designed to replicate the factor exposures of a benchmark index like the S&P 500—in fact, a factor portfolio is just a special case of a tracking portfolio. One use of tracking portfolios is to attempt to outperform the S&P 500 by using the same factor exposures as the S&P 500 but with a different set of securities than the S&P 500.

7. **A** A *factor portfolio* is a portfolio with a factor sensitivity of 1 to a particular factor and zero to all other factors. It represents a *pure bet* on that factor. For example, a portfolio manager who believes GDP growth will be greater than expected, but has no view of future interest rates and wants to hedge away the interest rate risk in her portfolio, could create a *factor portfolio* that is only exposed to the GDP factor and not exposed to the interest rate factor.

8. **C** A tracking portfolio is deliberately constructed to have the same set of factor exposures to match (track) a predetermined benchmark. The strategy involved in constructing a tracking portfolio is usually an active bet on asset selection (the manager claims to beat the S&P 500). The manager constructs the portfolio to have the same factor exposures as the benchmark, but then selects superior securities (subject to the factor sensitivities constraint), thus outperforming the benchmark without taking on more systematic risk than the benchmark. Therefore, a tracking portfolio, with active asset selection but with factor sensitivities that match those of the benchmark, will have little or no active factor risk, but will have high active specific risk.

9. **B** Multifactor models enable investors to zero in on risks that the investor has a comparative advantage in bearing and avoid the risks that the investor is unable to take on. Multifactor models are preferred over single factor models like CAPM in cases where the underlying asset returns are better described by multifactor models. Allocation of an investor's portfolio between the market portfolio and the risk-free asset is part of CAPM, not multifactor models.

The following is a review of the Portfolio Management principles designed to address the learning outcome statements set forth by CFA Institute. Cross-Reference to CFA Institute Assigned Reading #49.

MEASURING AND MANAGING MARKET RISK

EXAM FOCUS

This topic review discusses different approaches to risk measurement as well as mechanisms to manage and control risk. VaR is an important risk metric, and you should know different ways to compute it as well as pros and cons of different approaches. Also know the limitations of VaR as a risk metric and the variations of VaR. The discussion on scenario and sensitivity analysis is mostly qualitative. Finally, know the risk measures that are more relevant for different asset managers, such as banks, pension funds, et cetera.

LOS 49.a: Explain the use of value at risk (VaR) in measuring portfolio risk.

CFA® Program Curriculum, Volume 6, page 315

Value at risk (VaR) measures downside risk of a portfolio. It has three components: the loss size, the probability (of a loss greater than or equal to the specified loss size), and a time frame. Consider the statement: "There is a 5% probability that the company will experience a loss of $25,000 or more in any given month." This is same as stating that the monthly 5% VaR is $25,000. In the above statement, the probability is 5%, the loss size is $25,000, and the time frame is one month.

Note that $25,000 is a *minimum* loss amount, so we can state, "5% of the time the minimum monthly loss that the company will experience is $25,000."

VaR can also be expressed in percentage terms so that for a portfolio, we could state that the 5% monthly VaR is 3%, meaning that 5% of the time the monthly portfolio value will fall by *at least* 3%. We can also state VaR as a confidence level: we are 95% (i.e., 100% − 5%) confident that the portfolio will experience a loss of no more than 3%.

To estimate a VaR, we must specify the time period and the size of the loss, so there is significant judgment involved in VaR estimation. If we choose the size of the loss, we will estimate the probability of losses of that size or larger; but, if we choose the probability of the loss, we will estimate the minimum size of the losses that will occur with that probability.

Figure 1 shows the 5% VaR for a given probability distribution of monthly returns. *The 5% left-hand tail of the distribution of possible monthly outcomes is bounded by the 5% VaR; VaR is the upper limit of the specified left tail.*

Figure 1: Distribution of Monthly Returns

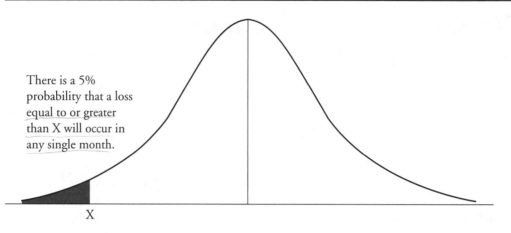

There is a 5% probability that a loss equal to or greater than X will occur in any single month.

X

While any probability can be specified, VaR is typically expressed for 1%, 5%, or 16% (one standard deviation below the mean for a normal distribution) probability. The time frame specified also varies; we could estimate VaR for a day, a week, a month, or any other relevant period.

LOS 49.b: Compare the parametric (variance–covariance), historical simulation, and Monte Carlo simulation methods for estimating VaR.

LOS 49.c: Estimate and interpret VaR under the parametric, historical simulation, and Monte Carlo simulation methods.

CFA® Program Curriculum, Volume 6, page 320

The first step in estimating the VaR for a portfolio is to identify the risk factors that enter into the determination of portfolio returns. These risk factors might include market risk, interest rate risk, or currency risk, among others.

One method of estimating VaR is the **parametric** or **variance-covariance** method. Often we assume that the risk factors are distributed normally, but we could also assume other distributions. Assuming normality allows us to estimate the risk of the portfolio based only on the means, variances, and covariances (or correlations) of the various risk factors. An assumption that risk factor probabilities are non-normal would increase the complexity of the analysis and require that we estimate values for other parameters, such as skewness and kurtosis.

Assuming normality, we can use the portfolio variance formula to estimate the mean and variance of portfolio returns. Once we have estimated these parameters, we can identify portfolio VaR as the value bounding the left-hand tail of the distribution, as we illustrated in Figure 1. To simplify the explanation of the parametric method, we will consider a case of only two risk factors, both of which are normally distributed.

Consider two securities, asset A and asset B. For a portfolio with portfolio fraction W_A invested in asset A and the remaining portfolio fraction W_B invested in asset B, portfolio variance is given by the formula:

$$\sigma^2_{Portfolio} = W_A^2\sigma_A^2 + W_B^2\sigma_B^2 + 2W_A W_B Cov_{AB}$$

The returns period that we use to estimate the mean and standard deviation of returns for each risk factor (each fund in our example) is called the **lookback period.** For estimating the variance of daily returns, we might use the last two years; but, for estimating the variance of annual returns, we would choose a longer lookback period. The important point is that the parameter estimates we use should be those we expect over the period for which we are estimating the VaR. Estimates based on recent periods may be adjusted towards longer-term averages.

Example: Estimating VaR

Imagine that we are provided the following information about two assets, Security A and Security B:

Security	Standard deviation of daily returns	Mean daily return	Covariance of daily returns
Security A	0.0158	0.0004	0.000106
Security B	0.0112	0.0003	

How would we use this information to estimate the 5% annual VaR for a portfolio that is 60% invested in Security A and 40% invested in Security B?

Answer:

Mean daily portfolio return = 0.6(0.0004) + 0.4(0.0003) = 0.00036

Variance of portfolio return
= $(0.6)^2(0.0158)^2 + (0.4)^2(0.0112)^2 + 2(0.4)(0.6)(0.000106) = 0.000161$

Standard deviation of portfolio returns = $\sqrt{0.000161} = 0.012682$

For a 5% VaR we want 5% in the left-hand tail, so we calculate the value 1.65 standard deviations below the mean:

5% daily VaR = 0.00036 − 1.65(0.012682) = −0.0206

Assuming the distribution of daily returns is constant over the year, that there are 250 trading days in one year, and that daily returns are independently distributed, we can calculate the annual mean return as 250(0.00036) = 0.09.

Annualized σ

The annual standard deviation can be calculated as $\sqrt{250}\,(0.012682) = 0.20052$.

Based on these estimates, the *5% annual VaR* $= 0.09 - 1.65(0.20052) = -0.2409$. *daily VaR*

For a portfolio with a value of $10 million, the 5% daily and annual VaR are:

10 million (0.0206) = $206,000 and
10 million (0.2409) = $2,409,000.

The parametric method is relatively simple to apply under the assumption of normally distributed returns. Of course, its estimates will only be as good as the estimates of future mean returns and standard deviations. The calculated VaR is also very sensitive to the covariance estimate. The length of the lookback period will affect the parameter estimates, and care must be taken to adjust estimates based on recent results when they may not reflect the future distribution of returns. In cases where normality cannot be reasonably assumed, such as when the portfolio contains options, the parametric method has limited usefulness.

The **historical simulation method** of estimating VaR is based on the actual periodic changes in risk factors over a lookback period. For a daily VaR, the change in the value of the current portfolio is calculated for each day of the lookback period, using the actual daily changes in portfolio value. By ordering the changes in portfolio value from most positive to most negative, we can find the largest 5% of losses. The smallest of those losses is our estimate of the 5% VaR for the current portfolio.

Under the historical simulation method, no adjustments are made for the difference between the results for the lookback period and the results over a longer prior period.

One positive aspect of the historical simulation method is that we do not need the assumption of normality, or any other distributional assumption, to estimate VaR. Because the historical results for a portfolio containing options include the changes in option values, the historical simulation method can be used to estimate the VaR for portfolios that include options.

VaR estimates will depend on the lookback period and, as with any forecasts, will vary with the characteristics of the sample data used. VaR based on an unusually volatile lookback period will yield overestimates of VaR, just as VaR based on a lookback period with low volatility will likely underestimate the true VaR over subsequent periods.

A third method of VaR estimation is **Monte Carlo simulation**. Monte Carlo simulation is based on an assumed probability distribution for each risk factor. Additionally, an assumption must be made about the correlations between risk factors. Computer software is used to generate random values for each risk factor, and pricing models are used calculate the change in portfolio value for that set of risk factor changes.

This procedure is repeated thousands of times. Then, just as with historical simulation, we can order the outcomes and identify the fifth percentile (i.e., a value for which 5% of the outcomes will be lower) to estimate the 5% VaR. As with the other methods, the data used and the assumptions about the distributions of the risk factors will have significant effects on the estimated VaR. Assuming a large sample size, the Monte Carlo method will produce identical results as the parametric method if the distribution specified and the parameters are the same.

LOS 49.d: Describe advantages and limitations of VaR.

CFA® Program Curriculum, Volume 6, page 329

VaR, as a measure of portfolio risk, has many benefits but suffers from the same limitations as many other forward-looking estimates of portfolio risk.

ADVANTAGES OF VaR

- The concept of VaR is simple and easy to explain, although the details of the methodology can be complex.
- VaR allows the risk of different portfolios, asset classes, or trading operations to be compared to gain a sense of relative riskiness.
- VaR can be used for performance evaluation (i.e., returns generated vs. risk taken). Rather than evaluating a trading group's performance based only on returns, VaR allows calculation of the ratio of trading income to VaR.
- When allocating capital to various trading units, a firm's risk managers can also look at the allocation of VaR and optimize the allocation of capital given the firm's determination of the maximum VaR that the organization should be exposed to (sometimes referred to as *risk budgeting*). In the same manner, managers can estimate risk-adjusted performance of trading units or profits per dollar of VaR. For example, the equity trading desk may be assigned a maximum daily VaR of $5 million while the more profitable currency trading desk may be assigned a daily VaR of $15 million.
- Global banking regulators accept VaR as a measure of financial risk, although they do not prescribe estimation methods or impose a maximum VaR.
- Reliability of VaR as a measure of risk can be verified by backtesting.

LIMITATIONS OF VaR

- VaR estimation requires many choices (loss percentage, lookback period, distribution assumptions, and parameter estimates) and can be very significantly affected by these choices. An unscrupulous analyst can choose assumptions that lead to a low estimate of VaR.
- The assumption of normality leads to underestimates of downside (tail) risk because actual returns distributions frequently have "fatter tails" than a normal distribution. When this is the case, VaRs based on an assumption of normality tend to underestimate the probability of extreme outcomes. Although the assumption of normality is not a requirement of VaR, it is almost always used, especially with the parametric method.
- Liquidity often falls significantly when asset prices fall. A VaR which does not account for this will understate the actual losses incurred when liquidating positions that are under extreme price pressure.

- It is well known that correlations increase, or spike, during periods of financial stress. Increasing correlations mean that VaR measures based on normal levels of correlation will overestimate diversification benefits and underestimate the magnitude of potential losses.
- While VaR is a single number that can be used to quantify risk, as with any summary measure, many aspects of risk are not quantified or included. Users of VaR must understand the limitations of VaR as a measure of risk in order to use it appropriately.
- VaR focuses only on downside risk and extreme negative outcomes. Including consideration of right-hand tail values will give a better understanding of the risk-return trade-off.

LOS 49.e: Describe extensions of VaR.

CFA® Program Curriculum, Volume 6, page 332

Another measure based on VaR is the **conditional VaR** (CVaR). The CVaR is the expected loss, given that the loss is equal to or greater than the VaR. For this reason, the CVaR is also referred to as the *expected tail loss* or *expected shortfall*. The CVaR is expected loss given that the loss is in the left-hand tail past the VaR.

When the VaR is estimated using the historical simulation method or Monte Carlo simulation, we have all the values equal to or less than the VaR loss, so it is straightforward to take the average of these to get the CVaR. With the parametric method, we don't know the magnitude of losses greater than the VaR, so calculating the expected loss in the left-hand tail is mathematically complex.

Incremental VaR (IVaR) is the change in VaR from a change in the portfolio allocation to a security. If a 2% increase in the weight of a security in the portfolio increases the portfolio's VaR from $1,345,600 to $1,562,400, the IVaR for the 2% increase in the portfolio weight of the security is 1,562,400 – 1,345,600 = $216,800.

A related measure is the **marginal VaR** (MVaR). The MVaR is estimated as the slope of a curve that plots VaR as a function of a security's weight in the portfolio. The MVaR is calculated at the point on the curve corresponding to the security's current weight, so we can interpret it as the change in VaR for a 1% increase in the security's weight. This is not precisely correct because the MVaR is the slope at a point on the curve, not the slope for a 1% change in weight. It is, however, a reasonable approximation of the sensitivity of VaR to a 1% change in weight of a security. Thus, both the MVaR and IVaR can be used to estimate the change in VaR that will result from a change in the weight of a single security.

Ex ante tracking error, also referred to as **relative VaR**, measures the VaR of the difference between the return on a portfolio and the return on its manager's benchmark portfolio. A 5% monthly relative VaR of 2.5% implies that 5% of time, the portfolio's relative underperformance will be at least 2.5%. The relative VaR can be calculated as the VaR of a combination of a long position in the subject portfolio and a short position in the benchmark portfolio.

LOS 49.f: Describe sensitivity risk measures and scenario risk measures and compare these measures to VaR.

Scenario Analysis   *CFA® Program Curriculum, Volume 6, page 334*

Given the limitations of VaR as a risk measure, analysts should use other risk measures that complement VaR.

Risk assessment using sensitivity analysis focuses on the effect on portfolio value given a small change in one risk factor. By examining the sensitivity of a portfolio's value to several risk factors, portfolio risk can be better understood and more effectively managed. Sensitivity analysis complements VaR in understanding portfolio risk, but, unlike VaR, it does not involve any prediction of the probability of losses of any specific amount.

While sensitivity analysis provides an estimate of the change in portfolio value due to a small change in a single risk factor, **scenario analysis** provides an estimate of the effect on portfolio value of a set of changes of significant magnitude in multiple risk factors. The changes in risk factors used in scenario analysis are often a set of changes that are expected to result in a significant decline in portfolio value, although a scenario of changes in risk factors that would increase portfolio value may also be considered.

A **historical scenario** approach uses a set of changes in risk factors that have actually occurred in the past, especially changes during a period of financial disruption and stress such as the subprime mortgage crisis of 2008 or the equity market crash of 1987.

With a **hypothetical scenario** approach, any set of changes in risk factors can be used, not just one that has happened in the past. A hypothetical scenario could have more extreme changes in risk factors than those that have occurred in the past, but that have some non-zero probability of occurring in the future.

Stress tests examine the effect on value (or solvency) of a scenario of extreme risk-factor changes.

LOS 49.g: Demonstrate how equity, fixed-income, and options exposure measures may be used in measuring and managing market risk and volatility risk.

CFA® Program Curriculum, Volume 6, page 335

The risk factors used to measure the risks of equities, fixed-income securities, and options are all different. For equities, the most often used risk factor is **beta**. Beta is a measure of how the returns of a security or a portfolio are expected to be affected by overall market returns. The capital asset pricing model (CAPM) is based on market risk as measured by beta and concludes that the expected return on an asset is equal to the risk-free rate plus beta times the market risk premium:

$$E(R_i) = R_f + Beta_i \, [E(R_{MKT}) - R_f]$$

For fixed-income securities and portfolios, **duration** provides an estimate of how market values are affected by changes in interest rates (yields to maturity). For larger changes in interest rates, including the effects of **convexity** on fixed-income security values improves estimates of the sensitivity of the values of fixed-income securities to changes in interest rates. Together, duration and convexity are used to estimate the sensitivity of the values of fixed-income securities (and portfolios) to changes in interest rates. An estimate of the percentage change in value of a fixed-income security or portfolio in response to a change in YTM (ΔY) is given by:

Change in price = $-$Duration (ΔY) + ½ Convexity (ΔY)^2

Modified ΔY
Macaulay $\left| \dfrac{\Delta Y}{1+Y} \right|$

> *Professor's Note: If duration in the above equation is Macaulay duration (rather than modified duration), ΔY is replaced by $\Delta Y/(1 + Y)$.*

Several risk factors affect the values of options positions. **Delta** is an estimate of the sensitivity of options values to changes in the value of the underlying asset. Delta is the ratio of the change in an option's value to a change in the price of the underlying security. A call delta of 0.6 means that for every $1 increase in the price of the underlying asset, the call value increases by $0.60. A put delta of -0.5 means that for every $1 increase the value of the underlying asset, the put value will decrease by $0.50.

Gamma is an estimate of how delta changes as the price of the underlying asset changes and is calculated as the ratio of the *change in delta* to a change in the price of the underlying asset. Just as convexity improves estimates of the impact of interest rate changes captured by delta, gamma improves estimates of the impact of a change in the price of the underlying asset on option values. Both convexity and gamma are considered *second-order effects,* while duration and delta measure first-order effects of risk factor changes.

Vega is a measure of the sensitivity of option values to changes in the expected volatility of the price of the underlying asset. We can incorporate all three of these option risk measures in the following equation:

Delta / GAMMA Vega

Change in call price = delta (ΔS) + ½ gamma (ΔS)^2 + vega (ΔV)

where ΔS is the change in the price of the underlying asset and ΔV is the change in future volatility.

LOS 49.h: Describe the use of sensitivity risk measures and scenario risk measures.

CFA® Program Curriculum, Volume 6, page 335

Sensitivity risk measures can inform a portfolio manager about a portfolio's exposure to various risk factors to facilitate risk management. Exposure to risks the manager believes are excessive can be reduced (i.e., hedged). Of course, eliminating all risk is not the goal; portfolios not exposed to risk can be expected to earn only the risk-free rate of return.

When using scenario analysis for a portfolio that contains options or fixed-income securities with embedded options, the individual options and bonds must be valued with a pricing model using scenario values for the risk factors. Factor sensitivities can be used to estimate the effects of small changes in risk factors for these securities; for larger risk factor changes, pricing models for portfolio securities must be used. Even combining first-order and second-order effects, such as duration and convexity, only provides an approximation of the change in value that would result from a relatively large change in a risk factor.

Pricing models can be quite accurate when all of the relevant characteristics of a security are specified. With scenario analysis, each portfolio security is model-priced using the risk factor values of a particular scenario in order to estimate the scenario impact on portfolio value.

Scenario analysis is often performed as if the scenario changes were instantaneous. In some cases, scenario changes are modeled as incremental changes, and the scenario includes portfolio manager actions in response to each, perhaps daily, incremental change in the set of risk factors. The idea is to allow for the reduction or closing of some positions or adjusting hedges appropriately. Because such actions will reduce the overall impact of the scenario changes, scenario analysis based on an instantaneous change in risk factors is considered more conservative. It is also more realistic in circumstances where, for example, counterparties are unable or unwilling to provide additional collateral required or lack of liquidity makes changing portfolio positions very costly or impossible.

In reverse stress testing, the first step is to identify a portfolio's largest risk exposures. Then an unacceptable outcome is determined (usually one that would threaten the survival of the organization), and scenarios of changes in risk factors that would result in such an outcome are identified. The question then becomes how likely such scenarios are. Using scenario analysis in this way can be beneficial in helping risk managers identify the vulnerabilities of a portfolio and perhaps mitigate the risk exposures identified.

Scenario analysis can be seen as the final step in the risk assessment and management process, after performing sensitivity analysis. For a firm that has limited its risk through a maximum VaR, limits on position sizes, limits on specific risk exposures, and so on, scenario analysis can provide additional information on a portfolio's vulnerability to a set of events or changes in correlations that would significantly reduce the value of the portfolio.

Firms that use leverage, especially banks and hedge funds, often use stress tests involving a single risk factor to determine the size of change in that factor that could cause such losses that the firm's sustainability is compromised.

LOS 49.i: Describe advantages and limitations of sensitivity risk measures and scenario risk measures.

CFA® Program Curriculum, Volume 6, page 345

VaR, sensitivity analysis, and scenario analysis complement each other, and a risk manager should not rely on only one of these measures. VaR provides a probability of loss. Sensitivity analysis provides estimates of the relative exposures to different risk factors, but no estimate of the probability of any specific changes in risk factors. Scenario analysis will provide information about exposure to simultaneous changes in several risk factors or changes in risk correlations, but, again, there is no probability associated with a specific scenario other than the empirical probability of a historical scenario over the lookback period.

As an example of the limitations of sensitivity analysis, consider two bond portfolios that both have the same duration, so that the change in value resulting from a one basis point change in yield is the same for both portfolios. The problem with using duration as the risk measure is that the yield volatility of one portfolio may be quite different from the yield volatility of the other. The yield volatilities of government bonds, investment-grade bonds, corporate bonds, and high-yield bonds may be quite different from each other so that the probabilities of a given percentage decrease in value are quite different as well. Similarly, option delta (or delta and gamma) may be an appropriate measure of the risk for small changes in the price of the underlying, but the volatility of the prices of the underlying may be quite different for different options.

LOS 49.j: Describe risk measures used by banks, asset managers, pension funds, and insurers.

CFA® Program Curriculum, Volume 6, page 349

The risk measures used by an organization will depend on the types of risks it is exposed to, the regulations that govern it, and whether the organization uses leverage. For each type of organization, differences among firms will result in differences in the risk measures used. In what follows, we focus on similarities of risk measures used among organizations of the same type and typical differences between the risk measures used by different organizations.

Banks typically use sensitivity measures (duration of held-to-maturity securities and foreign exchange risk exposure), scenario analysis and stress testing (for their full balance sheets), leverage risk measures, and VaR (especially for trading securities). Banks also estimate risk from asset-liability mismatches, estimate VaR for economic capital, and disaggregate risk by both geographic location and business unit type.

Traditional (long-only) asset managers typically focus on relative risk measures unless their goal is an absolute return target. Typical risk measures used include the size of positions, sensitivity measures of interest rate and market risk, historical and hypothetical scenario analysis, and options risk. A risk measure more specific to asset management is **active share**: the difference between the weight of a security in the portfolio and its weight in the benchmark.

Ex-post tracking error (backward looking) and **ex-ante tracking error** (forward looking) measures provide different information. Ex-post tracking error is a measure of a portfolio's tracking error relative to a benchmark portfolio over a lookback period. Ex-post tracking error is used for performance attribution and to assess manager skill over prior periods. Traditional asset managers mostly use ex-ante tracking error for risk estimation, which focuses on the potential underperformance of the current (rather than a historical) portfolio. Managers with an absolute return target may use VaR instead.

For **hedge funds**, the risk measures used depend, to some extent, on the strategy employed. For hedge funds in general, the risk measures used include sensitivity analysis, leverage measures, scenario analysis, and stress tests. Funds with both long and short positions will estimate risk measures for long positions and short positions, as well as for the overall portfolio (gross exposure). Hedge funds that use VaR focus on VaR measures of less than 10% for short periods.

Hedge funds with significantly non-normal returns distributions use a risk measure referred to as *maximum drawdown;* the largest decrease in value over prior periods of a specific length. As we have noted, sensitivity measures based on standard deviation or beta may be misleading for large changes in risk factors when returns are non-normal.

Defined benefit pension funds calculate the difference between the present value of their assets (often market values) and the present value of their estimated future liabilities (payments to retirees and heirs). A risk measure used by pension funds is **surplus-at-risk**, a VaR for plan assets minus liabilities. A negative surplus must be made up by the firm if higher-than-expected asset returns do not reduce it significantly over time. The term *glide path* refers to a multi-year plan for adjusting pension fund contributions to reverse a significant overfunded or underfunded status. To reduce surplus uncertainly, a pension fund may match its assets to its liabilities. A related risk measure is an estimate of the hedged exposure and unhedged (returns-generating) exposure of the fund.

Insurance companies are often subject to significant regulation of their products and their investment portfolios (reserves). **Property and casualty insurers** sell auto, home, boat, liability, and health insurance. The insurance risks of a P&C company are not highly correlated with the market risk of their investment portfolios. Insurance risks are reduced by purchasing reinsurance (from another insurance company) and by geographical diversification. **Life insurers** primarily sell life insurance policies and annuities, some of which make payments until the death of the annuity owner.

P&C insurers use sensitivities of their exposures to market risk factors in their investment portfolios for risk management. Premium income is expected to cover the cost of insurance claims in a typical year, with the investment portfolio available to cover extraordinary claim losses, such as those in a year with a natural disaster.

P&C insurers use VaR and capital at risk as measures of their risk exposure in their investment accounts. They also use scenario analysis, often combining portfolio risk factors and insurance risk factors in a scenario. Regulations may require specific amounts of reserves (based on policies issued), and regulators discount the values of riskier assets held as reserves in determining their adequacy.

The insurance risk of life insurers is more highly correlated with the market risk exposures of their investment portfolios than it is for P&C insurers. Because annuities pay over relatively long periods into the future, the present values of these liabilities are quite sensitive to the discount factors used, although they have significant mortality risk factors as well. (The longer a life annuity pays, the larger the current liability.) For this reason, life insurers estimate the sensitivities to market risk factors for both their investment portfolios and their annuity liabilities.

Because life insurers are able to somewhat match the market risk of their portfolio assets to their liabilities, they must consider the risk of the remaining mismatch between assets and liabilities. Life insurers also use scenario analysis that includes both nonmarket (insurance) risk factors and market risk factors.

LOS 49.k: Explain constraints used in managing market risks, including risk budgeting, position limits, scenario limits, and stop-loss limits.

CFA® Program Curriculum, Volume 6, page 357

Constraints imposed to limit risk can be too restrictive, impairing profitability, or not restrictive enough, leading to financial stress, corporate reorganization, or bankruptcy. Imposing restrictions at the business-unit level may be too restrictive to the extent diversification benefits or offsetting positions across business units are not taken into account. Risk limits that are often imposed include the following.

Risk budgeting refers to a risk management process that first determines the acceptable total risk for an organization, and then allocates that risk to different activities, strategies, or asset classes as appropriate. An example would be first determining the maximum allowable 5% VaR amount, then allocating that VaR across various business units. A portfolio manager may set a limit for total risk relative to a benchmark and then allocate that risk to deviations from the portfolio's target asset allocations, deviations from benchmark weights in specific industries, and deviations from benchmark weights for firms within a specific industry.

Position limits are one way to limit risk because they ensure some minimum level of diversification by limiting risk exposures. For example, position limits may be imposed on allocations to individual securities within an asset class, asset classes such as equities or high-yield bonds, investments in a single country, securities in a single currency or the differences between long and short positions for a hedge fund manager.

Position limits can be expressed as currency amounts or as percentages of a portfolio's value. Position limits can also be based on a liquidity measure, such as average daily or weekly trading volume.

Scenario limits are limits on expected loss for a given scenario.

Stop-loss limits require that a risk exposure be reduced if losses exceed a specified amount over a certain period of time. An example of a simple stop-loss limit is a requirement to reduce the portfolio allocation to a stock or asset class (by a given amount) if it declines in value by more than a specified percentage (or currency amount). A slightly more complex type of stop-loss limit is a requirement that a risk exposure be hedged as the value of a security or index falls. This is referred to as **portfolio insurance** when the value of a portfolio is hedged by index puts.

LOS 49.l: Explain how risk measures may be used in capital allocation decisions.

CFA® Program Curriculum, Volume 6, page 360

Capital allocation decisions refer to how the capital of a firm is used to fund its various business units or activities, analogous to asset allocation for a portfolio manager. The optimal capital allocation, ignoring risk, would be the allocation that maximizes the expected return on the firm's invested capital. Risk management, however, requires that the risk exposure for each use of firm capital be considered.

One way to introduce risk exposures to various activities into the capital allocation decision is to limit the overall risk of all the activities. By calculating a VaR for each activity or business unit, the maximum acceptable VaR can be allocated across the activities or business units in a process similar to risk budgeting for a portfolio manager. This is but one method of considering risk exposures when determining the optimal allocation of firm capital to various activities.

KEY CONCEPTS

LOS 49.a

Value at risk (VaR) is an estimate of the minimum loss that will occur with a given probability over a specified period expressed as a currency amount or as percentage of portfolio value.

LOS 49.b

Value at risk estimation methods:
- Parametric method—uses the estimated variances and covariances of portfolio securities to estimate the distribution of possible portfolio values, often assuming a normal distribution.
- Historical simulation—uses historical values for risk factors over some prior lookback period to get a distribution of possible values.
- Monte Carlo simulation—draws each risk factor change from an assumed distribution and calculates portfolio values based on a set of changes in risk factors; repeated thousands of times to get a distribution of possible portfolio values.

LOS 49.c

The x% VaR is calculated as the minimum loss for the current portfolio, x% of the time, based on an estimated distribution of portfolio values.

LOS 49.d

Advantages of VaR:
- Widely accepted by regulators.
- Simple to understand.
- Expresses risk as a single number.
- Useful for comparing the risk of portfolios, portfolio components, and business units.

Disadvantages of VaR:
- Subjective in that the time period and the probability are chosen by the user.
- Very sensitive to the estimation method and assumptions employed by the user.
- Focused only on left-tail outcomes.
- Vulnerable to misspecification by the user.

LOS 49.e

Conditional VaR (CVaR) is the expected loss given that the loss exceeds the VaR.

Incremental VaR (IVaR) is the estimated change in VaR from a specific change in the size of a portfolio position.

Marginal VaR (MVaR) is the estimate of the change in VaR for a small change in a portfolio position and is used as an estimate of the position's contribution to overall VaR.

Ex ante tracking error, also referred to as relative VaR, measures the VaR of the difference between the return on a portfolio and the return on the manager's benchmark portfolio.

LOS 49.f

Sensitivity analysis is used to estimate the change in a security or portfolio value to an incremental change in a risk factor.

Scenario analysis refers to estimation of the effect on portfolio value of a specific set of changes in relevant risk factors.

A scenario of changes in risk factors can be historical, based on a past set of risk factors changes that actually occurred, or hypothetical (based on a selected set of significant changes in the risk factors of interest).

LOS 49.g

Equity risk is measured by beta (sensitivity to overall market returns).

The interest rate risk of fixed-income securities is measured by duration (sensitivity to change in yield) and convexity (second-order effect, change in duration).

Options risk is measured by delta (sensitivity to asset price changes), gamma (second-order effect, change in delta), and vega (sensitivity to asset price volatility).

Market risk can be managed by adjusting portfolio holdings to control the exposures to these various risk factors.

LOS 49.h

A stress test based on either sensitivity or scenario analysis uses extreme changes to examine the expected effects on a portfolio or organization, often to determine the effects on a firm's equity or solvency. A reverse stress test is designed to identify scenarios that would result in business failure.

Sensitivity analysis can give a risk manager a more complete view of the vulnerability of a portfolio to a variety of risk factors. Sensitivity and scenario risk measures provide additional information about portfolio risk but do not necessarily provide probabilities or, in the case of sensitivity measures, the sizes of expected changes in risk factors and portfolio value.

Sensitivity and scenario analysis provide information that VaR does not and are not necessarily based on historical results. A historical scenario will not necessarily be repeated. Hypothetical scenarios may be misspecified, and the probability that a scenario will occur is unknown.

LOS 49.i

VaR, sensitivity analysis, and scenario analysis complement each other, and a risk manager should not rely on only one of these measures.
- VaR provides a probability of loss.
- Sensitivity analysis provides estimates of the relative exposures to different risk factors, but does not provide estimates of the probability of any specific movement in risk factors.
- Scenario analysis provides information about exposure to simultaneous changes in several risk factors or changes in risk correlations, but there is no probability associated with a specific scenario.

LOS 49.j

Banks are concerned with many risks including asset-liability mismatches, market risk for their investment portfolio, their leverage, the duration and convexity of their portfolio of fixed-income securities, and the overall risk to their economic capital.

Asset managers are most concerned with returns volatility and the probability distribution of either absolute losses or losses relative to a benchmark portfolio.

Pension fund managers are concerned with any mismatch between assets and liabilities as well as with the volatility of the surplus (assets minus liabilities).

P&C companies are concerned with the sensitivity of their investment portfolio to risk factors, the VaR of their economic capital, and scenarios that incorporate both market and insurance risks as stress tests of the firm.

Life insurers are concerned with market risks to their investment portfolio assets and liabilities (to make annuity payments), any mismatch between assets and liabilities, and scenarios that would lead to large decreases in their surplus.

LOS 49.k

Risk budgeting begins with determination of an acceptable amount of risk and then allocates this risk among investment positions to generate maximum returns for the risk taken.

Position limits are maximum currency amounts or portfolio percentages allowed for individual securities, securities of a single issuer, or classes of securities, based on their risk factor exposures.

A stop-loss limit requires that an investment position be reduced (by sale or hedging) or closed out when losses exceed a given amount over a specified time period.

A scenario limit requires adjustment of the portfolio so that the expected loss from a given scenario will not exceed a specified amount.

LOS 49.l

Firms use risk measures by adjusting expected returns for risk when making capital allocation decisions.

CONCEPT CHECKERS

1. Weekly 5% VaR of £1 million indicates:
   A. a maximum allowable loss of £1 million in 5% of weeks.
   B. that the largest weekly loss is £1 million or 5% of portfolio value.
   C. a 5% probability of a loss greater than £1 million in any given week.

2. A lookback period is *least likely* to be specified when estimating VaR using:
   A. historical simulation.
   B. the parametric method.
   C. Monte Carlo simulation.

3. Which of the following is a limitation of VaR?
   A. VaR focuses on downside risk.
   B. Use of VaR is discouraged by banking regulators.
   C. Estimates of VaR for different asset classes are not comparable.

4. The expected amount of a loss, given that it is equal to or greater than the VaR, is the:
   A. marginal VaR.
   B. conditional VaR.
   C. incremental VaR.

5. The sensitivity of an option value to changes in volatility of the underlying asset price is measured by:
   A. beta.
   B. vega.
   C. gamma.

6. Which of the following risk measures is *most likely* to be used by a traditional asset manager?
   A. Active share.
   B. Surplus at risk.
   C. Maximum drawdown.

7. The risk committee of an investment management firm believes high-yield bonds will decrease in value if the economy goes into recession, and the committee decides to limit exposure to this asset class to 10% of assets under management. This constraint is *best* described as a:
   A. position limit.
   B. scenario limit.
   C. stop-loss limit.

8. A portfolio manager expects to earn a return of 6.5% over the next year with a standard deviation of 9%. The portfolio is currently valued at $6.4 million. What is the 5% annual VaR of the portfolio?
   A. $83,500.
   B. $160,000.
   C. $534,400.

9. The risk measure of volatility of surplus would most likely be used by a:
    A. bank.
    B. pension fund.
    C. life insurance company.

To access other content related to this topic review that may be included in the Schweser package you purchased, log in to your Schweser.com online dashboard. Schweser's OnDemand Video Lectures deliver streaming instruction covering every LOS in this topic review, while SchweserPro™ QBank provides additional quiz questions to help you practice and recall what you've learned.

ANSWERS – CONCEPT CHECKERS

1. **C** Weekly 5% VaR of £1 million indicates that there is a 5% probability that a loss during any given week will be greater than £1 million.

2. **C** Monte Carlo simulation uses estimated statistical properties for each of its risk factors. The parametric method and historical simulation both use a lookback period.

3. **A** Because VaR focuses on negative (left-tail) outcomes, it does not provide a complete view of the trade-off between risk and return. Advantages of VaR include its acceptance by global banking regulators and its usefulness in comparing risk across different asset classes.

4. **B** Conditional VaR is the expected amount of a loss, given that it is equal to or greater than the VaR. Marginal VaR is the slope of a curve of VaR as a function of a security's weight in a portfolio. Incremental VaR is the change in VaR resulting from changing the portfolio weight of a security.

5. **B** Vega is a measure of the sensitivity of an option value to changes in volatility of the underlying asset price.

6. **A** Active share is the difference between the weight of a security in an asset manager's portfolio and its weight in a benchmark index. Maximum drawdown is a risk measure often used by hedge funds. Surplus at risk is a risk measure used by defined benefit pension plans.

7. **A** Limiting the allocation to an asset class is an example of a position limit.

8. **C** % VaR = 0.065 − 1.65(0.09) = −0.0835

    $ VaR = (0.0835) × ($6,400,000) = $534,400

9. **B** Pension fund managers are concerned with any mismatch between assets and liabilities as well as with the volatility of the surplus (assets minus liabilities).

ECONOMICS AND INVESTMENT MARKETS

EXAM FOCUS

This topic review links real rate of return to investors' inter-temporal rate of substitution. It further uses utility theory to derive risk premium for consumption hedging properties of assets. Be able to identify appropriate risk premiums for different asset classes.

LOS 50.a: Explain the notion that to affect market values, economic factors must affect one or more of the following: 1) default-free interest rates across maturities, 2) the timing and/or magnitude of expected cash flows, and 3) risk premiums.

CFA® Program Curriculum, Volume 6, page 376

The value of any asset can be computed as the present value of its expected future cash flows discounted at an appropriate risk-adjusted discount rate. The more uncertain the cash flows, the higher the discount rate.

Notional R = Real R + Inflation

Components of the discount rate are: (R)

1. Real risk-free discount rate (R).

2. Expected inflation (π).

3. Risk premium reflecting the uncertainty about the cash flow (RP).

The value of an asset will change if either the cash flow forecasts change or any of the components of the discount rate changes. Risk premiums not only vary across assets (and asset classes), but also vary with changes in investors' perception of risk. We will examine the decomposition of risk premiums for several asset classes in the remainder of this topic review.

LOS 50.b: Explain the role of expectations and changes in expectations in market valuation.

CFA® Program Curriculum, Volume 6, page 379

The value of an asset depends on (1) its expected future cash flows and (2) the discount rate used to value those cash flows. As market participants receive new information, the timing and amounts of expected future cash flows are revised and valuations change as a result.

The impact of new information will depend on its effect on current expectations so that an earnings report of 53% growth in earnings may have a positive or negative effect on the firm's value, depending on whether expectations were for slower or more rapid growth.

LOS 50.c: Explain the relationship between the long-term growth rate of the economy, the volatility of the growth rate, and the average level of real short-term interest rates.

CFA® Program Curriculum, Volume 6, page 388

Even in a world of no inflation, a default-free bond has to compensate an investor for forgoing their current consumption. The investor evaluates the disutility of forgoing current consumption relative to the utility of obtaining future consumption.

The real risk-free rate of interest derives from the inter-temporal rate of substitution, which represents an investor's trade-off between real consumption now and real consumption in the future. Based on utility theory, we can represent this trade-off as:

$$\text{inter-temporal rate of substitution} = m_t = \frac{\text{marginal utility of consuming 1 unit in the future}}{\text{marginal utility of current consumption of 1 unit}} = \frac{u_t}{u_0}$$

For a given quantity of consumption, investors always prefer current consumption over future consumption ($u_0 > u_t$) and $m_t < 1$ as a result.

The current price (P_0) of a zero-coupon, inflation-indexed, risk-free bond that will pay $1 at time *t* can be expressed as:

$$P_0 = E(m_t)$$

in which case, the real risk-free rate of return is:

$$R = \frac{1 - P_0}{P_0} = \left[\frac{1}{E(m_t)} \right] - 1$$

> *Professor's Note: We have been considering an inflation-indexed bond in this example because we do not want to consider the effects of inflation in our analysis yet.*

Some key points to keep in mind:

- The higher the utility investors attach for current consumption relative to future consumption, the higher the real rate.
- Diminishing marginal utility of wealth means that an investor's marginal utility of consumption declines as wealth increases. This suggests that marginal utility of consumption is higher during periods of scarcity, such as during economic contractions.

- If investors expect higher incomes in the future, their expected marginal utility of future consumption is decreased relative to current consumption. When investor expectations about the economy change to better economic times ahead, the expectation of higher incomes in the future will lead to an increase in current consumption and a reduction in savings. Investors will derive greater utility from current consumption relative to future consumption and would, therefore, save less. Conversely, investors expecting worse times ahead would prefer to increase future consumption by reducing current consumption and saving more.
- Investors increase their savings rate when expected returns are high or when uncertainty about their future income increases.

Risky Cash Flows and Risk Premiums

The risk aversion of investors can be explained by the covariance of an investor's inter-temporal marginal rate of substitution and expected returns on savings. Our discussion so far was limited to risk-free investments. However, if the underlying cash flows are uncertain, investors demand a risk premium for bearing the risk that comes with such uncertainty. The investor's expected marginal utility of a payoff is inversely related to the level of uncertainty of the payoff. Investors experience a larger loss of utility for a loss in wealth as compared to a gain in utility for an equivalent gain in wealth. This property is called as **risk-aversion**.

An investor's absolute risk-aversion declines with their wealth; wealthier investors are less risk-averse and more willing to take risk relative to their poorer counterparts. However, the marginal utility of holding risky assets declines as an investor holds more risky assets in her portfolio. When the markets are in equilibrium, wealthy and poorer investors would have the same willingness to hold risky assets.

Consider a risk-free, inflation-indexed, zero-coupon bond that an investor will sell prior to maturity. The uncertainty about the sale price gives rise to a risk premium. The price of the bond will be lower than the expected sale price discounted at the real risk free rate. We can model this risk premium as:

$$P_0 = \frac{E(P_1)}{(1+R)} + cov(P_1, m_1)$$

where:

R = the real risk-free rate

The covariance between the expected future price of the bond and the investor's inter-temporal rate of substitution can be viewed as a risk premium. Now imagine this relationship in the context of a risky asset (e.g., stocks). For risk-averse investors, the covariance is negative; when the expected future price of the asset is high, the marginal utility of future consumption relative to current consumption is low. This is because during good economic times, both investors' labor incomes and most risky asset values are high. However, with higher future labor incomes, the marginal utility of future consumption is lower. The resulting negative covariance between the marginal utility of consumption and asset prices reduces the value of the asset for a given expected sale price, P_1. Everything else constant, the lower current price (P_0) increases expected return. This higher expected return is due to a positive risk premium.

For a single-period risk-free bond, the covariance is zero as there is no uncertainty about the terminal value; there is no risk premium.

GDP Growth Rates

If GDP growth is forecast to be high, the utility of consumption in the future (when incomes will be high) will be low and the inter-temporal rate of substitution will fall; investors will save less, increasing real interest rates. Therefore, real interest rates will be positively correlated with real GDP growth rates. This is consistent with the existence of high real rates in rapidly growing developing economies such as those of India and China. Interest rates are also positively correlated with the expected volatility in GDP growth due to higher risk premium.

LOS 50.d: Explain how the phase of the business cycle affects policy and short-term interest rates, the slope of the term structure of interest rates, and the relative performance of bonds of differing maturities.

CFA® Program Curriculum, Volume 6, page 398

So far we have not considered the implications of inflation in our analysis of the correlation between interest rates and GDP growth. Nominal risk-free interest rates include a premium for expected inflation (π). However, actual inflation is uncertain. This additional risk gives rise to an additional risk premium for the uncertainty about actual inflation (θ). This risk premium is higher for longer maturity bonds.

For short-term risk-free securities (e.g., T-bills), the uncertainty about inflation is negligible and, therefore, the nominal interest rate (r) would be comprised of real risk-free rate (R) and expected inflation (π):

$$r(\text{short-term}) = R + \pi$$

For longer term bonds, we add the risk premium for uncertainty about inflation, θ:

$$r(\text{long-term}) = R + \pi + \theta$$

Taylor Rule

Central banks are usually charged with setting policy rates so as to (1) maintain price stability and (2) achieve the maximum sustainable level of employment. The Taylor rule links the central bank's policy rate to economic conditions (employment level and inflation):

$$r = R_n + \pi + 0.5(\pi - \pi^*) + 0.5(y - y^*)$$

where:

r = central bank policy rate implied by the Taylor rule
R_n = neutral *real* policy interest rate
π = current inflation rate
π^* = central bank's target inflation rate
y = log of current level of output
y* = log of central bank's target (sustainable) output

Central banks can moderate the business cycle by making appropriate changes to the policy rate or can magnify the cycle by not responding appropriately to changing economic conditions (e.g., committing policy errors such as keeping rates too low).

Business Cycle and Slope of the Yield Curve

When the economy is in recession, policy rates tend to be low. Investors' improving expectations about future GDP growth and increasing inflation as the economy comes out of recession, leads to higher longer-term rates. This results in a positively sloped yield curve. Conversely, expectations of a decline in GDP growth results in a negatively sloped (inverted) yield curve. For this reason, an inverted yield curve is often considered a predictor of future recessions. Later stages of an economic expansion often are characterized by high inflation and high short-term interest rates, while longer term rates tend to be low, reflecting investor's expectation of decreasing inflation and GDP growth.

A **term spread** is the difference between the yield on a longer-term bond yield and the yield on a short-term bond. Evidence suggests that normal term spread is positive so the yield curve is upward sloping. Recall that the risk premium for uncertainty in inflation (θ) is higher for longer maturity bonds. Positive term spreads can be attributed to increasing θ for longer periods.

LOS 50.e: Describe the factors that affect yield spreads between non-inflation-adjusted and inflation-indexed bonds.

CFA® Program Curriculum, Volume 6, page 406

The difference between the yield of a non-inflation-indexed risk-free bond and the yield of an inflation-indexed risk-free bond of the same maturity is the **break-even inflation rate (BEI)**.

BEI = yield on non-inflation-indexed bond − yield on inflation-indexed bond

Recall that for longer maturity bonds, the nominal rate is composed of the real rate, expected inflation, and a risk premium for inflation uncertainty. Therefore, BEI is composed of two elements: expected inflation (π) and a risk premium for uncertainty about actual inflation (θ).

$$BEI = \pi + \theta$$

LOS 50.f: Explain how the phase of the business cycle affects credit spreads and the performance of credit-sensitive fixed-income instruments.

CFA® Program Curriculum, Volume 6, page 421

The required rate of return for bonds with credit risk includes an additional risk premium. This credit risk premium (credit spread) is the difference in yield between a credit risky bond and a default-free bond of the same maturity.

Required rate of return for credit risky bonds = $R + \pi + \theta + \gamma$

where:

γ = additional risk premium for credit risk = credit spread

Credit spreads tend to rise during times of economic downturns and fall during expansions. Research has shown that defaults increase, and recovery rates decrease, during periods of economic weakness. Both effects result in greater credit losses during economic downturns.

When credit spreads narrows, credit risky bonds will outperform default-free bonds. Overall, lower rated bonds tend to benefit more than higher rated bonds from a narrowing of credit spreads (their yields fall more). Conversely, when credit spreads widen, higher rated bonds will outperform lower rated bonds on a relative basis (because their yields will rise less).

LOS 50.g: Explain how the characteristics of the markets for a company's products affect the company's credit quality.

CFA® Program Curriculum, Volume 6, page 427

Analysis of credit spreads by industrial sectors reveals that spreads differ among sectors and over time. Differences in credit spreads are primarily due to differences in industry products and services and the financial leverage of the firms in the industry. Spreads for issuers in the consumer cyclical sector increase significantly during economic downturns compared to spreads for issuers in the consumer non-cyclical sector.

LOS 50.h: Explain how the phase of the business cycle affects short-term and long-term earnings growth expectations.

CFA® Program Curriculum, Volume 6, page 435

Corporate earnings may be related to the business cycle. Cyclical industries (e.g., durable goods manufacturers and consumer discretionary) tend to be relatively more sensitive to the phase of the business cycle. Companies in these industries have revenues and earnings that rise and fall with the rate of economic growth. Defensive or non-cyclical industries (e.g., consumer non-discretionary) tend to be relatively immune to fluctuations in economic activity; their earnings tend to be relatively stable throughout the business cycle.

LOS 50.i: Explain the relationship between the consumption-hedging properties of equity and the equity risk premium.

CFA® Program Curriculum, Volume 6, page 434

The discount rate used to value equity securities includes an additional risk premium, the equity risk premium. This risk premium is in addition to the risk premium on credit risky bonds because equity is more risky than debt.

Discount rate for equity $= R + \pi + \theta + \gamma + \kappa$ → *Additional Risk Premium* [handwritten: *uncertainty of Inflation*, *Real*, *inflation*, *Credit Spread*]

where:

κ = additional risk premium relative to risky debt for an investment in equities

λ = equity risk premium $= \gamma + \kappa$ → [handwritten: *Credit spread of Risk Bond + risk Prem for Equity*]

Assets that provide a higher payoff during economic downturns are more highly valued because of the *consumption hedging property* of the asset. This property reduces the risk premium on an asset. Equity prices are generally cyclical, with higher values during economic expansions when the marginal utility of consumption is lower. Equity investments, therefore, are not the most effective hedge against bad consumption outcomes. Because of this poor consumption hedging ability, equity risk premium is positive.

LOS 50.j: Describe cyclical effects on valuation multiples.

CFA® Program Curriculum, Volume 6, page 441

Price multiples such as P/E and P/B are often used in determining the relative values of companies, of sectors, or of the overall market from a historical perspective. However, it is inappropriate to judge the multiple in a historical context only. If the P/E ratio for S&P 500 is above historical standards, it could be that the index is overvalued, but it also could be that the index level is justified by current conditions.

Price multiples are positively correlated with expected earnings growth rates and negatively correlated to required returns. Therefore, price multiples rise with increases in expected future earnings growth and with a decrease in any of the components of the required rate of return (the real rate, expected inflation, the risk premium for inflation uncertainty, or the equity risk premium). As a result, the equity risk premium declines during economic expansions and rises during recessions.

Shiller's CAPE (real cyclically adjusted P/E) ratio reduces the volatility of unadjusted P/E ratios by using real (i.e., inflation-adjusted) prices in the numerator and a 10-year moving average of real earnings in the denominator.

LOS 50.k: Describe the implications of the business cycle for a given style strategy (value, growth, small capitalization, large capitalization).

CFA® Program Curriculum, Volume 6, page 444

Growth stocks are characterized by high P/Es and by low dividend yields and tend to be in immature markets with high growth prospects. Value stocks tend to have low P/Es, have high dividend yields, and are generally found in established and mature markets. Value stocks tend to have stable earnings. A growth investing strategy means investing in growth stocks, while a value strategy means investing in value stocks. Historically, there have been periods when one strategy distinctly outperforms the other. A value strategy performs well during recessionary conditions, while growth strategy performs well during economic expansions.

Stocks are also categorized by company size as measured by market capitalization (e.g., small-cap, mid-cap, and large-cap). Small-cap stocks tend to have higher volatility and command a higher risk premium.

LOS 50.l: Describe how economic analysis is used in sector rotation strategies.

CFA® Program Curriculum, Volume 6, page 446

Ex post risk premiums on equity sectors can be computed as the difference between the average return on a sector and the short-term risk free rate. Consider two sectors: cyclical and non-cyclical industries. There are periods during which one sector outperforms the other; one sector generates a higher risk premium relative to the other. If investors could rotate out of the under-performing sector and into the better performing sector right before the change in performance, they would generate superior returns. Getting the timing right is of course very difficult. The point, however, is that understanding and forecasting the relationship between the equity market performance of different sectors and the business cycle would help analysts enhance their sector rotation strategies.

LOS 50.m: Describe the economic factors affecting investment in commercial real estate.

CFA® Program Curriculum, Volume 6, page 448

Commercial real estate investments have:

- Bond-like characteristics. The steady rental income stream is similar to cash flows from a portfolio of bonds. Furthermore, just as the credit quality of issuers affects the value of a bond portfolio, the credit quality of tenants affects the value of commercial real estate.
- Equity-like characteristics. The value of commercial real estate is influenced by many factors, including the state of the economy, the demand for rental properties, and property location. Uncertainty about the value of the property at the end of the lease term gives commercial properties an equity-like character.
- Illiquidity. Real estate as an asset class is characterized by illiquidity; it could take years to exit a real estate investment at its fair value.

Valuation

When estimating the value of real estate investment, the discount rate includes an additional risk premium for the lack of liquidity:

Discount rate for commercial real estate = $R + \pi + \theta + \gamma + \kappa + \phi$

where:

κ = risk premium for uncertainty about terminal value of property (similar to the equity risk premium)

ϕ = risk premium for illiquidity

While rental income from commercial properties seems to be more or less steady across business cycles, commercial property values tend to be very cyclical. Because of this, the correlation of commercial property values with those of other asset classes (e.g., equities) tends to be positive. Similar to equities, real estate provides a poor hedge against bad consumption outcomes. Therefore, the risk premium required by investors for investment in commercial properties will be relatively high and often close to the risk premium required for equity investments.

KEY CONCEPTS

LOS 50.a
The value of any asset can be computed as present value of its expected future cash flows discounted at an appropriate risk-adjusted discount rate. Risky cash flows require the discount rate to be higher due to inclusion of a risk premium.

LOS 50.b
Market prices reflect current expectations. Only changes in expectations cause a change in market price.

LOS 50.c
Interest rates are positively related to GDP growth rate and to the expected volatility in GDP growth due to a higher risk premium.

LOS 50.d
When the economy is in recession, short-term policy rates tend to be low. Investor expectations about higher future GDP growth and inflation as the economy comes out of recession lead to higher longer-term rates. This leads to positive slope of the yield curve. Conversely, an inversely sloping yield curve is often considered a predictor of future recessions.

LOS 50.e
Break-even inflation rate (BEI)
= yield on non-inflation-indexed bonds − yield on inflation-indexed bonds

BEI is comprised of two elements: expected inflation (π) and risk premium for uncertainty in inflation (θ).

LOS 50.f
Credit spreads tend to rise during times of economic downturns and shrink during expansions. When spreads narrow, lower-rated bonds tend to outperform higher-rated bonds.

LOS 50.g
Spreads for issuers in consumer cyclical sector widen considerably during economic downturns compared to spreads for issuers in the consumer non-cyclical sector.

LOS 50.h
Cyclical industries (e.g., durable goods manufacturers and consumer discretionary) tend to be extremely sensitive to the business cycle; their earnings rise during economic expansions and fall during contractions. Non-cyclical or defensive industries tend to have relatively stable earnings.

LOS 50.i
Equities are generally cyclical; they have higher values during good times and have poor consumption hedging properties. Therefore, the risk premium on equities should be positive.

LOS 50.j
Price multiples tend to follow the business cycle: multiples rise during economic expansions (as analysts revise growth estimates upward) and fall during contractions (as growth estimates are revised downward).

LOS 50.k
Empirical evidence shows that there are periods during which one style strategy (e.g., growth) will outperform others. However, timing the style strategy is the tricky part.

LOS 50.l
Relative outperformance of sectors can be discerned ex post. Ex ante forecasting of this outperformance is the objective of active managers.

LOS 50.m
Commercial real estate has equity-like and bond-like characteristics. The valuation depends on the rental income stream, the quality of tenants, and the terminal value at the end of the lease term. The discount rate for commercial real estate includes a risk premium for uncertainty in terminal value and also for illiquidity.

CONCEPT CHECKERS

1. Carrier, Inc.'s stock price fell last week, which was contrary to the movement in the industry index. Which of the following is *most likely* a valid reason for that to occur?
   A. An increase in the real risk-free rate.
   B. Inflation is expected to be higher.
   C. Investors are demanding a higher risk premium on Carrier.

2. Sonic, Inc., reported 12% earnings growth year-over-year, but its stock price fell. Which of the following is *most likely* a valid reason for that to occur?
   A. The market's expectation for Sonic was to report an earnings growth of less than 12%.
   B. The market's expectation for Sonic was to report an earnings growth of more than 12%.
   C. The market expected Sonic to outperform its competitors.

3. Which of the following statements is *most accurate*? Higher expected GDP growth would:
   A. lower the utility of future consumption and reduce the inter-temporal rate of substitution.
   B. increase the utility of future consumption and reduce the inter-temporal rate of substitution.
   C. lower the utility of future consumption and increase the inter-temporal rate of substitution.

4. Break-even inflation rate is comprised of the:
   A. real rate and unexpected inflation.
   B. expected inflation and risk premium for inflation uncertainty.
   C. inter-temporal rate of substitution and expected inflation.

5. An economy just getting out of recession would *most likely* have:
   A. high short-term rates and an inverted yield curve.
   B. low short-term rates and an inverted yield curve.
   C. low short-term rates and an upward sloping yield curve.

6. Zeon Corp's 10-year bonds are currently yielding 7.50%. The real rate is 3% and expected inflation is 2%. Which of the following is *most accurate*? Credit spread on Zeon bonds is:
   A. equal to 2.50%.
   B. less than 2.50%.
   C. greater than 2.50%.

7. Credit spreads on issuers classified as consumer cyclical are *most likely* to :
   A. widen during economic downturns.
   B. narrow during economic downturns.
   C. remain stable during the entire business cycle.

8. Earnings of companies in the consumer staples industry are *most likely* to:
   A. fluctuate with the business cycle.
   B. remain stable over the business cycle.
   C. fluctuate more than companies in consumer discretionary industries.

9. Which of the following statements is *most accurate*? Equity as an asset class provides:
   A. good consumption hedging properties and, therefore, commands a positive risk premium.
   B. poor consumption hedging properties and, therefore, commands a positive risk premium.
   C. good consumption hedging properties and, therefore, commands a negative risk premium.

10. Analysis of price multiples is *most likely* to indicate that the equity risk premium:
    A. declines during economic downturns.
    B. is stable over the business cycle.
    C. declines over economic expansions.

11. Growth stocks are *least likely* to be characterized by high:
    A. dividend yield.
    B. price multiple.
    C. expected earnings growth rate.

12. Relative to other asset classes, investors in commercial real estate are *least likely* to require a risk premium for:
    A. uncertainty in inflation.
    B. illiquidity.
    C. uncertainty in terminal value.

To access other content related to this topic review that may be included in the Schweser package you purchased, log in to your Schweser.com online dashboard. Schweser's OnDemand Video Lectures deliver streaming instruction covering every LOS in this topic review, while SchweserPro™ QBank provides additional quiz questions to help you practice and recall what you've learned.

ANSWERS – CONCEPT CHECKERS

1. **C**   If the real risk-free rate had increased or expected inflation had been higher, the discount rate would have been higher and would have lowered both Carrier's stock price and industry index. Given the divergence between Carrier's stock price and the industry index, a higher risk premium for Carrier's stock is the only valid reason from the choices provided.

2. **B**   Market prices embed current expectations. If the market reaction to earnings growth of 12% was negative, it would mean that the market prices were based on a higher earnings growth rate expectation.

3. **A**   A higher GDP growth rate would mean higher incomes in the future. Due to the principle of diminishing marginal utility, the utility of future consumption would, therefore, be lower. Lower future utility relative to the utility of current consumption lowers the inter-temporal rate of substitution.

4. **B**   BEI = expected inflation + risk premium for uncertainty in inflation.

5. **C**   An economy just getting out of recession is more likely to have low short-term rates, as the central bank policy rate would be low. Higher future GDP growth prospects would mean higher real rates and higher expected inflation over the longer term, so long-term rates would be high, leading to an upward sloping yield curve.

6. **B**   Yield on risky corporate debt = real risk-free rate + expected inflation + risk premium for inflation uncertainty + credit spread. 2.50% = risk premium for inflation uncertainty + credit spread. Given that the bond is long term, the risk premium for inflation uncertainty must be positive and credit spread must be less than 2.50%.

7. **A**   Credit spreads on consumer cyclical issuers widen during economic downturns and narrow during economic expansions.

8. **B**   Earnings of consumer staples companies tend to be relatively stable over the entire business cycle.

9. **B**   Stocks in general tend to perform well during economic expansions and, therefore, pay off during good economic times. The property of performing poorly during bad economic times implies that equities are a poor consumption hedge. Because they are a poor consumption hedge, investors demand a positive risk premium for investing in equities.

10. **C**   Price multiples tend to expand during economic expansions, suggesting that the equity risk premium declines during expansions. This is because investors become less risk averse during economic expansions and demand a lower premium for taking risk.

11. **A**   Growth stocks tend to have a low dividend yields, high price multiples, and high expected earnings growth rates.

12. **A**   Two risk premia that are unique to real estate as an asset class are the risk premium for illiquidity and the risk premium for uncertainty in terminal value (similar to the equity risk premium).

ANALYSIS OF ACTIVE PORTFOLIO MANAGEMENT

Study Session 17

EXAM FOCUS

The information ratio is used to evaluate active managers and can be used to make portfolio allocation decisions for an investor. There are lots of formulae and linkages to be on top of for this reading. Understand the differences between the Sharpe ratio and the information ratio. Be able to describe the full fundamental law and what influences each of the components. Understand the application of the fundamental law in the context of market timing and sector rotation strategies. Finally, be aware of the limitations of the fundamental law.

LOS 51.a: Describe how value added by active management is measured.

CFA® Program Curriculum, Volume 6, page 468

Active management seeks to add value by outperforming a passively managed benchmark portfolio.

Professor's Note: In this topic review, we are going to assume that the systematic risk of the active portfolio is the same as the systematic risk of the benchmark portfolio (i.e., the beta of the active portfolio relative to the benchmark is 1). If the beta of the actively managed portfolio is different than the beta of the benchmark, active return is computed as the difference in risk-adjusted returns and is known as alpha.

Active Return

Active return (R_A) is the value added by active management. Active return can be measured ex-ante (i.e., based on expectations) or ex-post ("after the fact"). Ex-ante active return is the difference between the expected return of an actively managed portfolio and the expected return of its benchmark:

$$E(R_A) = E(R_P) - E(R_B)$$

Active weights in a portfolio determine the amount value added. Active weight is the difference between a security's weight in an actively managed portfolio and its weight in the benchmark portfolio. Overweighted (underweighted) securities have positive (negative) active weights. Active weights must sum to zero.

For an active portfolio of N securities:

$$E(R_A) = \sum \Delta w_i E(R_i)$$

where:
$\Delta w_i =$ active weight $= w_{Pi} - w_{Bi}$

Ex-post active return is the difference between the realized return of the actively managed portfolio and its benchmark portfolio.

Example: Active return

The following information is available for an actively managed portfolio and its benchmark.

Security (i)	Portfolio Weight (W_{Pi})	Benchmark Weight (W_{Bi})	Expected Return $E(R_i)$
A	22%	25%	12%
B	20%	25%	–6%
C	21%	25%	4%
D	37%	25%	19%

Calculate the ex-ante active return.

Answer:

Active return = $E(R_P) - E(R_B)$

$E(R_P) = \sum w_{Pi}(R_i) = (0.22)(0.12) + (0.20)(-0.06) + (0.21)(0.04) + (0.37)(0.19) = 0.0931$ or 9.31%

$E(R_B) = \sum w_{Bi}(R_i) = (0.25)(0.12) + (0.25)(-0.06) + (0.25)(0.04) + (0.25)(0.19) = 0.0725$ or 7.25%

$E(R_A) = 0.0931 - 0.0725 = 0.0206$ or 2.06%

Alternatively:

Security (i)	Portfolio Weight (W_{Pi})	Benchmark Weight (W_{Bi})	Return R_i	Active Weight (ΔW_i)
A	22%	25%	12%	–3%
B	20%	25%	–6%	–5%
C	21%	25%	4%	–4%
D	37%	25%	19%	12%

$E(R_A) = \sum \Delta w_i E(R_i) = (-0.03)(0.12) + (-0.05)(-0.06) + (-0.04)(0.04) + (0.12)(0.19) = 2.06\%$

Given an investment strategy involving multiple asset classes, expected returns on the active and benchmark portfolios can be computed as the weighted average of securities returns:

$$E(R_P) = \sum w_{P,j} E(R_{P,j}) \text{ and } E(R_B) = \sum w_{B,j} E(R_{B,j})$$

Ex-ante active return is the expected return on the active portfolio minus the expected return on the benchmark:

$$E(R_A) = \sum w_{P,j} E(R_{P,j}) - \sum w_{B,j} E(R_{B,j})$$

Alternatively, active return can be decomposed into two parts:

1. Asset allocation return (from deviations of asset class portfolio weights from benchmark weights).

2. Security selection return (from active returns within asset classes).

$$E(R_A) = \sum \Delta w_j E(R_{B,j}) + \sum w_{P,j} E(R_{A,j})$$

where:

$\sum \Delta w_j E(R_{B,j}) = $ return from asset allocation

$\sum w_{P,j} E(R_{A,j}) = $ return from security selection

$E(R_{A,j}) = $ expected active return within asset classes $= E(R_{Pj}) - E(R_{Bj})$

Consider an active portfolio manager with a benchmark portfolio composed of 25% stocks and 75% bonds. The portfolio manager could overweight stocks (and underweight bonds), resulting in a difference in return relative to the benchmark; this is the asset allocation return. The manager can also choose to have higher weight to a specific stock within the allocation to stocks (and correspondingly underweight some other stocks). This contributes to the security selection return.

Example: Active return

Optoma Fund invests in three asset classes: U.S. equities, U.S. bonds, and international equities. The asset allocation weights of Optoma and the expected performance of each asset class and the benchmark are shown below.

Asset Class (i)	Portfolio Weight (W_{Pi})	Benchmark Weight (W_{Bi})	Portfolio Return $E(R_{Pi})$	Benchmark Return $E(R_{Bi})$
U.S. equities	45%	40%	11%	12%
U.S. bonds	30%	30%	6%	5%
International equities	25%	30%	14%	12%

Calculate the expected active return.

Answer:

Asset Class (i)	Portfolio Weight (W_{Pi})	Bench-mark Weight (W_{Bi})	Portfolio Return $E(R_{Pi})$	Bench-mark Return $E(R_{Bi})$	Active Weight (ΔW_i)	$(\Delta W_i) \times E(R_{Bi})$	$E(A_i) = E(R_{Pi}) - E(R_{Bi})$	$(W_{Pi}) \times E(A_i)$
U.S. equities	45%	40%	11%	12%	5%	0.60%	−1%	−0.45%
U.S. bonds	30%	30%	6%	5%	0%	0.00%	1%	0.30%
International equities	25%	30%	14%	12%	−5%	−0.60%	2%	0.50%
Total						0.00%		0.35%

$$E(R_A) = \sum w_{P,i} E(R_{P,i}) - \sum w_{B,i} E(R_{B,i}) = 10.25\% - 9.90\% = 0.35\%$$

Alternatively,

$$E(R_A) = \sum \Delta w_i E(R_{B,i}) + \sum w_{P,i} E(R_{A,i}) = 0.00\% + 0.35\% = 0.35\%$$

It can be seen that all of the expected active return is attributable to security selection. The active weights do not contribute to any asset allocation return.

LOS 51.b: Calculate and interpret the information ratio (ex post and ex ante) and contrast it to the Sharpe ratio.

CFA® Program Curriculum, Volume 6, page 473

The information ratio and the Sharpe ratio are two different methods of measuring a portfolio's risk-adjusted rate of return.

The **Sharpe ratio** (SR) is calculated as excess return per unit of risk (standard deviation):

$$SR = \frac{R_P - R_F}{\sigma_P}$$

An important attribute of the Sharpe ratio is that it is *unaffected by the addition of cash or leverage* in the portfolio. A 50% allocation to the risk-free asset would reduce both the excess return and standard deviation of returns by half.

The **information ratio** (IR) is the ratio of the active return to the standard deviation of active returns, which is known as **active risk**:

$$IR = \frac{R_P - R_B}{\sigma_{(R_P - R_B)}} = \frac{R_A}{\sigma_A} = \frac{\text{active return}}{\text{active risk}}$$

Handwritten margin notes:
Ex ante IR Normally positive
Ex-Post IR is Normally Negative

Some important points:

- In this topic review, the information ratio that we are considering is usually the ex-ante information ratio (i.e., the information ratio based on expectations). The ex-ante information ratio is generally positive (otherwise active management is not worth pursuing), while ex-post information ratios will often turn out to be negative.

- A *closet index fund* is a fund that is purported to be actively managed but in reality closely tracks the underlying benchmark index. These funds will have a Sharpe ratio similar to that of the benchmark index, a very low information ratio, and little active risk. After fees, the information ratio of a closet index fund is often negative.

- A fund with zero systematic risk (e.g., a market-neutral long-short equity fund) that uses the risk-free rate as its benchmark would have an information ratio that is equal to its Sharpe ratio. This is because active return will be equal to the portfolio's return minus the risk-free rate, and active risk will be equal to total risk.

Margin note: Sharpe Ratio is constant if we use leverage. IR is constant if we change weight

- Unlike the Sharpe ratio, the information ratio will change with the addition of cash or the use of leverage.

- The information ratio of an unconstrained portfolio is unaffected by the aggressiveness of the active weights. If the active weights of a portfolio are tripled, the active return and the active risk both triple, leaving the information ratio unchanged.

Margin note: If Return Risk ↑ or ↓ by same amount

- If we combine an actively managed portfolio with an allocation to the benchmark portfolio, the resulting blended portfolio will have the same information ratio as the original actively managed portfolio. As we increase the weight of the benchmark portfolio, the active return and active risk decrease proportionately, leaving the information ratio unchanged.

- Investors can select an appropriate amount of active risk by investing a portion of their assets in the active portfolio and the remaining portion in the benchmark. For example, if the active risk of a fund is 10%, an investor seeking to limit active risk to 6% can do so by investing 60% in the active portfolio and the remaining 40% in the benchmark portfolio.

Margin note: Active Risk. So Risk of Benchmark is Considered Zero

For an unconstrained active portfolio, the optimal amount of active risk is the level of active risk that maximizes the portfolio's Sharpe ratio. This optimal amount of active risk can be calculated as:

$$\sigma_A^* = \frac{IR}{SR_B}\sigma_B$$

Margin note: Optimal Risk to get highest SR
(annotations: Benchmark; Sharpe Ratio Benchmark)

> *Professor's Note: Unconstrained active portfolios have optimal weights for each of the securities in the portfolio based on (ex ante) expectations of active return and active risk. Sometimes constraints (e.g., long only positions) are imposed on active portfolios, resulting in less-than-optimal weights. We will discuss this in detail later in this topic review.*

The Sharpe ratio of a portfolio with optimal level of active risk can be calculated as:

$$SR_P = \sqrt{SR_B^2 + IR^2}$$

Furthermore, the total risk of the portfolio is given by:

Margin note: Diversification

$$\sigma_P^2 = \sigma_B^2 + \sigma_A^2$$

Example: Optimal active risk

Omega fund has an information ratio of 0.2 and active risk of 9%. The benchmark portfolio has a Sharpe ratio of 0.4 and total risk of 12%. If a portfolio (portfolio P) with an optimal level of active risk has been constructed by combining Omega fund and the benchmark portfolio, calculate:

1. Portfolio P's Sharpe ratio.

2. Portfolio P's excess return (i.e., return above the risk-free rate).

3. The proportion of benchmark and Omega fund in portfolio P.

Answer:

1. Optimal active risk = $\sigma_A{}^* = \dfrac{IR}{SR_B}\sigma_B = \dfrac{0.2}{0.4}(12\%) = 6\%$

   Based on Omega's information ratio of 0.2, the Sharpe ratio of portfolio P with an optimal level of active risk will be $(0.4^2 + 0.2^2)^{1/2} = 0.4472$

2. The expected active return given an active risk of 6% is:

   $E(R_A) = IR \times \sigma_A = 0.2 \times 0.06 = 1.2\% = (R_P - R_B)$

   Given the benchmark Sharpe ratio of 0.4 and a benchmark total risk of 12%,

   $$0.40 = \dfrac{R_B - R_F}{\sigma_P} = \dfrac{R_B - R_F}{0.12}$$

   Therefore, $(R_B - R_F) = 4.8\%$,

   portfolio P's excess return = $(R_P - R_F) = (R_P - R_B) + (R_B - R_F) = 1.2\% + 4.8\% = 6.0\%$,

   and $\sigma_P{}^2 = 0.12^2 + 0.06^2 = 0.018$ and $\sigma_P = 0.134$

   The Sharpe ratio of portfolio P then is: SR = 6% / 13.4% = 0.4472 (as calculated before).

3. The optimal level of active risk is 6% and Omega fund has an active risk of 9%, so we can calculate that 6% / 9% = 67% of portfolio P's allocation will be to the Omega fund and 33% will be to the benchmark portfolio.

Riskweighted Correlation
> IC
Actual correlation of Active Return

Correlation of weight ←

LOS 51.c: State and interpret the fundamental law of active portfolio management including its component terms—transfer coefficient, information coefficient, breadth, and active risk (aggressiveness).

CFA® Program Curriculum, Volume 6, page 483

$\frac{R_P - R_B}{\sigma(R_P - R_B)}$

There are three factors that determine the information ratio:

- The **information coefficient** (IC) is a measure of a manager's skill. IC is the *ex-ante* (i.e., expected) risk-weighted correlation between active returns and forecasted active returns. The *ex-post* information coefficient, IC_R measures *actual* correlation between active returns and expected active returns.

- The **transfer coefficient** (TC) can be thought of as the correlation between actual active weights and optimal active weights. The optimal active weight for a security is positively related to its expected active return and negatively related to its expected active risk. For an unconstrained active portfolio, the active weights will be equal to the optimal weights and TC = 1. For a constrained portfolio (e.g., constraints on short positions or active risk), TC may be less than 1.

More precisely, transfer coefficient is the cross-sectional correlation between the forecasted active returns and the actual weights adjusted for risk:

$$TC = CORR(\mu_i / \sigma_i, \Delta w_i \sigma_i) = CORR(\Delta w_i * \sigma_i, \Delta w_i \sigma_i)$$

where:
μ_i = the ex-ante active return for security i

- **Breadth** (BR) is the number of independent active bets taken per year. For example, if a manager takes active positions in 10 securities each month, then BR = 10 × 12 = 120.

The **Grinold rule** allows us to compute the expected active return based on the information coefficient, active risk, and a standardized score:

$$\mu_i = IC\sigma_i S_i$$

where:

S_i = score of security *i* (standardized with an assumed variance of 1)

The expected value added by active management is:

$$E(R_A) = \sum \Delta w_i \mu_i$$

For an unconstrained portfolio, TC = 1 and optimal values are denoted by asterisks (*):

TC =1 is

$$IR^* = IC\sqrt{BR}$$
$$E(R_A)^* = IC\sqrt{BR}\sigma_A$$

So TC ≠ 1 Normally TC < 1
→ IR = TC × IC √BR
E(R_A) = TC × IC √BR σ_A
E(R_A) = IR × σ_A

For constrained portfolios, the actual active weights (Δw_i) will differ from the optimal active weights (Δw_i^*), and the transfer coefficient will be less than 1. In this case, we have:

$$IR = (TC)IC\sqrt{BR}$$
$$E(R_A) = (TC)IC\sqrt{BR}\sigma_A$$

Because transfer coefficients are always less than one (TC<1), the information ratio must be less than the optimal information ratio (IR<IR*), and the expected active return must be less than the optimal expected active return $E(R_A)<E(R_A)^*$.

Recall that the optimal level of active risk (in an unconstrained portfolio) is a function of the information ratio, the Sharpe ratio of the benchmark, and the standard deviation of the benchmark return:

$$\sigma_A^* = \frac{IR}{SR_B}\sigma_B$$

For a constrained portfolio, the optimal level of active risk (σ_{CA}^*) is calculated as:

$$\sigma_{CA}^* = TC\frac{IR^*}{SR_B}\sigma_B$$

where:

IR* = the information ratio of an unconstrained portfolio

This implies that the optimal active risk of a constrained portfolio will be less than the optimal active risk of an unconstrained portfolio. Similarly, the Sharpe ratio of a constrained portfolio is lower than the Sharpe ratio of an unconstrained portfolio and is given by:

$$SR_{PC} = \sqrt{SR_B^2 + TC^2 \times IR^{*2}}$$

Ex-Post Performance Measurement

Realized value added from active management is the ex-post alpha that the manager achieves. Using the ex-post information coefficient IC_R, the fundamental law can be written as:

$$E(R_A | IC_R) = (TC)IC_R\sqrt{BR}\sigma_A$$

The actual return on the active portfolio can be expressed as its conditional expected return and a noise term:

$$R_A = E(R_A | IC_R) + noise$$

where $E(R_A | IC_R)$ represents the expected value added, given the realized skill of the investor that period.

The proportion of realized variance attributed to variation in the realized information coefficient is TC^2.

$\frac{R_P - R_B}{\sigma(R_P - R_N)}$

LOS 51.d: Explain how the information ratio may be useful in investment manager selection and choosing the level of active portfolio risk.

CFA® Program Curriculum, Volume 6, page 476

Portfolio theory concludes that investors will choose some combination of the risk-free asset and an optimal risky portfolio, with the weights determined by their preferences (risk tolerance). The optimal risky portfolio is the portfolio with the highest Sharpe ratio. The Sharpe ratio of an actively managed portfolio is higher than the Sharpe ratio of the benchmark based on the information ratio of the actively managed portfolio. **The portfolio with the highest information ratio will also be the portfolio with the highest Sharpe ratio,** so investors will choose the active manager with the highest information ratio; the actively managed portfolio with the highest information ratio is the optimal (active) portfolio for all investors regardless of their risk tolerance.

The information ratio can be used to determine the expected active return for a given target level of active risk:

$$E(R_A) = IR \times \sigma_A$$

LOS 51.e: Compare active management strategies (including market timing and security selection) and evaluate strategy changes in terms of the fundamental law of active management.

CFA® Program Curriculum, Volume 6, page 495

Market timing is simply a bet on the direction of the market (or a segment of the market). For example, an active manager may rotate money out of equities and into cash based on an expected decline in stock prices. For a market timer, the information coefficient is based on the proportion of correct calls:

$$IC = 2(\% \text{ correct}) - 1$$

If the manager is correct 50% the time, the IC will equal zero.

> ### Example: Market timer vs. security selector
>
> Darsh Bhansali is a manager with Optimus Capital. Bhansali, a market timer, makes quarterly asset allocation decisions based on his forecast of the direction of the market. Bhansali's forecasts are right 55% of the time.
>
> Mike Neal is an equity analyst focusing on technology stocks. Neal, a security selector, typically makes 50 active stock selections annually. Neal has an information coefficient of 0.04.
>
> Compute the information ratios of Bhansali and Neal assuming that both managers construct unconstrained portfolios.

Answer:

Because both portfolios are unconstrained, TC = 1.

Bhansali's IC = 2(0.55) − 1 = 0.10

Bhansali's IR = $IC\sqrt{BR}$ = (0.10) $\sqrt{4}$ = 0.20   ← *Number of Bets*

Neal's IR = $IC\sqrt{BR}$ = (0.04) $\sqrt{50}$ = 0.28

Sector Rotation

Market timing can also be used to make sector rotation decisions. For example, an active manager may allocate assets into sectors that are expected to outperform. Consider a two sector market made up of sectors X and Y. Assume the expected sector return and volatility of returns are $E(R_X)$ and σ_X for Sector X, and $E(R_Y)$ and σ_Y for Sector Y.

If the correlation between the returns of sectors X and Y is given by r_{XY}, the active risk of this strategy is the standard deviation of differential returns of the two sectors (i.e., R_X − R_Y) and is given by σ_C:

$$\sigma_c = \left[\sigma_X{}^2 - 2\sigma_X\sigma_Y r_{XY} + \sigma_Y{}^2\right]^{1/2}$$

The annualized active risk is a function of the number of bets made during the year. If, for example, the active manager makes quarterly bets, BR = 4:

$$\text{annualized active risk} = \sigma_A = \sigma_C \times \sqrt{BR}$$

and the annualized active return = $E(R_A) = IC \times \sqrt{BR} \times \sigma_A$

Example: Sector rotation

12 BR

Hwang Soi makes monthly allocation decisions between consumer discretionary and consumer staples based on a proprietary model. The historical correlation between the returns of the two sectors is 0.30 and Soi's bets have been correct 60% of the time. Further information is below.

Sector	E(R)	σ	Benchmark Weight
Consumer staples	10.8%	3.0%	65%
Consumer discretionary	13.2%	5.0%	35%

1. What is the annualized active risk of Soi's sector rotation strategy?

2. What is the expected annualized active return of Soi's sector rotation strategy?

3. What will be the allocation to the consumer discretionary sector if Soi feels that consumer staples will outperform the consumer discretionary sector over the next month and if the active risk is limited to 5.20%?

Answers:

SD

1. Monthly active risk = $\sigma_c = \left[\sigma_X^2 - 2\sigma_X\sigma_Y r_{XY} + \sigma_Y^2\right]^{1/2}$

    Variance

    $= [0.03^2 - 2(0.03)(0.05)(0.30) + 0.05^2]^{1/2} = 0.05$ or 5%

    Annualized active risk = $0.05 \times (12)^{1/2} = 0.1732$ or 17.32%

IR = IC√BR

IC = (2×0.6)−1

2. IC = 2(0.60) − 1 = 0.20

    Annualized active return = $IC \times \sqrt{BR} \times \sigma_A = 0.20 \times (12)^{1/2} \times 0.1732 = 0.12$ or 12%

    Alternatively, active return from this strategy using a probability weighted average (given that Soi makes correct calls 60% of time) of combined risk is:

    $(0.60)(0.05) + (0.40)(-0.05) = 0.01$ or 1% per month.

    Annual active return = 1% × 12 = 12%.

3. If active risk is limited to 5.20%, the deviation from the benchmark weights of 65% and 35% is limited to (5.20% / 17.32%) = 30%. When Soi feels that consumer staples will outperform, the allocation to that sector will be 65% + 30%, or 95%, and the allocation to consumer discretionary will be 5%.

LOS 51.f: Describe the practical strengths and limitations of the fundamental law of active management.

CFA® Program Curriculum, Volume 6, page 508

As we previously demonstrated, the fundamental law can be used to evaluate a range of active strategies, including security selection, market timing, and sector rotation. The practical limitations of the fundamental law of active management can be summarized as "garbage in, garbage out:" poor input estimates lead to incorrect evaluations. In the case of unconstrained optimization, the two components (inputs) that determine the information ratio are (1) the information coefficient (IC) and (2) the breadth (BR) of the manager's strategy.

The limitations are generally derived from inaccurate estimates of the two inputs:

- *Ex-ante measurement of skill:* The information coefficient is an estimate of the accuracy of an active manager's forecasts on an ex-ante basis. One problem with this is that managers tend to overestimate their ability to outperform the market and, hence, overestimate their IC. Regardless of the bias, the accuracy of the IC determines the accuracy of the ex-ante information ratio.
- *Independence:* The breadth of a strategy is meant to measure the number of truly independent decisions that an active manager makes. If two or more decisions rely on same (or similar) information, then they are not independent. If individual decisions are correlated, then the breadth can be estimated as:

$$BR = \frac{N}{1 + (N-1)r}$$ if it is correlated

where:

N = number of decisions

r = correlation between the decisions

Decision independence may be compromised by systemic influences within a strategy, the cross-sectional dependency. For example, a value strategy applied to different stocks within an industry may not be truly independent (most stocks will have similar fundamentals, such as P/E ratio). Similarly, decision independence can be compromised by time-series dependency. Monthly rebalancing decisions may not be truly independent from period to period.

KEY CONCEPTS

LOS 51.a

Value added = active return = active portfolio return – benchmark return

portfolio active return = Σ (active weight of security i × return of security i).

Active return is composed of two parts: asset allocation return plus security selection return:

$$E(R_A) = \sum \Delta w_i E(R_{B,i}) + \sum w_{P,i} E(R_{A,i})$$

where:

$E(R_{A,j})$ = expected active return within asset classes = $E(R_{Pi}) - E(R_{Bi})$

LOS 51.b

Sharpe ratio = $SR = \dfrac{R_P - R_F}{\sigma_P}$

Information ratio = $IR = \dfrac{R_P - R_B}{\sigma_{(R_P - R_B)}} = \dfrac{R_A}{\sigma_A} = \dfrac{\text{active return}}{\text{active risk}}$ → Tracking Error

unconstrained portfolio optimal active risk = $\sigma_A^* = \dfrac{IR}{SR_B} \sigma_B$

The Sharpe ratio of a portfolio comprised of an optimal proportion of benchmark portfolio and active portfolio is $SR_P = \sqrt{SR_B^2 + IR^2}$

LOS 51.c

The three components of the information ratio are the information coefficient (measure of manager's skill), the breadth (number of independent active bets), and the transfer coefficient (the degree of constraints on manager's active management).

$IR = (TC)IC\sqrt{BR}$

$E(R_A) = (TC)IC\sqrt{BR}\sigma_A$ → Active Risk

For an unconstrained portfolio, TC = 1.

LOS 51.d

An investor will always choose the active manager with the highest information ratio regardless of her risk aversion. The investor will combine this optimal active portfolio with the benchmark to create a portfolio with a suitable level of optimal risk based on her risk preferences.

LOS 51.e

The information coefficient of a market timer = $IC = 2(\% \text{ correct}) - 1$

The fundamental law can also be used to evaluate active sector rotation strategies.

LOS 51.f

While the fundamental law can be used for evaluating market timing, security selection, and sector rotation strategies, one has to be aware of its practical limitations. The limitations of the fundamental law include bias in measurement of the ex-ante information coefficient and lack of true independence while measuring breadth of an active strategy.

independent

CONCEPT CHECKERS

1. When measuring value added by active management, it is *most accurate* to state that the active weights in an actively managed portfolio:
    A. must add to 100%.
    B. are the differences between an individual asset's weight in the actively managed portfolio versus the corresponding weight in an equally-weighted portfolio.
    C. must be positively correlated with realized asset returns for value added to be positive.

2. Which of the following statements regarding the ex-post and ex-ante information ratio and Sharpe ratio is *most accurate*?
    A. The Sharpe ratio measures reward per unit of risk in benchmark relative returns.
    B. The information ratio measures reward per unit of absolute risk.
    C. The information ratio can be applied either ex ante to expected returns or ex post to realized returns.

3. Investors that are constrained by regulation or investment policy may find that some of the important variables identified by the fundamental law of active portfolio management are out of their control. The element that is *most likely* to still be within the investor's control is the:
    A. information coefficient.
    B. transfer coefficient.
    C. benchmark tracking risk.

4. The information ratio is *least appropriate* as a criterion for:
    A. quantifying an actively managed portfolio's return in excess of the risk-free rate.
    B. constructing an actively managed portfolio.
    C. evaluating the past performance of actively managed portfolios.

5. Breadth is *most likely* to be equal to the number of securities multiplied by the number of decision periods per year if active returns are correlated:
    A. cross-sectionally.
    B. over time.
    C. with active weights.

6. Which of the following factors *least accurately* identifies one of the major limitations of the fundamental law of active management?
    A. Ex ante measurement of skill using the information coefficient.
    B. Assumption of independence in forecasts across assets and over time.
    C. Attribution of value added to a small number of inputs.

To access other content related to this topic review that may be included in the Schweser package you purchased, log in to your Schweser.com online dashboard. Schweser's OnDemand Video Lectures deliver streaming instruction covering every LOS in this topic review, while SchweserPro™ QBank provides additional quiz questions to help you practice and recall what you've learned.

ANSWERS – CONCEPT CHECKERS

1. **C** Value added will be positive only when end-of-period realized asset returns are positively correlated with the asset weights that the manager selected at the beginning of the period. Active weights are defined as the differences between an asset's weight in a managed portfolio versus its weight in the benchmark portfolio. Active weights in a portfolio must add up to zero, not 100%.

2. **C** The information ratio can be applied either ex ante to expected returns or ex post to realized returns. The Sharpe ratio measures reward per unit of absolute (or total) risk. The information ratio measures reward per unit of risk in benchmark relative terms.

3. **A** The information coefficient represents an active manager's own skill and ability to forecast returns accurately. The other three of the four elements of the fundamental law of active portfolio management (transfer coefficient, breadth of the strategy, and benchmark tracking risk) may be beyond investors' control if they are constrained by investment policy or regulation.

4. **A** The information ratio evaluates risk-adjusted return in relation to a benchmark-investment baseline, rather than in relation to a risk-free investment. Expected information ratio is the single best criterion for building an actively managed portfolio. The ex-post information ratio is the best criterion for evaluating the past performance of actively managed funds.

5. **C** Breadth (BR) is intended to measure the number of independent decisions that an investor makes each year. Breadth is equal to the number of securities multiplied by the number of decision periods per year only if (1) active returns are cross-sectionally uncorrelated and (2) active returns are uncorrelated over time.

6. **C** The fundamental law of active management's usefulness stems from its ability to separate the expected value added of a portfolio into the contributions of the few basic elements of the strategy. Limitations of the fundamental law of active management concern uncertainty about the ex-ante information coefficient, as well as the definition of breadth as the number of independent decisions.

The following is a review of the Portfolio Management principles designed to address the learning outcome statements set forth by CFA Institute. Cross-Reference to CFA Institute Assigned Reading #52.

ALGORITHMIC TRADING AND HIGH-FREQUENCY TRADING

EXAM FOCUS

After completing this reading, you should understand what algorithmic trading is and how it is defined. Be able to describe the different types of execution algorithms and high-frequency trading algorithms. You will want to be able to describe market fragmentation and its effects on how trades are placed. Also, be able to describe the use of technology in risk management and regulatory oversight. Finally, be sure that you are familiar with the issues and concerns related to the impact of algorithmic and high-frequency trading on securities markets.

LOS 52.a: Define algorithmic trading.

CFA® Program Curriculum, Volume 6, page 530

ALGORITHMIC TRADING

An algorithm is a set of rules or a process followed by a computer to reach an end result. **Algorithmic trading** thus is a trading strategy that has been automated through the use of a computer.

While computers and trading algorithms make decisions and execute trades thousands of times *faster* than a human trader could, an algorithm generally makes the same *kinds* of decisions that a human trader would make.

LOS 52.b: Distinguish between execution algorithms and high-frequency trading algorithms.

CFA® Program Curriculum, Volume 6, page 530

Trading algorithms can be broken down into the following two primary categories.

EXECUTION ALGORITHMS

The objective of an **execution algorithm** is to execute large orders with minimal price impact (and without other market participants taking notice). These algorithms are especially important for large buy orders. Execution algorithms generally slice a large order into smaller pieces and execute them in a way that minimizes price impact.

HIGH-FREQUENCY TRADING ALGORITHMS

High-frequency trading algorithms are used to analyze real-time market data in search of patterns that can be profitably traded. (The "high frequency" in high-frequency trading refers to the frequency with which data gets updated.) These algorithms identify and execute trades in milliseconds. Usually the securities are held only for a short time (generally less than a day and sometimes less than a second).

LOS 52.c: Describe types of execution algorithms and high-frequency trading algorithms.

CFA® Program Curriculum, Volume 6, page 530

TYPES OF EXECUTION ALGORITHMS

Execution algorithms take a large order and break it down into smaller orders.

There are several types of execution algorithms, including:

- **Volume-Weighted Average Price (VWAP) Algorithms**—VWAP algorithms consider a security's historical trading patterns over a typical day and split a large order into pieces sized proportionally to this historical distribution so that larger pieces get executed during times of the day when market depth is greater.
- **Implementation Shortfall Algorithms**—These algorithms attempt to strike a balance between minimizing the potential market drift that may happen if an order takes a long time to execute (i.e., minimize the opportunity cost of unfilled orders) and minimizing the negative price impact that will result when an order is executed too quickly. In this way, implementation shortfall algorithms attempt to reduce the difference between the price at which the order actually executes and the price at which the decision was made to buy or sell the security.

  execution Price and analysed price

- **Market Participation Algorithms**—These algorithms cut a large order into slices that vary in size proportionally with actual trading volume.

TYPES OF HIGH-FREQUENCY TRADING ALGORITHMS

One major class of high-frequency trading algorithms is **statistical arbitrage** (or "stat arb") algorithms. Statistical arbitrage algorithms are used to identify securities that have historically moved together but have diverged recently. The algorithm will buy one security and sell the other so as to realize a profit when they eventually converge.

Types of statistical arbitrage algorithms include:

- **Pairs trading**—When the prices of two securities diverge from their historically correlated movements, the outperforming security is shorted while the underperforming security is purchased. If the relative prices of these securities later converge, a profit will be earned.
- **Index arbitrage**—These algorithms seek out temporary differences in price performance between securities and the sector to which they belong. For example, the price of McDonald's Corporation stock should be correlated with the price of a restaurant sector index.

- **Basket trading**—Basket trading is applying statistical arbitrage strategies to groups of securities, rather than to individual securities. Instead of trading one individual security against another as in pairs trading, we trade one basket of securities versus another basket.

- **Spread trading**—Spread trading is a type of statistical arbitrage that takes long and short positions in two closely-related futures contracts, on the notion that the spread between the two will change. Traders use tools called **spreaders** to manage these trades.

  Types of spread trades include:

  - **Intra-market spread**: A long position in one contract month and a short position in the same futures contract in another contract month. For example, purchasing near futures and selling later futures on the same exchange for the same commodity.
  - **Inter-market spread**: Purchasing a futures contract in one market and selling futures on the same commodity and delivery month in a different market.
  - **Inter-exchange spread**: Buying a commodity future on one exchange and selling a similar commodity future on a different exchange.
  - **Multilegged inter-exchange spreads:**
    - **Crack spread**—crude oil vs. petroleum products.
    - **Spark spread**—price of electricity from a gas-fired power plant vs. fuel prices.
    - **Crush spread**—soybean futures vs. soybean oil futures and soybean meal futures.

- **Mean reversion**—These algorithms are based on the idea that when the price of a security drifts away from its recent historical mean, its price will likely move back towards that mean.

- **Delta neutral strategies**—These arbitrage strategies are designed to produce a small profit regardless of whether the market goes up or down. By combining securities such as stocks and options in such a way that the total delta of all of the securities is zero, the strategy may be able to earn a profit from volatility changes or simply as the options approach maturity.

Apart from stat arbitrage, other broad uses of high-frequency algorithms include:

- **Liquidity aggregation and smart order routing**. The trading of securities has become more dispersed as the number of venues in which an individual security might be traded has proliferated. This phenomenon, known as **market fragmentation**, can lead to price differences across markets and a lack of liquidity within an individual market. By using a **liquidity aggregation** algorithm, a trader can gain a fuller picture of liquidity over multiple trading venues. These algorithms direct each order to the market that offers the best price and liquidity. We will discuss this algorithm in more detail in the next section.

- **Real-time pricing of securities**. Traditional techniques to value securities, such as fundamental analysis, can be slow, and the results may not correspond with market values. An alternative to such methods is to use algorithmic trading to price such instruments in real time by deriving instantaneous price and liquidity information from the market. Real-time pricing information can, for example, help a dealer adjust the width of their bid-ask spread to reflect what the market will bear.

- **Trading on news.** Securities traders have always made trades based on their reaction to breaking news stories such as unusual weather reports or the release of economic data. More recently, traders have attempted to create high-frequency algorithms that execute the same types of trades, but near-instantaneously and without human intervention. These efforts have been boosted by the increasing availability of high-frequency news feeds, including feeds that contain tags that identify key statistics.

- **Genetic tuning.** Genetic tuning refers to a self-evolving ("Darwinian trading") system that tests the performance of many different strategies by feeding live market data to each. Seemingly profitable strategies are deployed in the markets while money-losers are killed off. Strategies that earn profits are allowed to continue to evolve and pursue emerging opportunities. (The holy grail of algorithmic trading is a "money machine" that will evolve and profit without human oversight.)

LOS 52.d: Describe market fragmentation and its effects on how trades are placed.

CFA® Program Curriculum, Volume 6, page 533

MARKET FRAGMENTATION

Market fragmentation refers to when the same security is traded in multiple financial markets. For example, Hewlett-Packard stock trades simultaneously on the NASDAQ, the New York Stock Exchange, and several alternative trading systems. The downside of market fragmentation is the potential for price and liquidity differences across markets. Furthermore, the liquidity of a security in any individual market may represent only a fraction of that security's total liquidity across all markets.

Some of the drawbacks of market fragmentation can be addressed by using algorithmic methods, including smart order routing and liquidity aggregation. These methods can help traders to execute large trades effectively despite fragmented markets.

Liquidity aggregators make use of a concept called a "super book," which adds up the liquidity available for an individual instrument across multiple markets. **Smart order routing** is then used to direct orders to the market with the best combination of liquidity and price.

In order for these algorithmic methods to be effective in addressing market fragmentation, liquidity information needs to be current. To achieve this, timely updates and low latency are necessary. Latency refers to the time lag between market data being released (or generated) and a corresponding trade being placed: traders seek out the shortest possible end-to-end latency times.

LOS 52.e: Describe the use of technology in risk management and regulatory oversight.

CFA® Program Curriculum, Volume 6, page 538

While algorithmic trading has, in some cases, created new challenges in terms of risk management and regulatory oversight, the same kinds of tools (alerts, data analysis tools, and graphical dashboards) have also been useful in addressing these challenges.

THE USE OF TECHNOLOGY IN RISK MANAGEMENT

High-frequency trading has revolutionized the securities markets and has allowed trading at volumes and speeds unimaginable before. High-frequency trading can also increase trading risk dramatically.

Two methods of using algorithmic techniques to mitigate trading risk are as follows:

1. **Real-time pre-trade risk firewall.** One method of ensuring that existing risk limits are not exceeded is to continuously calculate risk exposures on the trading positions being taken, and block those trades that would exceed the limits. Furthermore, the tools can be used to block erroneous trades (such as placing an order at an irrational quantity or price, e.g., "**fat finger**" trades). These automated monitoring tools can also help protect brokers that offer clients "sponsored access" to the broker's exchange membership.

2. **Back testing and market simulation.** Another method of using algorithmic techniques to mitigate trading risk is to test algorithms to see how they perform under various offline scenarios. Market simulators are used, along with either historical data or some invented scenarios.

The stock market crash of 2008–2009 and the resulting increase in regulatory scrutiny helped to convince traders that pre-trade risk management was worth the potential increased in latency.

THE USE OF TECHNOLOGY IN REGULATORY OVERSIGHT

Regulatory Oversight: Real-Time Market Monitoring and Surveillance

Global financial regulators have realized that real-time market monitoring and surveillance may allow those regulators to detect and respond to market issues more quickly and effectively. By using the same tools that are used in high-frequency trading, regulators have a better chance to police high-frequency markets.

Real-time market monitoring and surveillance refers to the practice of scrutinizing markets continuously in order to identify abnormal movements. Unusual and dramatic changes in volume or price for a security can provide advanced warning of issues in the markets.

Examples of suspicious trading that such regulators are on the lookout for include:

- **Insider trading.** When a trader makes a large transaction in a security that they do not trade regularly and the trade turns out to be profitable due to news that breaks later, the trader may come under suspicion of insider trading. If this pattern repeats, it is likely to attract the attention of regulators, who may investigate whether the trader was behaving improperly or simply lucky.
- **Front running.** Somewhat similar to insider trading, **front running** is when a trader has advance knowledge of a large buy order and trades slightly earlier than that large order to profit from the price movement that the large transaction will cause. Algorithms can be used to detect such a situation where a trader has made a transaction just before another market participant's large trade.
- **"Painting the tape".** In this scenario, a trader who wishes to sell a large quantity of a security first buys small quantities of the same security in order to drive up the market price. A trader often needs to purchase only a small strategic quantity of shares in order to move the market price significantly.
- **Fictitious orders.** Traders submit fictitious orders to move the market price or to induce other algorithms to make unwise trades.
  - **Quote stuffing:** The algorithm injects a larger number of orders into the market and then almost immediately cancels them. These bogus orders distract other market participants, giving the originating algorithm an opportunity to trade ahead of others or take advantage of mispricing that the false orders cause.
  - **Layering:** In this strategy, the algorithm places genuine orders on one side of the market but also places layers of fake orders on the other side of the market. The purpose of the false orders is to induce market participants to transact with the genuine orders.
  - **Spoofing:** In spoofing, the algorithm places orders between the bid and ask price with the intention of canceling these trades before they execute. These fake orders are intended to create false pessimism or optimism about the security and move the market price in advance of the trader placing a bona fide order.
- **Wash trading.** The algorithm buys and sells the same securities repeatedly, in order to create false trading volume and increase buyer interest in a security that the trader wishes to sell.
- **Trader collusion.** In this category of manipulation, multiple traders conspire to sway markets in a direction that is favorable to them. One relatively recent example of collusion was the Libor scandal of 2012, where it was alleged that traders manipulated interest rates in order to turn their derivatives trades profitable. In response to such scandals, communications between traders have received greater scrutiny.

Similar to the monitoring and surveillance activities by regulators, many exchanges use the same tools to detect abuses or problems on their own trading venue. Brokers that wish to take steps to protect their reputation may also monitor their clients' activities.

LOS 52.f: Describe issues and concerns related to the impact of algorithmic and high-frequency trading on securities markets.

CFA® Program Curriculum, Volume 6, page 541

While news stories in the popular press have focused on the potential negative aspects of algorithmic and high-frequency trading, a closer examination shows both negative and positive effects of this technology on the markets.

POSITIVE IMPACTS OF ALGORITHMIC AND HIGH-FREQUENCY TRADING

Some of the positive impacts include:

- **Facilitates large trades.** Without algorithmic trading, large orders will move markets and execute at a disadvantageous price. Algorithmic trading allows a market participant to divide an order into small pieces that, when executed over time, will have minimal impact on execution price. These algorithms have resulted in a *simultaneous* increase in the number of trade orders globally, and a decrease in the size of the average order.

    [handwritten: higher volume, less order sized]

- **Increased liquidity.** When challenged to defend the actions of their firms, executives from high-frequency trading firms often point out that they are contributing liquidity to other market participants via the firms' willingness to buy and sell securities.

- **Lower costs.** Using well-paid human traders to execute trades can be expensive. Trading using algorithms can minimize manual labor and help to lower transaction costs.

- **Tighter bid–ask spreads.** High-frequency traders that act as market makers demand only a fraction of a cent per share profit to transact with other market participants. The actions of such high-frequency traders help to reduce the gap (margin) between bid prices and ask prices.

- **Improved pricing efficiency.** Prices are said to be efficient when they reflect all available information and there are no trading strategies that produce positive excess returns. Trading algorithms act to increase pricing efficiency by quickly identifying and eliminating any opportunities for statistical arbitrage.

- **Promotes open and competitive markets.** Despite public perception that the largest firms rule trading in the financial markets, the proliferation of technology for analyzing and trading on high-frequency market data has helped small players to compete on a relatively even footing.

- **Increased competition between trading venues.** Securities exchanges have felt pressure from their customers to improve trading technology offerings. In response to these demands, these venues have raced to provide greater order throughput, lower matching latency, and other services such as **co-location** (whereby traders are permitted to bring their own hardware inside the trading venue).

CONCERNS REGARDING THE IMPACTS OF ALGORITHMIC AND HIGH-FREQUENCY TRADING

Among the general public and politicians, there is a general belief that high-frequency trading and algorithmic trading have a negative impact on the markets. Specific concerns include:

- **Unfair speed advantages.** High-frequency traders attempt to locate themselves as physically close as possible to trading venues in order to gain microseconds of head start over other market participants. This allows traders to learn of market movements before other traders, and may even provide the opportunity to "front run" the orders of other market participants.

- **Magnification of market movements.** It is generally believed that the 2010 Flash Crash was sparked by a large mutual fund selling $4.1 billion worth of S&P 500 futures contracts. Trading algorithms, however, likely did much to amplify and intensify the plunge. Trading algorithms use only the logic programmed into them (e.g., to short falling securities), and will continue to execute these instructions in a situation that might otherwise give a human trader pause.

- **Market manipulation.** High-frequency trading tools can be used in abusive ways to game the market and disadvantage other market participants. Examples of market manipulation include spoofing, quote stuffing, wash trades, painting the tape, et cetera.

- **Risk of trading errors.** The speed of algorithmic trading can be a double-edged sword: while a computer can place thousands of trade orders in the time that a human trader could place only one, the results can be disastrous if those trades are not exactly what was intended. Without effective safeguards in place, a simple "**fat finger** error" can quickly cause havoc and huge losses.

- **Out-of-control algorithms.** If a trading algorithm has been tested inadequately, or if it encounters a scenario that it was not programmed to contend with, the algorithm may "go wild" and place illogical orders that could result in a large loss for the firm. One recent example of such an "algorithm gone wild" is the Knight Capital incident of 2012, where a defective algorithm bought and sold millions of shares in the first 45 minutes of the trading day. Unwinding these trades cost Knight $440 million in losses.

- **Denial-of-service.** In a few recent instances, trading algorithms directed thousands of orders into a market in a short time, either because the algorithm had gone out of control, or because a trader was trying to manipulate the market (e.g., "quote stuffing"). In face of such a deluge, a market may be unable to deal with all of the incoming orders, and will struggle to separate legitimate orders from bogus orders. This result is similar to a "denial-of-service" attack in computing, where a network becomes unavailable due to a flood of false data.

- **Slowed markets due to excessive orders.** The transition from human trading to algorithmic trading has resulted in an exponential increase in the total number of orders placed. Orders originating from high-frequency algorithms are often placed, modified, and canceled rapidly, even when the market moves only slightly. This volume of orders has the potential to slow down trading venues to the point where some exchanges have considered charging for canceled orders to try to keep loads under control.

- **Increased difficulty of policing the market.** Market regulators have struggled to "keep up" with advances in trading technology. In addition to the rapid increase in the use of trading algorithms, regulators have struggled to deal with the proliferation of trading venues, including "dark pools." **Dark pools** are non-public trading venues, where trades are confidential and not visible to the public.

- **Unequal access to information.** Articles in the mainstream press often focus on the way that high-frequency trading provides larger trading firms an advantage over smaller firms. Indeed, while high-frequency trading techniques are theoretically accessible to all market participants, these programs are expensive to develop and implement. Thus, smaller investors and individuals may have a disadvantage in terms of unequal access to information.

Despite the negative press, a broader analysis suggests that the advent of high-frequency trading has brought constructive changes to markets overall.

KEY CONCEPTS

LOS 52.a

An algorithm refers to a set of steps used to reach some result.

Algorithmic trading means automating a trading strategy by using a computer.

Algorithmic trading generally replicates the decisions a human trader would make and the orders they would place, but at speeds thousands of times faster.

LOS 52.b

There are two broad categories of trading algorithms:

- **Execution algorithms.** Institutions that need to place large orders will use execution algorithms to break an order down into smaller pieces. These smaller orders are then placed strategically over time in order to minimize negative price impact.
- **High-frequency algorithms.** These are rules for trading on real-time market data that a computer uses to pursue profit opportunities. "High frequency" refers to the rapidly-updated information sources that these algorithms rely on, such as market data feeds and news feeds.

LOS 52.c

Types of execution algorithms include:

- Volume-weighted average price ("VWAP") algorithms—Split an order into pieces sized proportionally to the security's historical trading pattern over a day.
- Implementation shortfall algorithms—Continually adjusts the speed at which a trade executes as market conditions change in an attempt to minimize the difference between the decision price and the final execution price.
- Market participation algorithms—A large order is sliced into smaller pieces that are then entered in the market at a pace that matches the pace of overall trading of the security.

Types of high-frequency trading algorithms include:

- Statistical arbitrage algorithms—Used to trade securities that have historically have moved together. Types include (1) pairs trading, (2) index arbitrage, (3) basket trading, (4) spread trading, (5) mean reversion, and (6) delta-neutral strategies.
- Liquidity aggregation and smart order routing—Deal with market fragmentation by sending each order to the market with the best combination of price and liquidity ("smart order routing"), or by spreading the order over several trading venues ("liquidity aggregation").
- Real-time pricing of instruments—Uses algorithmic trading tools to derive instantaneous price and liquidity information from the market itself.
- Trading on news—Algorithms that react (in fractions of a second, and without human intervention) to breaking news stories and new economic data.
- Genetic tuning—A self-evolving ("Darwinian trading") system that tests many different strategies, implements profitable strategies in the markets, and kills off money-losers.

LOS 52.d

Market fragmentation refers to the situation where a single financial instrument is traded in multiple venues, such as a stock trading on both the NASDAQ and the NYSE. The result is the liquidity of a security in any individual market may represent only a fraction of that security's total liquidity across all markets.

"Liquidity aggregators" use a "super book" to add up liquidity for a security across multiple markets.

"Smart order routing" is used to direct orders to the market with the best combination of liquidity and price.

LOS 52.e

Two methods of using algorithmic techniques to mitigate trading risk are as follows:
- Real-time-trade risk firewalls. Constantly calculate risk exposures on the trades to ensure that risk limits are not exceeded. Trades that would exceed limits are blocked.
- Back testing and market simulation. Testing algorithms to see how they perform under various offline scenarios or historical data.

Regulatory oversight of financial markets can be provided by real-time market monitoring and surveillance to identify unusual changes in volume or price. Kinds of suspicious trading that such regulators might be looking for include (1) insider trading, (2) "front running," (3) "painting the tape," (4) fictitious orders (e.g. quote stuffing, layering, or spoofing), (5) wash trading, and (6) trader collusion.

LOS 52.f

Algorithmic and high-frequency trading has been found to have a mostly-positive impact on securities markets.

Positive impacts include smaller bid-ask spreads, lower costs, greater liquidity, and superior pricing efficiency.

Concerns about algorithmic and high-frequency trading include: the possibility of amplifying market movements, the prospect of an "algorithm gone wild," the possibility of market manipulation using algorithmic tools, increased difficulty of regulatory oversight, and the potential for smaller market participants to be disadvantaged in terms of access to information.

Zuhir Al Sadi, CFA

19:26
25/04/2018

Beauderc Advisory Services
LONDON

CONCEPT CHECKERS

1.   Algorithmic trading:
     A. is used to execute strategies that are too sophisticated for a human trader to understand.
     B. operates entirely autonomously of any human intervention.
     C. means automating a trading strategy by using a computer.

2.   An algorithm that minimizes the market impact of a large order by breaking the order down into smaller pieces is *best* described as a(n):
     A. execution algorithm.
     B. high-frequency trading algorithm.
     C. fragmentation algorithm.

3.   An algorithm that continuously analyses real-time market data in search of patterns that can be traded profitably is *most accurately* described as a(n):
     A. execution algorithm.
     B. scouring algorithm.
     C. high-frequency trading algorithm.

4.   An execution algorithm that automatically adjusts the pace of the trade in reaction to market conditions to minimize the difference between the decision price and the final execution price is *best* described as a(n):
     A. volume-weighted average price (VWAP) algorithm.
     B. implementation shortfall algorithm.
     C. market participation algorithm.

5.   Algorithms are *least likely* to adapt to market fragmentation by incorporating:
     A. liquidity aggregation capabilities.
     B. intelligent smart order routing capabilities.
     C. market quantity reconstruction capabilities.

6.   An investor that repeatedly buys and sells the same security in an attempt to boost perceived trading volume for a security that the investor is trying to sell is *most likely* engaging in:
     A. front running.
     B. painting the tape.
     C. wash trading.

7.   Which of the following is *least likely* to represent a concern related to the impact of algorithmic and high-frequency trading on securities markets?
     A. Increased complexity of regulatory oversight.
     B. The impact of unequal access to information.
     C. Widening bid–ask spreads.

To access other content related to this topic review that may be included in the Schweser package you purchased, log in to your Schweser.com online dashboard. Schweser's OnDemand Video Lectures deliver streaming instruction covering every LOS in this topic review, while SchweserPro™ QBank provides additional quiz questions to help you practice and recall what you've learned.

ANSWERS – CONCEPT CHECKERS

1. **C** Algorithmic trading simply refers to using a computer to automate trading strategies. Generally, trading algorithms analyze the same information and make the same decisions as a human trader, but in a much shorter period of time. Some trading algorithms operate almost completely autonomously of a human; however, others trade on behalf of a trader.

2. **A** Execution algorithms break down large orders into several smaller orders in order to lessen the market impact. High-frequency trading algorithms continuously monitor market data in search of patterns that can be traded profitably.

3. **C** High-frequency trading algorithms continuously monitor market data in search of profitable trade opportunities. Execution algorithms break down large orders into several smaller orders in order to lessen the market impact of the order.

4. **B** Implementation shortfall algorithms dynamically adjust the trade schedule in reaction to market conditions in order to minimize the difference between the decision price and the final execution price. An implementation shortfall algorithm attempts to balance the negative impact of executing an order too quickly against the market drift that will occur when an order takes too long to execute. VWAP algorithms divide an order into slices proportional to historical daily trading volume. Market participation algorithms cut an order into slices that are used throughout the execution period to participate with volume on a pro rata basis.

5. **C** Market fragmentation refers to a situation where the same financial security is traded in multiple markets. Algorithms can mitigate the problem of market fragmentation through the use of intelligent smart order routing capabilities, and by liquidity aggregation capabilities. Liquidity aggregation means compiling a comprehensive record of a security's availability in the various global markets in which it trades. Smart order routing means dynamically sending each order to a market based on price and quantity.

6. **C** Wash trading refers to an individual or firm repeatedly buying and selling the same security to make it appear that that there is more trading volume in that security than there actually is. Front running is when a trader learns of a large order that a firm is planning to place, and the trader trades ahead of the firm in order to benefit from the market movement that the large trade causes. "Painting the tape" is when a trader makes small trades in one direction to move the market price, and then a larger trade in the other direction in order to benefit from the altered price.

7. **C** Research has shown that high-frequency trading has resulted in tighter (rather than wider) bid–ask spreads. In fact, algorithmic trading has been found to have had a positive impact on markets overall. Other benefits attributed to high-frequency trading are increased liquidity, lower transaction costs, and more efficient pricing. Two of the major concerns that have been raised regarding high-frequency trading are increased difficulty of implementing regulatory oversight and the potential impact of unequal access to information. Other possible downsides of high-frequency trading include algorithms' potential for magnifying market swings, the possibility of algorithms going out-of-control, and the ability of traders to manipulate markets through fictitious orders.

You have now finished the Portfolio Management topic section. The following self-test will provide immediate feedback on how effective your study of this material has been. The test is best taken timed; allow 3 minutes per subquestion (18 minutes per item set). This self-test is more exam-like than typical Concept Checkers or QBank questions. A score less than 70% suggests that additional review of this topic is needed.

Use the following information to answer Questions 1 through 6.

Faster Analytics Capital Management makes portfolio recommendations using various factor models. Bill Adams, chief economist at Faster Analytics, is responsible for providing macroeconomic and capital market forecasts. Mauricio Rodriguez, a Faster Analytics research analyst, is examining the prospects of several portfolios: the FACM Century Fund (CF), the FACM Esquire Fund (EF), the FACM Zeta Fund (ZF), and the FACM Delta Benchmark (DB).

Figure 1: Selected Data for CF, ZF and Their Benchmark

Information ratio (CF)	0.12
Information ratio (ZF)	0.25
Benchmark Sharpe ratio	0.30
Benchmark total risk(s)	20%

Rodriguez's supervisor, Barbara Woodson, asks Rodriguez to use the capital asset pricing model (CAPM) and a multifactor model (APT) to make a decision about whether to continue or terminate the Esquire Fund. The two factors in the multifactor model are not identified. To help with the decision, Adams provides Rodriguez with the capital market forecasts shown in Figure 2: Capital Market Forecasts.

Figure 2: Capital Market Forecasts

Risk-free rate	4%
Market portfolio risk premium	8%
APT factor 1 risk premium	5%
APT factor 2 risk premium	2%
Inflation rate	3%

After examining the prospects for the EF portfolio, Rodriguez derives the forecasts in Figure 3: EF Data.

Figure 3: EF Data

Expected Return	12%
CAPM beta	0.80
APT factor 1 risk sensitivity	1.50
APT factor 2 risk sensitivity	2.00

Rodriguez also develops a 2-factor macroeconomic factor model for the EF portfolio. The two factors used in the model are the surprise in GDP growth and the surprise in investor sentiment. The equation for the macro factor model is:

$$R_{EF} = a_{EF} + b_{EF,1}F_{GDP} + b_{EF,2}F_{IS} + \varepsilon_{EF}$$

During an investment committee meeting, Woodson makes the following statements related to the 2-factor macroeconomic factor model:

Statement 1: An investment allocated between CF and EF that provides a GDP growth factor beta equal to one and an investor sentiment factor beta equal to zero will have lower active factor risk than a tracking portfolio consisting of CF and EF.

Statement 2: When markets are in equilibrium, no combination of CF and EF will produce an arbitrage opportunity.

Rodriguez says to Woodson that for a long-term, default-risk-free bond, if the covariance between the bond's price and investors' inter-temporal rate of substitution is positive, the bond will trade at a lower price than it otherwise would, and that covariance will capture the risk premium on the bond.

In their final meeting, Rodriguez informs Woodson that the DB portfolio consistently outperformed its benchmark over the past five years. "The consistency with which DB outperformed its benchmark is amazing. The difference between the DB monthly return and its benchmark's return was nearly always positive and varied little over time," says Rodriguez.

1. The highest possible Sharpe ratio for a portfolio consisting of a combination of the CF fund and the benchmark is *closest* to:
    A. 0.32.
    B. 0.35.
    C. 0.38.

2. For an investor in the ZF, the optimal level of active risk, and the corresponding total excess return (over risk-free rate), are respectively *closest* to:

Optimal active risk	Total excess return
A. 12.0%	9.2%.
B. 16.7%	10.2%.
C. 18.6%	11.9%.

3. Considering the data provided in Figure 2: Capital Market Forecasts and Figure 3: EF Data, should Rodriguez recommend that Faster Analytics continue to invest in the EF fund using an analysis based on the CAPM or 2-factor APT?

CAPM?	2-factor APT?
A. Yes	Yes
B. Yes	No
C. No	Yes

4.   Rodriguez's statement regarding default risk-free bonds is *most likely*:
     A. correct.
     B. incorrect about the existence of a risk premium on a default-risk-free bond.
     C. incorrect about the covariance being positive.

5.   Are Woodson's statements 1 and 2 regarding the macro factor model correct?
     A. Both statements are correct.
     B. Only statement 1 is correct.
     C. Only statement 2 is correct.

6.   The historical performance of the DB portfolio is *best* summarized as:

     A. high active risk.
     B. high tracking risk.
     C. high information ratio.

1. **A** The optimal combination of the CF and the benchmark portfolio will result in highest possible Sharpe ratio.

   The Sharpe ratio for the optimal portfolio consisting of the benchmark and the CF can be calculated using the following equality: $SR_P^2 = SR_B^2 + IR^2$.

   $$SR_P = \sqrt{SR_B^2 + IR_{CD}^2}$$
   $$= \sqrt{0.30^2 + 0.12^2}$$
   $$= 0.3231$$

2. **B** Optimal active risk $= \sigma_{ZF}^* = \left(\dfrac{IR_{ZF}}{SR_B}\right)\sigma_B = \left(\dfrac{0.25}{0.30}\right)0.20 = 0.1667 = 16.67\%$

   Expected excess return for ZF (active return):
   $E(R_A) = IR \times \sigma_A = (0.25) \times (0.1667) = 4.17\%$

   Benchmark excess return = $(0.30) \times (0.20) = 6\%$

   Total excess return = $4.17\% + 6\% = 10.17\%$

3. **B** The equations for required rate of return using the CAPM and a 2-factor APT are respectively:

   CAPM: $R_{EF} = RF + \beta_{EF}[E(R_M) - RF]$

   2-factor APT: $R_{EF} = RF + \beta_{EF,1}(\lambda_1) + \beta_{EF,2}(\lambda_2)$

   Using the data provided in Figures 2 and 3:
   CAPM required rate of return = $0.04 + 0.80(0.08) = 0.104 = 10.4\%$
   2-factor APT required rate of return = $0.04 + 1.5(0.05) + 2(0.02) = 0.155 = 15.5\%$

   The expected return for the EF is 12%, which exceeds the CAPM required return. Therefore, Rodriguez predicts that the EF portfolio return will exceed its CAPM required return; a signal to continue investing in EF. However, the forecasted EF return of 12% is less than the 2-factor APT model required return of 15.5%; this is a signal to not invest in EF.

4. **C** The covariance between the uncertain future price of a default-risk-free bond and the investor's intertemporal rate of substitution is negative, resulting in a positive risk premium for a longer-term, default-risk-free bond.

5. **C** A portfolio that has a factor beta equal to one for one factor and factor betas equal to zero for all other factors is called a factor portfolio. In contrast, a portfolio that has factor betas equal to the benchmark factor betas is called a tracking portfolio. Unlike the tracking portfolio, the factor portfolio betas are not identical to the benchmark betas. As a result, factor portfolios have higher active factor risk (which refers to the deviations of a portfolio's factor betas from those of the benchmark). Therefore, Woodson's first statement is not correct.

   Her second statement is correct. When markets are in equilibrium, all expected (i.e., forecast) asset returns are equal to their required returns. An arbitrage opportunity refers to an investment that requires no cost and no risk yet still provides a profit. If markets are in equilibrium, no profits can be earned from a costless, riskless investment.

6. **C** The information ratio equals active return divided by active risk. Active return equals the average difference between the CF portfolio return and the benchmark return. Active risk equals the standard deviation of the CF return minus benchmark return. From the comments made by Rodriquez about the historical performance of the CF portfolio, we know that the numerator of the information ratio is positive and that the denominator is very close to zero. Therefore, the information ratio will be high.

The fund standard deviation is very close to that of its benchmark (since its returns were nearly always a constant percentage above the benchmark). The CF rose and fell with the benchmark (same risk as the benchmark) but always beat the benchmark (outperformed the benchmark). Therefore, tracking risk (which is also referred to as active risk) is low.

Formulas

Study Session 15: Alternative Investments

net operating income:

rental income if fully occupied
<u>+ other income</u>
= potential gross income
<u>− vacancy and collection loss</u>
= effective gross income
<u>− operating expense</u>
= net operating income

capitalization rate:

cap rate = discount rate − growth rate

$$\text{cap rate} = \frac{NOI_1}{\text{value}} \quad \text{or} \quad \text{cap rate} = \frac{NOI_1}{\text{comparable sales price}}$$

value of a property using direct capitalization:

$$\text{value} = V_0 = \frac{NOI_1}{\text{cap rate}} \quad \text{or} \quad \text{value} = V_0 = \frac{\text{stabilized NOI}}{\text{cap rate}}$$

value of a property based on net rent and "all risks yield": $\text{value} = V_0 = \dfrac{\text{rent}_1}{\text{ARY}}$

value of a property using gross income multiplier:

$$\text{gross income multiplier} = \frac{\text{sales price}}{\text{gross income}}$$

value = gross income × gross income multiplier

term and reversion property valuation approach:

total value = PV of term rent + PV reversion to ERV

layer approach:

total value = PV of term rent + PV of incremental rent

NCREIF Property Index (NPI) calculation:

$$\text{return} = \frac{\text{NOI} - \text{capital expenditures} + \left(\text{end market value} - \text{beg market value}\right)}{\text{beginning market value}}$$

debt service coverage ratio (DSCR): $\text{DSCR} = \dfrac{\text{first-year NOI}}{\text{debt service}}$

loan-to-value (LTV) ratio: $\text{LTV} = \dfrac{\text{loan amount}}{\text{appraisal value}}$

capitalization rate based on comparable recent transactions:

$$\text{capitalization rate} = \frac{\text{net operating income}}{\text{property value}}$$

capitalization of a property's rental stream: $\text{property value} = \dfrac{\text{net operating income}}{\text{capitalization rate}}$

Net Asset Value approach to REIT share valuation:

estimated cash NOI
$\div$ assumed cap rate
= estimated value of operating real estate
+ cash and accounts receivable
$-$ debt and other liabilities
= net asset value
$\div$ shares outstanding
= NAV/share

price-to-FFO approach to REIT share valuation:

funds from operations (FFO)
$\div$ shares outstanding
= FFO/share
$\times$ sector average P/FFO multiple
= NAV/share

price-to-AFFO approach to REIT share valuation:

funds from operations (FFO)
$-$ non-cash rents:
$-$ recurring maintenance-type capital expenditures
= AFFO
$\div$ shares outstanding
= AFFO/share
$\times$ property subsector average P/AFFO multiple
= NAV/share

discounted cash flow approach to REIT share valuation:

value of a REIT share
= PV(dividends for years 1 through n) + PV(terminal value at the end of year n)

exit value:

$$\frac{\text{investment}}{\text{cost}} + \frac{\text{earnings}}{\text{growth}} + \frac{\text{increase in}}{\text{price multiple}} + \frac{\text{reduction}}{\text{in debt}} = \text{exit value}$$

NAV before distributions:

$$= \frac{\text{NAV after}}{\text{distributions in}} + \frac{\text{capital called}}{\text{down}} - \frac{\text{management}}{\text{fees}} + \frac{\text{operating}}{\text{results}}$$
prior year

NAV after distributions:

$$= \frac{\text{NAV before}}{\text{distributions}} - \frac{\text{carried}}{\text{interest}} - \text{distributions}$$

venture capital method:

the post-money portion of a firm purchased by an investment is:

$$f_1 = \frac{\text{investment 1}}{\text{PV}_1(\text{exit value})}$$

the number of new shares issued is:

$$\text{shares}_{VC} = \text{shares}_{EQUITY}\left(\frac{f_1}{1-f_1}\right)$$

where shares$_{EQUITY}$ is the pre-investment number of shares, and share price is:

$$\text{price 1} = \frac{\text{investment 1}}{\text{shares}_{VC}}$$

Theory of Storage:

commodity futures price = spot price + storage costs − convenience yield

STUDY SESSIONS 16 & 17: PORTFOLIO MANAGEMENT

APT equation

$$E(R_P) = R_F + \beta_{P,1}(\lambda_1) + \beta_{P,2}(\lambda_2) + \ldots + \beta_{P,k}(\lambda_k)$$

expected return = risk free rate + Σ(factor sensitivity) × (factor risk premium)

active return = factor return + security selection return

mutifactor model return attribution:

$$\text{factor return} = \sum (\beta_{pi} - \beta_{bi}) \times (\lambda_i)$$

active risk squared = active factor risk + active specific risk

active factor risk = active risk squared − active specific risk

active specific risk = $\displaystyle\sum_{i=1}^{n} (W_{pi} - W_{bi})^2 \sigma_{\varepsilon i}^2$

portfolio variance for W_A% in fund A and W_B% in fund B:

$$\sigma_{Portfolio}^2 = W_A^2 \sigma_A^2 + W_B^2 \sigma_B^2 + 2 W_A W_B Cov_{AB}$$

annualized standard deviation = $\sqrt{250} \times$ (daily standard deviation)

percentage change in value due to a change in yield to maturity (ΔY):

% change in price = −duration (ΔY) + ½ convexity (ΔY)^2

Note: For Macaulay duration rather than modified duration), ΔY is replaced by $\Delta Y / (1 + Y)$.

option value versus future volatility:

change in call price = delta (ΔS) + ½ gamma (ΔS)^2 + vega (ΔV)

where ΔV is the change in future volatility

inter-temporal rate of substitution:

$$\text{inter-temporal rate of substitution} = m_t = \frac{\text{marginal utility of consuming 1 unit in the future}}{\text{marginal utility of current consumption of 1 unit}} = \frac{u}{u_{\bullet}}$$

real risk-free rate of return = $R = \dfrac{1 - P_0}{P_0} = \left[\dfrac{1}{E(m_t)}\right] - 1$

price of a default-free, inflation-indexed, zero-coupon bond:

$$P_0 = \frac{E(P_1)}{(1+R)} + cov(P_1, m_1)$$

nominal short term interest rate (r) = real risk-free rate (R) + expected inflation (π)

r(long-term) = R + π + θ

where θ = risk premium for uncertainty about inflation

Taylor rule

$$r = R_n + \pi + 0.5(\pi - \pi^*) + 0.5(y - y^*)$$

break-even inflation rate (BEI):

BEI = yield on non-inflation-indexed bond – yield on inflation-indexed bond

BEI for longer maturity bonds = expected inflation (π) + risk premium for uncertainty about actual inflation (θ)

required rate of return for credit risky bonds = R + π + θ + γ

where:
γ = additional risk premium for credit risk = credit spread

discount rate for equity = R + π + θ + γ + κ

where:
κ = additional risk premium relative to risky debt for an investment in equities
λ = equity risk premium = γ + κ

discount rate for commercial real estate = R + π + θ + γ + κ + ϕ

where:
κ = risk premium for uncertainty about terminal value of property (similar to equity risk premium)
ϕ = risk premium for illiquidity

active return = portfolio return – benchmark return $R_A = R_P - R_B$

portfolio return = $R_P = \sum_{i=1}^{n} w_{P,i} R_i$

benchmark return = $R_B = \sum_{i=1}^{n} w_{B,i} R_i$

information ratio $= \dfrac{R_P - R_B}{\sigma_{(R_P - R_B)}} = \dfrac{R_A}{\sigma_A} = \dfrac{active\ return}{active\ risk}$

portfolio Sharpe ratio

$$SR = \frac{R_P - R_F}{\sigma_P}$$

information ratio = $IR = TC \times IC \times \sqrt{BR}$

expected active return = $E(R_A) = IR \times \sigma_A$

"full" fundamental law of active management:

$$E(R_A) = (TC)(IC)\sqrt{BR}\sigma_A$$

Sharpe-ratio-maximizing level of aggressiveness:

$$\sigma_A{}^* = \frac{IR}{SR_B}\sigma_B$$

portfolio total risk versus benchmark risk and active risk:

$$STD(R_P)^2 = STD(R_B)^2 + STD(R_A)^2$$

Index